Theatres of Thought:
Theatre, Performance and Philosophy

Edited by

Daniel Watt and Daniel Meyer-Dinkgräfe

Cambridge Scholars Publishing

Theatres of Thought: Theatre, Performance and Philosophy, Edited by Daniel Watt and Daniel Meyer-Dinkgräfe

This book first published 2007 by

Cambridge Scholars Publishing

15 Angerton Gardens, Newcastle, NE5 2JA, UK

British Library Cataloguing in Publication Data
A catalogue record for this book is available from the British Library

ISBN (10): 1-84718-424-3, ISBN (13): 9781847184245

TABLE OF CONTENTS

INTRODUCTION

DANIEL WATT
AND DANIEL MEYER-DINKGRÄFE

In the autumn of 2004, colleagues in the Department of Theatre, Film and Television Studies at the University of Wales Aberystwyth began their endeavours of spelling out common grounds and mutual interests in their wide-ranging research. *Theatre, Performance and Philosophy* emerged as one of the distinctive research groups, later formalised as a departmental research centre (*Centre for Theatre, Performance and Philosophy, CTPP*) The core members of that centre, with their research foci in the context of CTPP, are, in alphabetical order, **Alison Forsyth** (continental philosophy and the hermeneutics of performance: Gadamer, Benjamin, Weil, Sartre), **Richard Gough** (cultural theory of archives, food, cookery, travel and tourism), **Karoline Gritzner** (critical theory: Adorno and Lacan), **Daniel Meyer-Dinkgräfe** (CTPP chair, consciousness studies and Indian philosophy, especially Vedanta), **David Ian Rabey** (eroticism, death and time), and **Daniel Watt** (deconstruction, ethics, postmodernism and performance, especially puppet theatre). Under the auspices of CTPP, a series of research seminars were organised, with speakers from the universities of Reading, Lancaster Staffordshire Chester, London (Royal Holloway), Newcastle East Anglia and Liverpool (John Moores). CTPP was also involved in a number of conferences organised and hosted in Aberystwyth.

This local development at Aberystwyth coincided with a development across the UK: the establishment of the Theatre and Performance Research Association (TaPRA), in early 2005, and the establishment of a working group *Theatre, Performance and Philosophy* (TPP) within TaPRA, chaired by Meyer-Dinkgräfe and Watt. So far this working group has convened at the 2005, 2006 and 2007 annual TaPRA conferences in Manchester, London and Birmingham, respectively. At these conferences it has enjoyed wide participation from across the UK and beyond.

With Watt moving from Aberystwyth to Loughborough and Meyer-Dinkgräfe from Aberystwyth to Lincoln in 2005 and 2007, respectively,

CTPP expanded its base beyond Aberystwyth, in line with its founding statutes. This expansion included initiatives such as *Schismogenesis: An Unavowable Community*; a postgraduate and staff research group based in the English and Drama Department of Loughborough University. The aim of such a grouping is to provide an opportunity to discuss critical, theoretical and philosophical papers in relation to drama, performance and literature. Whilst primarily a forum for drama postgraduates this *schismogenesis*, or fracture, is not designed to divide but rather to complement the work in English. In such contexts philosophy forms the basis of continued interdisciplinary focus for theatre and performance studies.

Within the practice / theory divide there are frequent criticisms of the push to make the study of theatre articulate itself through the work of philosophical discourse. Certainly, theatre borrows heavily from the philosophical canon (and beyond) to transform its practice into words. However, this is not a simple deployment of philosophy to lend weight to a field of study. Theatre, fundamentally, makes things *appear*. Philosophy, fundamentally, makes things *appear*. Philosophy is at work in all disciplines. The issue is less about bringing them together but rather articulating the fact that they, like science and art, have never been truly apart.

Theatre has been gradually increasing its theoretical articulation over decades, fascinated by the possibility of transforming thought into spectacle. Many current publications are doing a welcome job of articulating such theoretical groundings, especially for the student of drama: Reinelt and Roach's *Critical Theory and Performance*, Buse's *Drama + Theory* and Fortier's *Theatre/Theory* are but a few. With the turn towards Performance Studies, philosophical trajectories of the 'performative' obviously supplied a core grounding to the 'paradigm' shift supposedly at work in such a turn; equally a broadening inter-disciplinarity infused the field with philosophical terms borrowed (twice) through such disciplinary encounters. More recently though there is an emerging desire to deal with philosophical issues in their own terms, and to clearly label them as such. A recent, and excellent, example would be Krasner and Saltz's edited collection *Staging Philosophy*, which offers a collection of essays that address philosophy and the theatre as kindred modes of questioning. Undoubtedly the 'thinking' of theatre cannot replace its actual practice, but it does offer means by which to consider the relevance of the form of theatre in the contemporary world. The 2007 TaPRA conference at the University of Birmingham saw many of the working groups considering the issue of ethics as a pressing issue in their diverse thematic areas of research. So perhaps philosophy – whilst a somewhat awkward and apparently abstracted companion to the theatre – is increasingly revealing itself as foundational to the continued importance of theatre and performance, both as entertainment and cultural criticism.

Perhaps a legitimate suspicion of philosophy arises from its occasional appropriation of the theatre to make manifest its own agendas (an appropriation that, in its reverse, has been noted above). There is in a sense no escaping this. But what does theatre benefit from when presented with a quintessentially expository work that delivers 'philosophy'? An example of this might be Sartre's *Kean*, recently staged at the Apollo Theatre in 2007. The endlessly self-reflective hall of mirrors that is the stage provides the perfect (or so one might think) environment for Sartre's preoccupations with authenticity. However, and this was not entirely the fault of the actors and the staging, the play disappoints with its clumsy unpacking of its philosophical issues in the context of a complex, and tempestuous, biography of a notorious actor. Little wonder that theatre finds itself unsure of the extent to which philosophical speculation has a home within its walls. Here we might also cite Brecht – whose theoretical writings, have provided the foundation for many philosophically grounded attempts to employ the theatre for various political agendas – and any number of directors and practitioners who have sought to locate a certain type of *thinking* at the heart of their practice. But at what point does theatre acquire its own ground – a 'thing-in-itself'?

In considering the question 'Why are there essents rather than nothing?', at the opening of *An Introduction to Metaphysics*, Martin Heidegger comments on the moments in which such a question arises:

> The question looms in moments of great despair, when things tend to lose all their weight and all meaning becomes obscured. Perhaps it will strike but once like a muffled bell that rings into our life and gradually dies away. It is present in moments of rejoicing, when all things around us are transfigured and seem to be there for the first time, as if it might be easier to think they are not than to understand that they are and are as they are. The question is upon us in boredom, when we are equally removed from despair and joy, and everything about us seems so hopelessly commonplace that we no longer care whether anything is or is not (1987: 1)

The passage is a particular concise description of that doubt that arises from extremes, and these extremes can arise at any moment. Some of the terms will be most familiar to theatre audiences: 'despair', 'rejoicing', 'transfigured', 'boredom' and 'joy', and might even describe the emotional journey of many productions. Philosophy does not sit outside of life, contentedly commenting on its minutiae, but rather figures itself as an event deeply structured within life, and theatre is also such an event. Particular philosophical methods will always seem both appropriate and inappropriate to theatre. They are only other means by which to ask theatre to *perform* itself. But it is not the task of this book to defend, or champion particular schools of thought, or particular aspects of practice for that matter. Perhaps it is the task of philosophy to only offer means by which questions can arise, issues such as ethics, existence and responsibility. Why is there *theatre*, rather than nothing? – a question which philosophy also asks of itself; a question unanswered (and unanswerable) here, in this book, but perhaps answered in myriad forms on the stage, if we give it a theatre to think the thought that is most proper to it, and to put that thought into play.

The essays collected in this volume arise from the 2005 and 2006 TaPRA conferences and papers presented under the auspices of CTPP at Aberystwyth. After careful consideration we have decided not to foist our editorial decisions on the sequence in which the papers are grouped for reading—instead, they appear in alphabetical order, allowing readers to make connections and associations based on their own reading.

The papers represent a wide range of approaches and ways in which philosophy may relate to theatre and performance. **Vasiliki Angelaki** considers phenomenology as a philosophical / theoretical approach to understanding theatre text, with reference to work by playwright Martin Crimp. **Carina Bartleet** explores Julia Kristeva's conceptual reworking of abjection and its implications for contexts of dramaturgy and theatre. **Lilja Blumenfeld** analyses five different productions of Shakespeare's *The Merchant of Venice* in the context of the real and imagined sites of Venice. **Elpida-Sophia Christianaki** goes back to Greek tragedy, the three versions of Socrates in Xenophon, Plato and Aristotle, and Nietzsche's views on Greek tragedy and philosophy. **Laura Cull** discusses the work of Chicago-based performance group *Goat Island* with reference, among others, to Deleuze. **Matthew Goulish**, artistic director of *Goat Island*, responds to Cull's intervention. **Dongning Feng** takes us beyond Europe and the USA to China: he describes and evaluates developments in contemporary Chinese performing arts against the backdrop of political developments in that country. **Elizabeth Jacobs** relates Chicana/o literature and criticism to the discourse of psychoanalysis. **Carl Lavery** offers an example of performative writing, reflecting on the practice itself while engaging in it, triggered by his experience of Graeme Miller's performance work *Linked*. **Chris Megson**'s contribution draws critical attention to the phenomenon of tribunal plays in the 1990s. **Daniel Meyer-Dinkgräfe** takes up Jill Dolan's concept of the *utopian performative* and develops it further in the context of current consciousness studies. **Michelle Piasecka** investigates ways in which performance (in the context of live art) may be used practically in primary school contexts. **Simon Piasecki** focuses his research on a specific historical period, that of early modernism, and the impact of the philosophical discourse of the time in particular on Meyerhold and Stanislavsky. **Jurriën Rood** turns the usual relation between philosophy and theatre, in which philosophy has the role of explaining, of helping to better understand phenomena and experiences of theatre, on its head, arguing that philosophy can in fact learn from Stanislavsky's practice about the relation between mind and body. **David Shirley**, finally, discusses the centrality, or otherwise, of *character* to drama and theatre.

Bibliography

Heidegger, Martin. 1987. *An Introduction to Metaphysics*. London: Yale University Press.

CHAPTER ONE

VASILIKI ANGELAKI

PERFORMING PHENOMENOLOGY: THE THEATRE OF MARTIN CRIMP

This paper is in part devoted to a brief understanding regarding the advantages of phenomenology as a philosophical/theoretical approach to the analysis of theatrical texts and in part to the brief application of phenomenological concepts to two recent plays by Martin Crimp, *The Country* and *Fewer Emergencies*. I aim to propose and demonstrate that phenomenology finds a natural partner in the medium of theatre, allowing for an incisiveness that complements the material being examined. My analysis will include references to pivotal philosophical texts within the phenomenological tradition and to studies which have adapted phenomenology to the needs of a theatre-related critical discourse. Specifically, I will discuss Gaston Bachelard's *The Poetics of Space* and Maurice Merleau-Ponty's *Phenomenology of Perception* and *Signs*, also referring to Stanton B. Garner's *Bodied Spaces: Phenomenology and Performance in Contemporary Drama* and Bert O. States' *Great Reckonings in Little Rooms: On the Phenomenology of Theater*.

Bachelard's *The Poetics of Space* is a unique text, which carries an almost poetic quality in its choice of vocabulary and grasps the intricacies of the individual's relationship with his/her private territory in a profundity that is captivating for the reader. The theoretical horizon of phenomenology is especially encouraging for such spatial analyses, as Bachelard's text proves through its account of the significance of the different locations in the house, which are examined in direct analogy to the consciousness of the inhabitant who perceives them. Bachelard's study indeed provides true insights into the corporeal and psychological relationship cultivated between the individual and his/her environment. Addressing the question "Why phenomenology," Bachelard suggests: "Only phenomenology—that is to say, consideration of the *onset of the image* in an individual consciousness—can help us to restore the subjectivity of images and to measure their fullness, their strength and their transsubjectivity" (xix). If we are to justify the purposefulness of a phenomenological approach to the study of a theatrical text, Bachelard's proposition helps us understand the affinities between this area of philosophy and performance analysis. Specifically, phenomenology enables the critic or academic researcher to account for more profound layers of meaning, appreciating the importance of the scenic image as it is placed before the spectators' consciousness and accounting for the complicated nature of the characters' motility and corporeality within their given stage habitat.

The Poetics of Space is a seminal work in the field of phenomenology in that it is devoted to one specific area, which is a main concern of the discipline, and which it navigates extensively. Space, of course has also been a primary focal point for the phenomenologist philosopher Maurice Merleau-Ponty, who devotes a lengthy chapter to it in his landmark work *Phenomenology of Perception*. Having referred to Bachelard's work though, I would like to especially concentrate on Merleau-Ponty's contribution in the field of a phenomenological account of language. Language is a major concern not only in *Phenomenology of Perception*, but in his work *Signs* as well. As is the case with the understanding of space, corporeality is the essential prism through which language is understood as well. That is, language is as much a mental process as it is a physical one. Expanding on the corporeality of language Merleau-Ponty proposes that, while speaking, the individual achieves intersubjectivity, simultaneously existing as a speaker and hearer of his/her own words, sharing this communal experience with any interlocutors and/or listeners. This communication process, as understood from a phenomenological viewpoint, enhances the sense of correlation between the producer and the receiver of an utterance. If we link this concept directly to the theatre, we understand its usefulness for the decoding of the relationship developed and sustained between the speaking character and the auditorium. Therefore, the prioritization of the sensory aspect of language, which becomes a physical entity when it is embodied in speech, is directly relatable to the critical analysis of theatre, as it helps us read the play beyond its written form. In this way, the critic is enabled to apprehend the essence of the play as a 'lived' text, one that belongs partially to the page and partially to the stage, meant to be voiced and not merely read. In other words, this aspect of phenomenology saves us from producing an analysis of a theatrical text which leans unevenly towards the literary, failing to adequately account for an essential feature of the play, which is only materialized in performance.

Although a phenomenological approach holds various advantages, the existing scholarship in the field of phenomenology and the theatre is not, to date, as wide as one might expect. It is not, of course, an unexplored territory, but it certainly lacks the prominence of other philosophical and theoretical approaches more commonly applied to theatre-related analysis. I would like to mention here two leading studies in the field, published in the mid 1980s and mid 1990s respectively. These are Bert O. States' *Great Reckonings in Little Rooms* and Stanton Garner's *Bodied Spaces*. States' work operates as an application of phenomenology to the theatre, but it is also, and perhaps primarily, a theoretical work, which contributes its own distinctive viewpoint to the area it investigates. States' critical incisiveness is undeniable and it is in part owing to the fact that he does not adopt a phenomenological frame of reference *de facto*, but he also takes into perspective the limitations of other approaches, which are surpassable in a phenomenological discussion. It might be suggested that *Great Reckonings in Little Rooms* remains to date the quintessential and most rewarding text, which a researcher focusing on phenomenology and the theatre might encounter.

Stanton Garner's *Bodied Spaces* acknowledges a debt to States' work, but it also makes a seminal contribution in its own right, especially in terms of its extensive and detailed application of phenomenological concepts to the work of contemporary influential playwrights. This makes the work a valuable point of reference for those focusing on post-war theatre. Moreover, the diversity of the text, demonstrated through the focus on playwrights ranging from Samuel Beckett to Sam Shepard and from Harold Pinter to Caryl Churchill, establishes *Bodied Spaces* as an inexhaustible source. The reason for this is that its case studies can function as paradigms for the fruitful application of phenomenological theory to the theatre, employed as references for the examination of the work of other playwrights with similar concerns. In both States' and Garner's texts questions of corporeality and space, as well as corporeality and language, also articulated by phenomenologist philosophers, are central. In the final part of my paper I will pursue an understanding of these issues in Martin Crimp's plays *The Country* and *Fewer Emergencies*.

In the majority of Crimp's writing spatiality is a recurring concern. This might be expressed in the depiction of the individual's relationship with his/her surroundings, the function of objects within a given locale, or the selection of vocabulary in the characters' dialogue, which brims with place names or metaphors. This is one of the factors that advocate a phenomenological approach to Crimp's work and *The Country* is a characteristic example for this observation. Opening at the Royal Court

Theatre Downstairs in May 2000, the play is a tale of marital dysfunction. The protagonists are Corinne and Richard, who move from the city to the country in an attempt to save their marriage. The basic problem is that Richard, a doctor, is a heroin addict. What Corinne is unaware of is that he is also adulterous and has supported this move to the country so as to resume his affair with the twenty-five year old Rebecca, another drug user, who has also relocated there. After Rebecca has taken an overdose, Richard brings the comatose Rebecca to the house and leaves shortly afterwards for house calls to his patients. When Rebecca regains consciousness she begins a tense conversation with Corinne.

As regards the issue of the subject and his/her *locus*, *The Country* offers itself to a phenomenological approach. First of all, the analogy can be supported in terms of the characters' territorial behaviour. No scene in the play is as exemplary of this territoriality as the one where Corinne encounters Rebecca. The young woman is the outsider who displays an assertive behaviour within Corinne's domestic environment and the attempt to establish herself as an equal or even superior interlocutor to Corinne triggers the latter's defence mechanism. As Corinne affirms:

> – This is where we live. This is where our children will live. This *is* our home. (35)

To which Rebecca replies:

> – Exactly. Well exactly: you and your children have nowhere to go / back to. (35)

Rebecca's questioning of the fact that Corinne is spatially rooted in her home and the overt challenging of her permanence in the familial *locus* instigates Corinne's firm response. As she asserts:

> – This is our home. We don't want to 'go back'. We are a family. We are here permanently. (35)

The assertion of authority within her space originates from Corinne's attachment to the home, which she views as the intimate territory where she can reclaim her marriage and build a prosperous life for her family. It is the place that has been chosen for precisely this purpose and has been invested with emotional expectations. In *The Poetics of Space*, Bachelard explores such intricate relationships by employing the analogy of the nest, suggesting that a home operates for the individual as a shelter does for an animal (90-104). The process of attachment to one's space then, from a phenomenological perspective, is in equal degrees mental and physical, reaching further than a mere psychological justification of the subject's behaviour (91). Regarding nests, or homes, Bachelard's text traces the crucial factor for the enhancement of their sheltering quality in their 'lived' nature, in their reciprocal rewarding relationship with their inhabitant (90-104). As a consequence, the domestic space, which bears its resident's projections of happiness, operates to instil confidence in the individual, who will be eager to defend his/her establishment within this space. As Bachelard concludes:

> Our house, apprehended in its dream potentiality, becomes a nest in the world, and we shall live there in complete confidence if, in our dream, we really participate in the sense of security of our first home. [. . .] The nest, quite as much as the oneiric house, and the oneiric house quite as much as the nest–[. . .] knows nothing of the hostility of the world. (103)

In Crimp's play this is precisely the quality with which Corinne endows her new home, which she views as the first step towards the fulfilment of her dream of an unperturbed family life. When Rebecca appears as a threat to what her house represents, Corinne becomes increasingly possessive, as demonstrated by her choice of vocabulary and by her attempts to obliterate the threat. By protecting the house, Corinne essentially protects herself and the family structure she strives to sustain.

Crimp's *Fewer Emergencies* staged at the Royal Court Theatre Upstairs in September 2005 is a quite different play from *The Country* in that, as opposed to the latter, it entirely disregards traditional narrative forms. *Fewer Emergencies* is the collective title of the play, taken from the third piece in order of performance. The other two are *Whole Blue Sky* and *Face to the Wall*, and, like *Fewer Emergencies*, their individual length in performance does not exceed twenty minutes. A small group of unnamed characters narrate, while place and time are only described in the stage directions as "blank" (5, 23, 39). The common denominator in the three pieces is the issue of social class in a capitalist society, its demands and its repercussions. The stage is almost bare, with a few white desks and chairs as the only set. Nothing actually happens on stage other than the narrating, and, yet, everything does, by virtue of the ability of language to create mental visualizations in the spectators' consciousness. The sparsely decorated set and the suspension of physical action create an ideal phenomenological theatrical environment, as language is enabled to emerge as the key component in the play. In order to grasp the importance of this it is necessary to follow a phenomenological approach where language, materialized through speech, is treated as a corporeal entity, which is as much physical and concrete as a practical enactment would be. It is difficult to find a text which more accurately accounts for this than Merleau-Ponty's "On the Phenomenology of Language," published in *Signs*. This is where the notion of language as a gesture is developed, phrased in these words:

> the spoken word is pregnant with a meaning which can be read in the very texture of the linguistic gesture [. . .] and yet is never contained in that gesture, every expression always appearing to me as a trace, no idea being given to me except in transparency, and every attempt to close our hand on the thought which dwells in the spoken word leaving only a bit of verbal material in our fingers. (89)

As Merleau-Ponty suggests, then, speech may not be tangible, but it has the power of generating imagery which lingers in thought as persistently as a physical depiction of events would. Consequently, speech *is* a gesture, as it is endowed with as much corporeality as a physical motion of the body. As a gesture affects its recipient, so speech achieves an effect on the listener. In the case of the theatre, and especially in a text such as *Fewer Emergencies*, where, unimpeded by a cluttered stage, language is elevated to the highest position in performance, Merleau-Ponty's text is particularly relevant. The characters' verbal behaviour not only compensates for the static nature of the play, it is also the essential factor for its effectiveness. By following the narration of images, to which a great amount of effort has been devoted in order to ensure precision, appropriate articulation and pace of delivery, the spectators of *Fewer Emergencies* remain alert, aware and connected with a spectacle which invites them in a journey of decoding and imagination.

My aim in this paper has been to suggest that phenomenology can be a highly rewarding approach for theatre-related analysis, as it helps us follow a trail from the page to the stage, accounting for vital aspects of the play(s) which we are discussing. In order to substantiate this I have considered seminal texts within the discipline, written by philosophers Maurice Merleau-Ponty and Gaston Bachelard. Moreover, in order to prove that the precepts of phenomenology translate to the requirements of theatre criticism, I have referred to works by Bert O. States and Stanton B. Garner, who have offered two compelling texts which apply phenomenology to the study of performance. Finally, I have applied the phenomenological writings of Bachelard and Merleau-Ponty to Crimp's *The Country* and *Fewer Emergencies* so as to demonstrate the complementation between the theatrical text and the theory, or the theory and the theatrical text. Of course, I have only examined a small fragment of the two plays, or a minute fragment of the totality of Crimp's theatre. There is a lot more to be said regarding the corporeality of language, the function of space and the objects within it, the performer's body, as well as about stage and soundscapes. It is not possible to visit all these considerations here. However, this paper has hopefully functioned to trace the extent of what it is possible to do with phenomenology in a theatrical analysis, especially when the texts discussed are as inviting as Crimp's work.

Bibliography

Bachelard, Gaston. 1994. *The Poetics of Space*. Trans. Maria Jolas. Boston: Beacon Press.
Crimp, Martin. 2000. *The Country*. London: Faber and Faber.
—. 2005. *Fewer Emergencies*. London: Faber and Faber.
—. *Fewer Emergencies*. 8 Sep. 2005. By Martin Crimp. Dir. James Macdonald. Perf. Rachael Blake, Neil Dudgeon, et al. Jerwood Theatre Upstairs Royal Court Theatre, London.
Garner, Stanton B. Jr. 1994. *Bodied Spaces: Phenomenology and Performance in Contemporary Drama*. Ithaca: Cornell University Press.
Merleau-Ponty, Maurice. [1945] 2002. *Phenomenology of Perception*. Trans. Colin Smith. New York: Routledge.
—. 1964. *Signs*. Trans. Richard G. McCleary. Evanston: Northwestern University Press.
States, Bert O. 1985. *Great Reckonings in Little Rooms: On the Phenomenology of Theater*. Berkeley: University of California Press.

CHAPTER TWO

CARINA BARTLEET

THE SCENE OF DISGUST: REALISM AND ITS MALCONTENTS, THE AUDIENCE AND THE ABJECT

The condition of abjection, from its etymological roots, contains the possibility of both the performative and the theatrical. According to the *Oxford English Dictionary*, at least in Anglophone parts of the world, the origin of "abject" is late Middle English from the Latin roots of "reject" – or *abjectus* – *ab* meaning "away" and *jacere* "to throw". In this sense, when something is abjected it is thrown away. Etymologically, abjection is potentially a gestural act – a pushing away, a deliberate rejection: semantically a method of putting something out as rubbish. This sense does not do justice to the nuance with which this word is used in an everyday context and still more with regard to its usage within a philosophical context. Julia Kristeva's study *Powers of Horror* is an important and useful interrogation of the term, which is also a significant reworking of it from a psychoanalytic perspective. It re-reads the term through Mary Douglas's *Purity and Danger*, and René Girard's discussion on the relationship between violence and the sacred. This chapter aims to explore Kristeva's conceptual reworking of abjection and consider the implications that this might have in dramaturgical and theatrical contexts. Illustration will be primarily through the consideration of the written text in performance, thus opening up the possibility of exploring literary contexts, alongside Kristeva's own but also an extension of it into the realm of performance.

Abjection: Non-object of the Enquiry

The abject, according to Kristeva, is located through its liminal status as neither a subject nor object. Thus, she asserts:

> The abject is not an ob-ject facing me, which I name or imagine [....] What
> is abject is not my correlative, which providing me with someone or
> something else as support, would allow me to be more or less detached and
> autonomous. The abject only has one quality of the object – that of being
> opposed to *I*. If the object, however, through its opposition, settles me
> within the fragile texture of a desire for meaning, which as a matter of fact,
> makes me ceaselessly and infinitely homologous to it, what is *abject*, on
> the contrary, the jettisoned object, is radically excluded and draws me
> toward the place where meaning collapses. (Kristeva 1982, 1—2)

Yet, at the same time, for Kristeva, "[o]n the edge of non-existence and
hallucination, of a reality that, if I acknowledge it, annihilates me. There,
abject and abjection are my safeguards" (2). In Kristeva's formulation, the
Cartesian *cogito ergo sum* becomes reformulated into I abject therefore I
am and, in being, I abject. This becomes clearer in her frequently-quoted
discussion of her own food loathing – that of the skin that forms on the
surface of milk.

> When the eyes see or the lips touch that skin on the surface of milk –
> harmless, [...] I experience a gagging sensation and, still further down,
> spasms in the stomach, the belly; and all the organs shrivel up the body,
> provoke tears and bile, increase heartbeat, cause forehead and hands to
> perspire. Along with sight-clouding dizziness, *nausea* makes me balk [...]
> separates me from the mother and father who proffer it. 'I' want none of
> that element, sign of their desire; 'I' do not want to listen, 'I' do not
> assimilate it, 'I' expel it. But since food is not an 'other' for 'me,' who am
> only in their desire, I expel *myself*, I spit *myself* out, I abject *myself* within
> the same motion through which 'I' claim to establish *myself*. (2—3)

Furthermore, it is "not lack of cleanliness or health that causes abjection
but what disturbs identity, system, order. What does not respect borders
positions, rules. The in-between, the ambiguous, the composite. The
traitor, the liar, the criminal with a good conscious [...]. Any crime
because it draws attention to the fragility of the law, is abject, but
premeditated crime, cunning murder, hypocritical revenge are even more
so because they heighten the display of such fragility" (4). Thus, abjection
"is immoral, sinister, scheming and shady: a terror that dissembles, a
hatred that smiles, a passion that uses the body for barter [...] a debtor
who sells you up, a friend who stabs you" (4). What can be discerned from
each of these examples is that, if abjection is an abstraction in the sense
that it is neither a subject nor an object, it is nonetheless manifest through
gestural and corporeal acts. The quotation lists acts that may be familiar
through metaphor in everyday life but they are also deeds and events that
can be constituents of Victorian melodrama, and evident in the plots of

Grand Guignol, realism, naturalism and Revenge Tragedy to list only a few examples. Like some aspects of Freudian psychoanalysis itself, many of these acts are commonplace plots for the dramatic text.

Realism and Naturalism's rose to prominence in the theatre during the second half of the nineteenth century and in the early twentieth and were broadly contemporary to the rise of psychoanalysis. In his study, *Modern Drama and the Rhetoric of Theater*, W. B. Worthen discusses what he terms the performance rhetoric of stage realism and observing that it embraces a number of difference dramatic genres, which:

> stage the text within its rhetorical priorities: a proscenium stage, often implying a box set, a fourth wall discrimination between stage and audience; objects that constitute both character and action; the necessary activities of production from the realm of the audience's legitimate interpretation. The rhetoric of realism opposes the visible and integrated scene onstage to the invisible indeterminate, absent scene of the spectator's interpretation. (Worthen 1992, 5)

Examples of dramatic realism and naturalism such as Ibsen's *Ghosts, Hedda Gabler* and Zola's stage version of (the infamous novel) *Thérèse Raquin* share a number of characteristics when considered in relation to Worthen's description. Although one should be wary of collapsing a discussion of the conventions of stage naturalism with realism, at first glance, all three plays appear to adhere to the convention of the illusion of the fourth wall between the audience and the action presented onstage. In incorporating a clear demarcation between the onstage action and the audience via the illusory fourth wall, such conventions appear to deny the possibility of a theatrical abject because they display a marked respect for and maintenance of a border. Worthen's description of the performance rhetoric of realism appears to endorse this reading when he notes that "The rhetoric of realism opposes the visible and integrated scene onstage to the invisible indeterminate, absent scene of the spectator's interpretation" (5). Such a reading is potentially a reductive one, however; it fails to take into account the role of the audience in constructing meaning within the theatre. If Worthen is correct in his assumption that the role of the audience in meaning making during performance in stage realism is minimized, it would seem that, at least in terms of individual performances of a play, the position of abjection, or non-objectival otherness, is not available.

Border Crossings: *Ghosts* and Ibsen's Devious Criminals

Ibsen's *Ghosts* (1881), written quickly during September and October 1881 and revised so it could be published before Christmas of the same year is one play that, famously, has been viewed as controversial, not so much for its performances, as for the outcry and protest its now somewhat oblique references to syphilis engendered (Watts in Ibsen 1964, 10—1). As Peter Watts, a twentieth-century translator of Ibsen's works into English, related:

> The uproar against *Ghosts* was the most violent of all the many storms that Ibsen raised. None of the Scandinavian theatres would stage it, and it was not till 1884 that anyone dared to translate it into German. In fact its first performance was not in Europe at all, but was given by a touring company in Chicago. When […] it was staged in London, the critics labelled it "putrid", "naked loathsomeness" and "an open sewer" (11).

It would seem, in this case, the audience or at least that part of it whose opinions were considered important enough to be committed to print, were far from being passive receivers of meaning made on stage. As Marker and Marker observe when reviewing the performance history of this play: "these early performances of *Ghosts* in London and in Paris at the beginning of the 1890s remain so enmeshed in the critical confusion and recriminations surrounding the play itself that an objective assessment of them in purely artistic terms is hardly possible now" (Marker and Marker 1989, 98). Rather instead, the initial audiences were as involved in the making of meaning within the performance contexts of *Ghosts* as Ibsen was. It is even arguable that the debates surrounding Ibsen's theatre and, especially, its spirited defence has been more important in forming present-day notions of Ibsen's secure place within the modern drama canon.[1]

Dramatic and performance conventions, content and theme all contribute to the making of meaning within the performance context and, in considering *Ghosts* in performance, it is the contention here that it is crucial to consider dramatic and theatrical conventions diachronically. It is one of the strengths of Ibsen's writing that he drew upon the conventions of previous drama and theatre sometimes not to reject but in order to subvert them. The character of Engstrand, with his crippled leg and obvious immorality is one aspect of Ibsen's dramaturgy where the conventions of nineteenth-century melodrama are evident. Whereas, in Victorian melodrama such facets of character can function to signify villainy to an audience, in Ibsen's dramaturgy Engstrand's status as a possible felon is equivocal. For example, it is unclear whether he was responsible for starting the fire that leads to the destruction of the orphanage Mrs Alving has built in memory of her husband. In this instance, a more nuanced reading of the character can be elucidated through knowledge of theatrical and dramatic conventions employed and rejected by Ibsen.

Thematically, Ibsen's play works within the conventions of realism and naturalism through the recognizably complex psychologies of the characters, most notably of Mrs Alving. Additionally, these conventions are reinforced through their incorporation of the classic realist detective narrative to reveal the shameful secret of Captain Alving's syphilis and the revelation that the son has inherited both this and his father's dissolute behaviour despite Mrs Alving's efforts to remove her son from his father's sphere of influence. Thus, it becomes apparent that Osvald has spent time away from his family at school and in Paris. Ibsen's narrative structure functions to reveal Mrs Alving's efforts to uphold the reputation of her dead husband, Captain Alving's as a good man, whilst simultaneously unravelling the details of his dissolute life: namely his affair with a maid and his syphilitic illness. In this play, syphilis functions as a metaphor for abjection in the sense that it does not respect borders. The narrative can be read as staging Mrs Alving's battle with the abject, from her attempt to reject, to throw away her recollection of her husband in favour of a purified public version. Thus, his fathering of bastards is abjected into an orphanage built in his memory. Ultimately, Mrs Alving's failure in this task is evident through the ambivalent manner in which she succumbs to the state of abjection by accepting the presence of her syphilitic son, urging him to stay with her despite her final act of screaming "I can't bear it [...] never! No, no, no... Yes! No, no" as she stares at him, hands in her hair – a gesture itself familiar to present-day audiences from Edvard Munch's famous *fin de siècle* work, the Scream (Ibsen 1964, 102). In this schema, the character of Engstrand becomes an analogue of the abjection. Ostensibly a villain *à la* melodrama, his status as felon, or victim of his social position, or neither remains unresolved. If we read the clues in Ibsen's play as suggestion of Engstrand's guilt in the burning down of the orphanage, then it is arguable that, the character represents what Kristeva describes as "the traitor, the liar, the criminal with a conscience", however, because he also functions as a means by which Mrs Alving slowly reveals the secret she has repressed, Engstrand is both a means by which the abject is unveiled and yet is and an actor in its expulsion or purgation.

Reading Ibsen's *Ghosts* alongside Kristeva's theorization of the abject, it becomes apparent that it contains a paradox: whereas, formally, the conventions the play draws upon, function through its staging rhetoric to create, and maintain the borders between the onstage performance and the audience of it, the play's content suggests that these borders are deceptive. Symbolically, *Ghosts*'s content or at least its subject matter and plotting, work to undermine the relationship that the play's realist stage rhetoric proclaims. In confronting its early audiences with the spectre of syphilis – a disease that could be passed unseen from person to person via sexual contact and was incurable – the play creates dis-ease in its suggestion that the borders so firmly established between audience, or the unseen, and the scenes enacted before them are themselves illusory. The outrage and disgust which surrounded *Ghosts* and its concomitant difficulty in finding a stage in the 1880s suggests that the fourth wall of realism and naturalism, in performance at the very least, is not just illusory but that illusionism is itself porous. In this play, the audience is never absent in performance but, in maintaining borders that are rendered porous as a result of the subject matter and Ibsen's *verisimilitude,* the audience as the unacknowledged component in the performance are themselves abjected and, confronted by their own effacement and replacement onstage, in being, must themselves abject.

Non-realist and Political Theatre in the Late 20th Century – Abjection and the Experiential

Distanced from the zenith of theatrical Naturalism and Realism by approximately a century, the dramas of Edward Bond and Sarah Kane nevertheless display the markers of influence (even if this is expressed as an emphatic rejection of both sets of conventions). Worthen has observed of Bond, who has worked within the constraints of realism, most notably in *Saved* (1965), that he is "oddly the inheritor of one strain of realistic theatricality deriving from Zola and the naturalists: the desire to analyze and expose the working of society through a 'scientific' or 'rational' art" (91). *Blasted*, Sarah Kane's first professionally-produced play, which must surely have a claim to be the most notorious British play since Howard Brenton's *Romans in Britain* (1980), is itself a play that starts in a realist vein that is exploded, both literally and metaphorically at the end of Scene Two (Kane 2001, 39).[2]

Bond – Confronting Abjection

Bond's *Lear*, a 1971 re-vision of Shakespeare's *King Lear*, is a fascinating text for a number of reasons not least because of its clear rejection of realism in favour of Epic form. Commenting on Shakespeare's play, Bond has observed that: "Shakespeare's *Lear* is usually seen as an image of high, academic culture. The play is seen as sublime action and the audience are expected to show the depth of their culture by the extent to which they penetrate its mysteries... But the social moral of Shakespeare's *Lear* is this: endure till in time the world will be made right. That's a dangerous moral for us. We have less time than Shakespeare" (Bond in Hay and Roberts 1978, 53, ellipsis in original). Bond's *Lear* covers the same period of time and action as *King Lear*, although it makes a number of alterations most notably reducing Lear's daughters to two, changing their names and reworking the character of Cordelia. Like Shakespeare's play, Bond's contains a number of violent and extremely brutal acts, however. In it people are raped, tortured grotesquely, have their eyes gouged out by a machine, and are killed, all in the name of social control as a civil war breaks out in Lear's former kingdom. The neo-Jacobean tag, which is associated with Bond's work more widely, appears to be justified in the "Preface" to this play through a concentration on violence that is on a far grander scale than is present in *Saved* and still more grotesque than in *King Lear*. Bond has observed somewhat disingenuously "I write about violence as naturally as Jane Austen wrote about manners" (Bond 1983, LVII). It is not clear whether Bond sees the irony in his selection of an example that displays clear social construction and nor does it matter especially. Later on in the "Preface" he argues:

> There is no evidence of an aggressive *need*, as there is of our sexual and feeding *needs*. We [humans] respond aggressively when we are constantly deprived of our physical and emotional needs, or when we are threatened with this; and if we are constantly deprived and threatened in this way – as human beings now are (sic) – we live in a constant state of aggression. (LVII—LVIII)

Bond's arguments in this preface would not be out of place in a foreword to one of the plays of Naturalism in the nineteenth century. What is significant in this and in the previous quotation from him is not its accuracy so much as the discursive strategies that he draws upon. Here, those discursive strategies attempt to give the feel of a writer who has researched the human condition from a standpoint of an observer and recorder of the behaviour of *Homo sapiens sapiens*. Individual humans are not, according to Bond, violent *per se,* but violent acts are manifest in responses to the environment in which they live. Bond's *Lear* is certainly successful in showing how an aggression-inducing environment might be created by the operations of the nation state and government in human

society. In so doing, however, Bond creates a war-torn state for which the
ruling classes, regardless of whether this is Lear, his daughters, or even
Cordelia as the leader of the freedom fighters: all display an obsession for
the proper respect for borders between nation states through the need to
continue with the wall that Lear is building at the start of the play.

The narrative arc in tandem with Bond's plotting of onstage action
suggests that the cost to society in creating and maintaining the proper
borders of state is too high to bear. In Act One, Scene One, Lear the ruler,
is accompanied by his daughters, Bodice and Fontanelle, on an inspection
of the wall-building project. The scene opens not on Lear, however, but
with the discovery of a dead man carried on by two workers, with building
materials in the background (1). The significance of the wall as a catalyst
creating disorder and chaos within the confines of Lear's kingdom is
reinforced by the selection of it as the location for the opening and closing
scenes, thus, framing the rest of the action.

One of Lear's early speeches provides an explanation for his wall-
building project. According to the character:

> I started this wall when I was young. I stopped my enemies in the field, but
> there were always more of them. How could we ever be free? So I built
> this wall to keep our enemies out. My people will live behind this wall
> when I am dead. You may be governed by fools but you'll always live in
> peace. My wall will make you free. That's why the enemies on *our* borders
> – the Duke of Cornwall and the Duke of North – try to stop us building it.
> (3-4)

Lear's speech displays a preoccupation with the creation of impermeable
borders in order to exclude his enemies. Through the speech, Bond reveals
Lear's contradictory logic; the wall may exclude Lear's enemies but it will
set the people he rules over free. Even in this first scene, events at the wall
reveal Lear's reasoning to be dubious. In order to accomplish the building
of the wall, workers are drafted in by removal from their farmland by
compulsion and then housed in sub-standard huts. Local farmers make
sorties on the wall overnight in order to sabotage it and Lear is in fear of
his own people disobeying him. The death of the man found at the
beginning of the play with a pickaxe blow to the head, is blamed on
another character, to whom Bond gives the representative title of "Third
Worker". Lear orders the Third Worker to be shot for the murder but is
interrupted by the announcement from his daughters, Bodice and
Fontanelle, that they are to marry Lear's enemies the Dukes of North and
Cornwall against their father's wishes and that the wall will be destroyed.
Lear's response to betrayal by his daughters is revealed in another long

speech that is worth quoting in its entirety. In the speech, directed at his daughters, Lear exclaims:

> My enemies will not destroy my work! I gave my life to these people. I've seen armies on their hands and knees in blood, insane women feeding dead children at their empty breasts, dying men spitting blood at me with their last breath, our brave young men in tears -. But I could bear all this! When I'm dead my people will live in freedom and peace and remember my name, no venerate it!... They are my sheep and if one of them is lost I'd take fire to hell to bring him out. I loved and cared for all my children, and now you've sold them to their enemies! (*He shoots* Third Worker, *and his body slumps forwards on the post in a low bow.*) There's no more time, it's too late to learn anything. (7, ellipsis in original)

The irony here is that the enemies are not being kept out of Lear's kingdom, they are inside it. For the people Lear rules over, the enemies are the kingdom's rulers. The juxtaposition of words and deeds in the above speech as Lear professes to love and care for his people whilst shooting dead the Third Worker suggests that the character is very far from being a reliable judge of his own nature at this point. The disjunction between the kingly and quasi-Christian discourse in which Lear frames his duty of care towards his subjects and the thoughtless violence that he subjects the Third Worker to, display a collapse of order and ambivalence in his role that becomes an abuse of power. The final line of the speech, "There's no more time, it's too late to learn anything," draws attention to the construction of character and positioning of the audience in Epic theatre as subject to and capable of change, however, in addition it reinforces prejudice of the elderly as being too confirmed in their habits to alter them. Spoken at the beginning of this play by Lear, who, during the course of the play, will undergo a *volte-face* regarding the wall as a consequence of his removal from power and exposure to the cruelties both petty and extreme to which the people in his kingdom are subjected. Lear's final visit to the wall at the play's end is not to inspect but an attempt to damage or destroy it. It is an act that results in Lear's death, shot by the Farmer's Son in order to protect the wall – an action that can be read doubly as a reversal of the action in the opening scene and a repetition of it. For the rulers, the maintenance of the wall as an impermeable border is paramount.

If Bond uses the wall as a material metaphor for the ways in which human rights and freedoms are eroded by the fear of attack (itself a timely notion and one that is in keeping with the manner in which the play has concretized many of the themes in its Shakespearean pre-text), it can also be read through Kristeva's work on the abject as a site of contestation or a border that is subject to unceasing attack.[3] The journey of Lear as a character in Bond's play is into a state of abjection as he fails to maintain the correct and proper borders between him and his people. In so doing, however, Bond suggests that Lear learns that suffering and abjection are constants within the bounded or guarded state regardless of who holds power. Bond achieves this through a series of encounters, most notably that of Cordelia and her husband, the Gravedigger's Boy.

In Bond's play, Cordelia is transformed from the beloved daughter who, although disowned, comes to her father's aid in Shakespeare's text, to a freedom fighter who eventually gains control of Lear's country in Bond's text, thus undergoing a reverse version of Lear's journey. The Gravedigger's boy who is, arguably, a figure analogous to the Fool in Shakespeare's play, transcends this in the role Bond forges for him. As the man who, like the Fool, is present while Lear is "displaced and threatened" he, as Patricia Hern has observed "shows pity to the old man, seeming to provide an alternative to the father-child bond which has proved so damaging both to Lear and to his daughters" (Hern in Bond 1983, XL). Moreover, because the Gravedigger's boy fails to recognize the man he rescues, he also helps Bond's Lear to a growing realization of the wrongs he has done for the sake of national security. When the soldiers of Bodice and Fontanelle arrive at the Gravedigger Boy's house, they murder him, capture Lear, slaughter the pigs and rape the Boy's pregnant wife, Cordelia, before a Carpenter attempts to intervene and kills at least one of the soldiers with a blow from a chisel.

The soldiers' acts of violence and brutality conclude Act One leaving it unclear whether or not Lear and Cordelia are rescued. The death of the Gravedigger's Boy who, stage directions indicate is shot as he is enfolded in a white sheet, so that the seeping red of the blood provides an emphatic and near clichéd image of his mortality, provides a highly significant turning point for the play. As the climax to Act One, the political point of the war crimes committed by the soldiers on behalf of Bodice and Fontanelle are demonstrated through the very material results of their actions. The death of Lear's saviour and destruction of his family would have made Bond's point about the over-arching and, often, brutal control states can exert over the people subject to the controlling forces, however, he sustains and widens his analysis though two strategies. The first is to reveal that the Gravedigger Boy's wife is Cordelia – that is a usurper of Lear's role – and to establish that this link is not through patrilineage as in *King Lear*, but because of her role as leader of the civil uprising, and eventual ruler of Lear's state. Second, Bond uses the figure of the Gravedigger's Boy as a means by which Lear and the audience are confronted by the consequences of state-sponsored brutality. When read through the abject, the implicit rejection of humanity and Bond's confrontation of it is manifest.

According to Kristeva the corpse "upsets even more violently [than food loathing] the one who confronts it [....] as in true theatre, without makeup or masks, refuse and corpses *show me* what I permanently thrust aside in order to live" (3). Furthermore, she adds that:

> These body fluids, this defilement [...] are what life withstands, hardly and with difficulty, on the part of death. There, I am at the border of my condition as a living being. My body extricates itself, as being alive, from that border. Such wastes drop that I might live, until, from loss to loss, nothing remains in me and my entire body falls beyond the limit [...]. [T]he corpse, the most sickening of wastes is a border that has encroached upon everything. It is no longer I who expel, 'I' is expelled. The border has become an object. (3-4)

Through the Gravedigger's Boy, Bond offers an alternative view of the abject that mirrors the character with the device of the wall. Despite or perhaps because of his onstage death at the end of Act One, the Gravedigger's Boy returns in Acts Two and Three as a Ghost who keeps Lear company. Act Two, Scene Two is central in the staging of Lear's abjection. Lear, a prisoner of his daughters' state, is held captive in a cell after a show trial when the ghost of the Gravedigger's Boy appears to him. After asking him if he is dead, a question to which the Ghost replies in the affirmative, Lear requests that he fetch his daughters to him. The Ghost brings the daughters but, unlike his real adult daughters, they are youthful phantoms. It is only after Lear is brought face to face with his now-estranged daughters as children that he is able to confront the borders of his own condition:

LEAR.	[...] What colour's my hair?
GHOST.	White.
LEAR.	I'm frightened to look. There's blood on it where I pulled it with these hands.
GHOST.	Let me stay with you, Lear. When I died I went somewhere. I don't know where it was. I waited and nothing happened. And then I started to rot, like a body in the ground. Look at my hands, they're like an old man's. They withered. I'm young but my stomach's shrivelled up and the hair's turned white. Look, my arms! Feel how thin I am. (LEAR *doesn't move*.) Are you afraid to touch me?
LEAR.	No.
GHOST.	Feel.

LEAR.   (*Hesitates. Feels*). Yes, thin.
GHOST.   I'm afraid. Let me stay with you, keep me here, please.
LEAR.   Yes, yes, poor boy. Lie down by me. Here. I'll hold you.
             We'll help each other. Cry while I sleep, and I'll cry and
             watch you while you sleep. We'll take turns. The sound of
             the human voice will comfort us. (Bond 1983, 42)

Lear, frightened to confront his own old age, is able to confront and
eventually to touch the ghost of the Gravedigger's Boy. Through the
conjuring of the rotting, post-mortem Ghost, Bond is able to postulate an
existence beyond subjectivity. In Kristevan terms, the Ghost (and the
change of the character's name from Gravedigger's Boy to Ghost after the
end of Act One is telling) becomes a border – and "I" who is expelled as
subject and object collapse into abjection. Through Lear's embrace of the
character, Bond shows that, at least for the former king, acknowledgement
of the repressed, of that which has been thrown away is a necessary
coming to consciousness. It is only after Lear has been remade into a
Christ-like figure, preaching in parables that the character is able to
dispense with this abjected double by killing him and being killed in turn
as he tries to destroy the wall/border.

In Bond's play, the unveiling of the abject and the ability to live
without borders is staged as a theatricalized return of the repressed.
Through this play's lesson in abjection, Bond shows that a dialectics of
violence, separation and subjugation is founded on material abjection.

Blasted: (Yet another) "Disgusting Feast of Filth"[4]

In contrast to Bond's text, which is played out on a grand scale, the
dramatist Sarah Kane's professional début, *Blasted*, features a cast of just
three characters confined to a Leeds hotel room. Premièred in 1995 to a
barrage of hostile and outraged reviews, *Blasted* has been the subject of
much general controversy and, since Kane's death, reassessment and the
beginnings of canonization. Seen by Aleks Sierz as one of the signature
plays of what he terms the "in-yer-face" theatre of the 1990s, the play has
become a locus for the discussion of the resurgence of British theatre
writing during the decade. *Blasted* appears, at least on a superficial level,
to be the degree zero of abjection within contemporary British theatre. On
the one hand, as an example of in-yer-face theatre, Sierz characterizes
Blasted, along with other theatre writing from the 1990s, as:

a theatre of sensation: it jolts both actors and spectators out of
conventional responses, touching nerves and provoking alarm. Often such

drama employs shock tactics or it is shocking because it is new in tone or structure, or because it is *bolder or more experimental* than what audiences are used to. *Questioning moral norms*, it affronts ruling ideas of what can or should be shown onstage; it also taps into more primitive feelings, *smashing taboos, mentioning the forbidden, creating discomfort*. Crucially, it tells us more about who we really are. Unlike the type of theatre that allows us to sit back and contemplate what we see in detachment, the best in-yer-face theatre takes us on an emotional journey, getting under our skin. In other words it is *experiential not speculative*. (Sierz 2001, 4)

On the other, in one of the earliest pieces of analytical writing to explore Kane's *Blasted*, Mark Ravenhill's *Shopping and Fucking* and Jez Butterworth's *Mojo* (all of which are mentioned in Sierz's study), Vera Gottlieb's "Lukewarm Britannia" offers a more sceptical perspective of new writing in the 1990s. Gottlieb remarks that "I... would suggest that anything that has happened in the Nineties was less creative, positive or radical than some critics might concede, and of mixed significance. 'Cool Britannia' feels decidedly 'lukewarm'"(Gottlieb 1999, 209). Gottlieb's comment highlights a weakness inherent in Sierz's analysis: that in claiming in-yer-face as the domain of new writing, it runs the risk of considering new writers in isolation. Ultimately, *Blasted*'s status as an important piece of theatre might lie in whether Sierz's or Gottlieb's opinions on it prevail, however, for the purposes of this article, it is noteworthy that Kane's special status is not located in sophisticated dramaturgical structure but in her work's potential to disturb its audience on an emotional level. Sierz argues that what makes in-yer-face theatre distinctive is that "it affronts ruling ideas of what can or should be shown onstage; it also taps into more primitive feelings, *smashing taboos, mentioning the forbidden, creating discomfort*. Crucially, it tells us more about who we really are" (Sierz 2001, 4). When read through Kristeva's examination of the abject, however, Sierz's description of 'in-yer-face' sounds very much like a manifesto for a theatre of abjection albeit one that confronts its audiences with that which society abjects.

Reading Kane with Kristeva, it is possible to see *Blasted*'s numerous similarities with Bond's *Lear*. For instance, thematically, both plays depict a society that is breaking down around them. Both plays stage scenes in which soldiers invade the private spaces of the main characters and, brutalized themselves, inflict war crimes on civilians such as rape and murder. Kane's play, set in an expensive hotel room the kind according to her that is "so expensive it could be anywhere in the world" has a cast of characters, that in contrast, suggest a geographical locus for the action (Kane 2001, 3). Immediately, *Blasted* presents its audience with a power dynamic that is demarcated along the lines of gender and age through the characters of Cate, who is 21, and Ian who is 45 and Welsh but with a northern accent. The introduction of the Soldier with his sniper's rifle, the final character, complicates this dynamic.

Although *Lear* can read as showing the multifarious ways in which the political is personal, Kane's work draws parallels between the crimes for which the soldier is responsible and Ian's behaviour towards Cate. Like Bond, Kane opts for linear plotting but, unlike the construction of *Lear*, at least for the realist first half of the play, hers is open to reading as causal. For Kane's characters, the old feminist adage that the "personal is political" can be rewritten to the circular, nuanced and more problematic the personal is political is personal as, first Cate and then Ian, become the victims of rape. Ian, a terminally-ill victim of his own addiction to tobacco, discovers at the end of the play that, even in death, there is no peace. The character, who dies only to discover that he is still sentient, provides another point of congruence between this play and *Lear*. Kane introduces a note of humour to an otherwise unremittingly bleak end to the play; Ian's first word after death is "Shit" (60).

IAN.   *Laughing hysterically.*
Darkness.
Light.
IAN.   *Having a nightmare.*
Darkness.
Light.
IAN.   *Crying huge, bloody tears.*
He is hugging the SOLDIER'S *body for comfort.*
Darkness.
Light.
IAN.   *Lying very still, weak with hunger.*
Darkness.
Light.
IAN.   *Tears the cross out of the ground, rips up the floor and lifts the baby's*
        body out.
        He eats the baby.
        He puts the remains back in the baby's blanket and puts the bundle
        back in the hole.
        A beat, then he climbs in after it and lies down, head poking out of the
        floor.
        He dies with relief.
        It starts to rain on him, coming through the roof.
        Eventually.
IAN.   Shit. (59—60)

If the main body of the play, and especially its second half, confronts its audience with many encounters with the abject, the pattern of occurrence differs from that of Bond. Whereas the first half of *Blasted* at least suggests the possibility of a return to normality and a life beyond the Leeds hotel room for Cate, the play's end closes this possibility down through its acceleration of pace and the depiction of the characters' inability to maintain the borders of abjection. Thus, in the final three scenes, that is, scenes Three, Four and Five, the soldier sucks out Ian's eyes and eats them before killing himself with the gun. The soldier remains on stage until the end of the play. Cate enters with a baby who is in need of food. Clueless in matters of childcare, she asks Ian what she should do to look after the child but he is more concerned with getting her to shoot him. When Cate relents and gives him the gun, she removes the bullets. His response to his own failure to commit suicide is the remark "fuck" and, on Cate discovering that, in the interim, the baby has died, to offer the comment "Lucky bastard" (56—7). Cate's attempt to respect the boundaries between life and death indicated in her prevention of Ian's suicide, surfaces once more in the manner in which she buries the baby under the floorboards and her regret in not knowing the child's name to mark the grave. Her abandonment of Ian, now blind and dying, to find food is a much more pragmatic move Kane implies, since it will involve Cate fraternizing with soldiers. Kane's stage directions at this point work to create a sense of time passing as Ian remains on stage through a series of lights up and down. In the moments between the blackouts, Ian masturbates, attempts to strangle himself, defecates, hugs the dead soldier's body for comfort, removes the body of the baby from under the floorboards and eats it. It is only after he has placed what remains of the baby back under the floorboards that he dies. On her return to the hotel room, Cate eats the food and drinks gin before passing the remainder to the dead but sentient Ian, who thanks her. The in-built ambiguity of Kane's stage directions in this concluding sequence mean that, in performance, Ian's death may not be conveyed to an audience since the character appears to be sentient and the actor continues to act after the event. Such a dramaturgical device, through its very ambiguity, opens up the possibility of a non-mimetic representation of abjection through its rejection of the very theatrical conventions that signal the border between being and non-being.

Moreover, this final section of *Blasted* presents an encounter with the abject that stages its threat towards individual life as a relentless onslaught. In it, Kane's characters display abjection as a state of mind, through humiliation and as the condition under which they only barely survive.

Like the Gravedigger's Boy, Ian is allowed no release from his suffering in death but, unlike Bond's Lear, Cate shows no recognition at the end of the play that Ian has made the transition from living being to "I" as border. In Ian, Kane has created a character whose rejection of the borders and ability to live beyond abjection is not so much transcendence but an acceptance of it. He departs from Kristeva's theorization of the corpse as abject because, in his sentience, he is both all border and unbounded. Unlike the Gravedigger Boy, Ian's state of utter abjection is not followed by catharsis but by further abjection. Cate's final act of feeding Ian – normally a life-giving act – at the play's end becomes an act of recognition or acceptance of the abjected as the human condition.

* * * * *

In her study, Kristeva identified literature as a privileged signifier of the abject (207—8). Her reason that "[b]ecause it occupies its [the sacred] place, because it decks itself out in the sacred power of horror, literature may also involve *not an ultimate resistance to* an unveiling of the abject: an elaboration, a discharge, and a hollowing out of abjection through the crisis of the Word" leaves itself open to elaboration (208). Theatre, because it works through numerous channels of communication and offers its audience the potential for a group or tribal experience as well an individual one, has an even greater potential as a safe site to unveil and negotiate the abject. Thus, if literature, according to Kristeva, offers "a hollowing out of abjection through the crisis of the Word", theatre has the potential to offer a simulation (and hence safe) or rehearsal of the human encounter with the abject. Like literature, theatre does not necessarily offer a site of resistance but, instead, has the potential to diminish or amplify its powers of horror through repetition. Theatre's visceral and live nature allows the unspeakable to be articulated and the inhuman to be embodied. Theatre opens up the potential for the ritualized encounter with the powers of horror a presentation of scenes of disgust. Its power of simulation as aural, visual and visceral offers the scene of disgust as a political, didactic or even emotional message. In confronting the simulation, theatre signals that the power of horror is best encountered through the rehearsal of its ritualized other of fictional representation and allows its audience, Like Bond's Lear, Ibsen's Mrs Alving and Kane's Cate the force of abjection.

Kane's bleak view of human existence and the pain of civil war presents a means by which to theorize the abject in the theatre more widely. Ultimately, the import of Kane's play is not simply the over-determination of the abject – an opportunity to confront and wallow in the powers of horrors *par excellence* although it can (and from the reviews of its première does fulfil this function). The special status of *Blasted* as a curious hybrid – at once half realist and a rejection of its conventions – means that it is a significant object of an enquiry in abjection and theatrical convention. Whereas, Ibsen's combination of subject matter and theatrical convention position the audience as the abjected non-other of performance that in turn abjects, Bond's Epic theatre model rejects the conventions of realism and naturalism implicitly. Kane, in contrast, draws attention to the constructedness of theatricality, that is, a ritualizing of representation. Within its superficially naïve construction, *Blasted* presents the potential for the simulation to itself become the power of horror through the classic realist narrative and conventions.[5] In Kane's dramaturgy – here and within the rest of her *œuvre* – realism and its conventions are positioned as the abject. In expelling realism in such an explosive fashion, Kane raises the spectre of a poetics of abjection and, in so doing, provides a bridge to, or permeable border between realism and non-realist representation.

Notes

1 See, for example George Bernard Shaw's *The Quintessence of Ibsenism*.
2 For a detailed discussion of the two-part nature of the play's construction, see, for example, Graham Saunders, *'Love Me or Kill Me': Sarah Kane and the Theatre of Extremes*, (Manchester: MUP, 2002) 40-50. Saunders also notes Kane's indebtedness to Ibsen's *Ghosts* and, in particular the manner that Osvald's illness is reworked in Ian's terminal cancer.
3 See, Jenny S. Spencer, *Dramatic Strategies in the Plays of Bond*, (Cambridge: Cambridge UP, 1992). Spencer's chapter on *Lear* discusses the various ways that Bond's play concretizes themes such as blindness and insight present in Shakespeare's play.
4 The quotation is from Jack Tinker's review of *Blasted* in the *Daily Telegraph*. For a discussion of the play's initial reception see Tom Sellar. 1996. 'Truth and dare: Sarah Kane's *Blasted* in *Theater* 1: 29—34.
5 For a discussion of the classic realist narrative structure see, Catherine Belsey, 'Constructing the Subject: Deconstructing the Text.' *Feminist Criticism and Social Change: Sex, Class and Race in Literature and Culture*. Ed. Judith Newton and Deborah Rosenfelt. London: Methuen, 1985.

Bibliography

Aristotle. 1999. *Poetics*. Trans. Kenneth McLeish. London: Nick Hern.
Belsey, Catherine. 1985. Construction the subject: Deconstructing the text.
    In *Feminist Criticism and social change: Sex, class, and race in
    literature and culture.* ed. Judith Newton and Deborah Rosenfelt.
    London: Methuen.
Bond, Edward. 1983. *Lear*. London: Methuen.
Gottlieb, Vera. 1999. Lukewarm Britannia. In *Theatre in a cool climate*.
    ed. Vera Gottlieb and Colin Chambers. Oxford: Amber Lane.
Hay, Malcolm, and Philip Roberts. 1978. *Edward Bond: A companion to
    the plays*. London: TQ Publications.
Ibsen, Henrik. 1964. *Ghosts.* In *Ghosts and other plays*. Trans. Peter
    Watts. Harmondsworth: Penguin.
Kane, Sarah. 2001. *Blasted*. In *Complete plays*. London: Methuen.
Kristeva, Julia. 1982. *Powers of horror: An essay on abjection*. Trans.
    Leon S. Roudiez. New York: Columbia University Press.
Marker, Frederick J. and Lise-Lone Marker. 1989. *Ibsen's lively art: A
    performance study of the major plays.* Cambridge: Cambridge
    University Press.
Saunders, Graham. 2002. *'Love me or kill me': Sarah Kane and the
    theatre of extremes*. Manchester: Manchester University Press.
Seller, Tom. 1996. Truth and dare: Sarah Kane's *Blasted. Theater* 1: 29-
    34. Sierz, Aleks. 2001. *In-yer-face theatre: British drama today*.
    London: Faber.
Girard, René. 1988. *Violence and the scared*. Trans. Patrick Gregory.
    London and New York: Continuum.
Spencer, Jenny S. 1992. *Dramatic strategies in the plays of Bond*.
    Cambridge: Cambridge University Press.
Worthen, W. B. 1992. *Modern drama and the rhetoric of theater*. Berkley
    and Los Angeles, USA and Oxford, UK: University of California
    Press.

CHAPTER THREE

LILJA BLUMENFELD

"SHAKESPEARE'S VENICE IMAGINED: BETWEEN LOCAL, FOREIGN, AND GLOBAL"

> "The act of imagination, [...], is a magical act. It is an incantation destined to make the object of one's thought, the thing one desires, appear in such a way that one can take possession of it. There is always, in that act something of the imperious and the infantile, a refusal to take account of distance and difficulties."
> —J. P. Sartre *The Imaginary*

If in general terms, 'local' means *here*, 'foreign' roughly signifies *there*, and 'global' refers *anywhere*, the city of Venice manifests itself as *in between*, it belongs to an unidentified *elsewhere*. There is no proper view we can define as Venice, its essence remains out of sight, unstable and utterly performative—the view of Venice is always already blurred. The city presents itself to the gaze of the spectator as an ongoing masquerade, manifesting its carnivalesque ambivalence. In the carnivalized world everything is suspended, everything already contains its potential opposite. I argue that in imaginary Venice, real Venice is always already included, just as the former is exclusively included in the latter; the 'local', the 'foreign' as well as the 'global' co-exist in different modalities of its being.

In *The Merchant of Venice* by Shakespeare, the enigmatic city of Venice is represented together with another imaginary place called Belmont. As a metadiegetic supplement and oppositional mirror image to the first, Belmont is included and needs some attention. In many ways, these places are bonded to each other as binary oppositions, and between them, there seems to exist what Emmanuel Levinas calls a 'bottomless difference.' Looking at some scenographic (re)-presentations of Venice and Belmont through the visual history of the play, I would like to focus on some aspects of 'imaginary' and 'real' in relation to the notions of 'local,' 'foreign,' and 'global'. I am applying Sartre's description of the 'imaginary' in order to see in what ways these notions are connected to each other in Shakespeare's Venice imagined.

I have chosen five productions to illustrate my argument. The first production presents the places of the play as embodied imaginary sites on a three-stage system in a conventional theatre space; the second is a site-specific performance located in real Venice—it applies the imaginary reality of the play to the real locale. The third production offers an imaginative theatrical setting of real Venice in a silent film format; the fourth is applying real, but imagined historical time to the imaginary reality of the play, suggesting a representation of Venice and Belmont as foreign places in a globally consumable format. The fifth production explores the ways in which the imaginary universe of the play is represented in the purpose-built theatre without visually representing the locale. In this paper, I am thus using examples from theatre as well as from film productions to illustrate the argument.

Venice: Imaginary, Imagined, and Real

Imaginary places do not exist anywhere else than in one's imagination, namely, 'elsewhere,' and it is difficult to capture the 'where'. An imaginary object does not have a substantial place of its own other than in the mind of the imager. An imaginary object itself is a kind of simulacrum, which simulates its very being, flattering the mind and undermining the sense of reality of the one who imagines.

In our imagination, we can travel far-and-wide without limits and imagine objects both imaginary and real. As Sartre in his *Imaginary*, a seminal insight to consciousness and imagination, has put it, "every consciousness posits its object, but each in its own way." Perception posits its object as existing and the image always includes an act of belief or a positional act. According to Sartre, such an **act** [my emphasis] can take four different forms: "it can posit the object as *non-existent*, as *absent*, or as existing *elsewhere*, [but] it can also *neutralize* itself, which is to say *not posit its object as existent*." (2004, 183)

The **non-existent object** is thus the one which does not exist, but which we can imagine using our imagination as a vehicle to create the most fantastic imaginary objects. This kind of object is for example Shakespeare's imaginary island in the *Tempest* or his imaginary Belmont in which the characters of *The Merchant of Venice* move and the famous casket scenes take place. Secondly, we can imagine objects which are **absent** from our perception and sight, and which we cannot reach because of their remoteness or our own limited access to these places. We can redeem our desire for these objects by positing them in our imagination. They are places we have seen or been to and which we want to recapture and hold. In our imagination these places appear as reality. A famous tourist site, for example, we can visit or revisit in our minds, but we can, similarly, imagine something which is missing from our lives and which we otherwise desire, a dinner at a very expensive restaurant, living in a *palazzo*, or a cruise to an exotic island. We can similarly imagine a special someone as an imaginary object of desire. The ideal object is not a real one and it exists in a magical elsewhere, and to this '*elsewhere*' we do not have any immediate access. *Elsewhere* transcends any places that are known, as it is mostly an unknown terrain; as imagers we have a very vague idea of *elsewhere* which must exist somewhere, but *where* exactly? Shakespeare's Illyria, Bithynia, and Bohemia have clearly a certain foreignness to them and seem to be displaced from their original sites. For example, Shakespeare's Bohemia has a seashore which real Bohemia could just dream of. The places of his plays appear both familiar and strange at the same time, positing themselves as what Freud called uncanny – the familiar transformed into the strange. This strangeness is common to all Shakespeare's plays in which the mythical, the imaginary and the real sites merge in a cunning way, creating another and scandalous imagery. Shakespeare's places are simultaneously existent and non-existent, foreign and local, imaginary and real. *Elsewhere* is the term which most precisely describes the task of scenography, it is to shift the locale from its origins and give it back to the spectator in a transformed imaginary format.

Finally, what Sartre means by *not positing its object as existent* describes an act of disbelief, which, in a way, is an intentional act of repression and silence: there is something to be denied, repressed, and silenced, which we would not like to be brought to mind, reminding us of the clinical state of aphasia.

I would now like to apply these notions to Venice and see if there is a pattern to follow. In order to say anything certain about Venice as a locale, we need to specify certain aspects of it. We can say that Venice exists in two distinct modes, first, as a real place, a well-known tourist attraction, and secondly as a famous fictional locale, which has caught the imagination of many artists and writers including Shakespeare, most prominently in *The Merchant of Venice*. We are conscious of Venice being there as such and we may well ask what it means.

As imagers, we can imagine and have a mental image of both, imaginary and real Venice. Being inhabitants of the real world, we can perceive the city of Venice on site through the intentional act of traveling there, or we can look at the images of Venice on photographs, drawings and paintings, capturing the place in imaginative mind. We have thus a good reason to believe that Venice *exists*. Through the act of visual perception, the real city of Venice offers itself to the one who perceives. There are a number of books written on Venice and dozens of films made on site, plus the infinite number of paintings, *capricci*, and photographs made on the theme: the mere body of work dedicated to Venice seems to prove its very existence.

Yet, one may also believe that Venice does not exist. Let us take the first of the four positional acts of belief, the *non-existence*, and look at Venice from without. It is somewhat hard to believe the city exists since it is springing up as if out of the blue [sea], and together with its mirror image in the lagoon, looks much more like a phantom of a city than a real one. Cities do not usually look like that. Venice thus undermines all our previous knowledge of cities as more or less stable entities, which should be somehow captured and measured.

On the other hand, the *absence* of Venice from its own site is rather obvious. The Venice trodden by its foreign visitors does not seem to be the real one. The houses suffer of severe dilapidation, the whole site is visibly falling apart and one knows that it is seriously sinking and will soon be taken over by sea. Once a year, at carnival time, the masked face of Venice in its motley and golden disguise is presented to the hungry eye of a tourist. The act of concealment of the other and the suspension of laws is reiterated year by year. From the very beginning of its history, Venice has been displaced from its *locale*, its own absence being disguised by its phantom-like presence.

The *neutralizing* act Sartre is telling us about is the most mysterious one; it is not to posit an object as existent. It is difficult to believe that something so well known as Venice does not exist; thus, by intentionally not thinking of Venice as existent it still exists. The mere negation of Venice thus becomes the very proof of its reality. As Edmund Husserl put it, "there exists nothing that does not exist." Positing Venice *elsewhere*, we also intentionally suspend our disbelief, transcending the possibility of the 'local' and entering into the impossibility of the 'foreign and strange'.

This Venice as *elsewhere* should interest us most. It is the Venice Shakespeare was writing about in his plays, most importantly in *The Merchant of Venice*. In Shakespeare's Venice, the notion of 'elsewhere' as 'foreign' manifests its presence through the famous stranger-characters, such as Shylock, Jessica, Morocco, and Arragon. Then there are the characters that do not personally appear on the scene, but are described to the audience in the mocking scene with Portia and Nerissa, namely, the unfortunate suitors who have to leave without the prize of Portia's hand. Not unlike in a popular joke, these characters are a German, an Englishman, and a Frenchman, explicitly despised by the leading lady. Those other characters, who could as well be called 'voyagers' (Gillies 1994, 3), come from the distant lands far outside the borders of fictional Venice. Their function in the play is to manifest the barbarian, the savage, and the wild as opposed to the local genteel best represented by the manically depressed homosexual Antonio and a young but handsome spendthrift Bassanio.

Antonio's yearnings for distant lands are fulfilled by his argosies, which travel far and wide, his maritime trade "hath an argosy bound to Tripolis, another to the Indies... a third/ at Mexico, a fourth for England, and other ventures" [...] (1.3.17-21), and he is defeated when learning that his ships do not return from "Lisbon, Barbary, and India, [...]"(3.2.265-9). As John Gillies has noted, *The Merchant of Venice* is centred roughly in the same Mediterranean geography, but not the same Mediterranean world. In order to understand the imaginary [fictional] Venice we will need to posit it on the mental map of the imagined universe of the play.

Venice: The Local

German director and theatre innovator Max Reinhardt staged *The Merchant of Venice* several times with different actors in the role of Shylock (Schildkraut, Basserman, Moissi, *et al*). The play underwent eight different productions between 1905 and 1934. Max Reinhardt, as the rest of theatre reformers of the day, wanted to re-theatricalize theatre and was dreaming of reuniting the actors and the spectators into "a one festive community." (Fischer-Lichte 1999, 169) Mysteriously, Reinhardt seemed to be openly obsessed with the play, which in German theatre was usually treated as the tragedy of a Jewish moneylender. However, these varied mountings of the play also demonstrate the development of Reinhardt as a director and the use of Venice as a scenographic site, and it seems that the major factor was the city of Venice itself. Arthur Kahane, Reinhardt's collaborator has written that:

> The hero, focal point, heart and essence of this performance is Venice. Not Shylock, but Venice. [...] A city, which believes it is a capital and centre of the world. The home of culture and intellectuals, university of *savoir vivre* and elegance, immersed in splendor and sun, flooded with music. And, of course, flooded with sadness and melancholy, since they are inseparably connected with joy, flooded with seriousness and sin, which

alas, though so beautiful, are so impregnated with inevitable fate. Venice with its hidden corners, bridges, squares and narrow alleyways, where cheerful calls echo across the water, is a loud, merry, humorous, wonderful being." (Fischer-Lichte 1999, 170)

Fischer-Lichte argues that instead of presenting a reading of the play, what Reinhardt presented and realized was a new concept of theatre. Yet, this new concept demanded a new way of perception and reception from the spectator. Everything had an immediate and strong appeal to the spectator's senses, so that they "sensed the atmosphere physically, they were drawn into it, became immersed in it." (Fischer-Lichte 1999, 175)

Reinhardt redefined theatre as "a game whose rules are set up by the stage director and the actors but which could be renegotiated by the spectators." The play is just "a material with which the actors and spectators play." A play is thus "just a trigger that sets the theatrical imagination of the stage director and the actors in motion without guiding, let alone controlling them in the ways they choose." (Fischer-Lichte 1999, 176) The spectators willingly accepted the rules of the game, the title of which was imaginary Venice—the absent Renaissance world was applied and superimposed to the present reality of the city.

According to Fischer-Lichte, Reinhardt used two devices to achieve his goals: the first one was to create an atmosphere and the second one to expose the performance's theatricality. The critics noted the "touch of Venice" and the "magic of atmosphere." An eyewitness, Alfred Klaar described "the narrow Venetian alleys with their atmospheric vistas, the mosaics and statues of saints at the front of gloomy palaces, the tight-packed architecture and the small daringly curved bridges." (Fischer-Lichte 1999, 172) Danish critic Georges Brandes wrote that the scenes made the audience realize "the impetuous festive spirit of the early Renaissance" and that "the stage pictures were reminders of paintings by Carpaccio, [...] Bellini, [...] Bordone, or [...] Veronese." (Fischer-Lichte 1999, 172)

Berliner Volks-Zeitung of the day wrote that:

"The Renaissance-it glowed everywhere in rich colours, in the fullness of life and happiness: Renaissance in the magnificent, cheery halls of Belmont castle, where the rich, graceful, brilliant Portia holds court surrounded by pleasure and games, and is hotly pursued by princes from all the nations in the world! Renaissance is the secluded corner of the lagoon city. Richly dressed Venetian youths warm themselves on sun-drenched piazzas; [...] the night throbs to the tempting sounds of the guitar, serenades sing out, carnivalesque and masked figures fit over jetties and bridges to the flickering light of torches...[...]"(Fischer-Lichte 1999, 172-3)

In various designs for the play Reinhardt continued to use the original concept of the stage, which he believed to be a realistic presentation of real Venice. In the first versions of the play designers Emil Orlik (1905) and Ernst Stern (1913) both made an attempt to create a 3-dimensional version of Venice and, using the system of the *Drehbühne*, to accommodate the whole universe of the play on the turntable of the proscenium arched theatre. Now not only the actors moved, but also the set. The revolving stage allowed quick change of scenes, and dictated the pace and rhythm of the performance. On the other hand, it was noted by critics that it was the acting that influenced the high temperature of performance mostly.

While Orlik's designs struggled with the logic of the sequence and failed to avoid multiple blackouts in order to rebuild the setting, Stern in his later design versions managed to develop a set that was penetrable all throughout the play without blackouts interrupting the flow of the scenes. According to Frederick Tollini it was "a moving cityscape through which the actors might wend their way from scene to scene." (Tollini 2004, 58) As a collage of realistic sites clustered unrealistically and in a somewhat impressionistic way on a *Drehbühne*, a threestage turntable, the setting continued the long tradition of *capricci*, a term that is normally applied to fantasy images of Venice by painters.

In Orlik's version, the "Venetian world was realistically presented, but not in historic detail, the design was not an attempt at historicism, but rather the three-dimensional Venice everyone imagined. [...] The partial view of "the Venice that was" evoked in its scenic integrity the entire imaginary world found in the eye and the mind of the beholder." (Tollini 2004, 60) In design versions by both designers, Reinhardt presented an imaginary and compressed city as the replica of both fantasy place and real Venice. In Orlik's case, "an attempt was made to represent the decadent state of Venetian buildings by painting bricks where plaster has fallen away, the weathering of stone, stains and cracks around windows, etc.," yet the scenes "do not form a continuous spatial composition." (Tollini 2004, 61) The imaginary Venice thus flirted with the real, without ever achieving the reality as well as ambiguity of the latter.

The imaginary Venice by Reinhardt was completed in the minds of the spectators, whose imagination already contained personal images of the city. That is why a critic Siegfried Jacobsohn was not happy with the setting by Ernst Stern and condemned it for being depressing; among his other accusations he complained that "the city seemed not like Venice but like Bruges, the City of the Dead." (Tollini 2004, 63-64) Despite all the critique towards Reinhardt, his staging was far ahead of his time and comparable with the experiments of Edward Gordon Craig and Adolphe Appia. His productions of the *MOV* influenced the silent films of the era without themselves being expressionistic but rather impressionistic in style. His introduction of a supplementary scene in which Shylock discovers his daughter's elopement and contemplates an empty house has become almost a natural part of productions ever since including the recent film by Michael Radford.

In 1934, Max Reinhardt, who already had a history of directing site specific productions in Germany, staged *The Merchant of Venice* in the real *locale* of Venice as part of the *Festival Internazionale del Teatro di Proza*. The setting was the Campo Santo Trovaso, which was arranged for the occasion, and in which "actual *palazzi,* canals, and bridges of Venice were used for the setting" (Tollini 2004, 59)The audience was seated on wooden benches facing the house of Shylock and had a church building of San Trovaso on the left hand side and Rio degli Ognisanti on the opposite. A small Venetian bridge led to the other side of the canal to the doorstep of Shylock. The performance took place at night using artificial light, [*a la*] Renaissance costumes, and featured all-Italian cast. The scenes were acted out both in the streets and within the interiors of the house. The spectators were thus positioned as voyeurs in the night peeping into the windows of a private property. They saw Shylock entering the house and then they saw the same character through the window opening the drawers and moving the furniture. In the next scene, he appeared at the balcony, tearing at his clothes and moaning "Jessica!!!" Then they saw him rushing back to the bridge agonizing for his daughter and his ducats until his breakdown. After the intermission, other parts of the environment were used and Belmont scenes were acted by setting out the table with the caskets and lining up the torchbearers along the canal; Prince Arragon arrived on a barque majestically gliding down the canal. The environment was artistically and performatively exhausted and every corner of the square was used. The spectators placed in a real environment of Venice had become an inevitable part of the imaginary locale. The performative element of Venice magnified the performative element of the play's setting. As Fischer-Lichte put it: "Performing Venice, here, meant to let the city take part in the performance, to let it – so to speak –act itself." (Fischer-Lichte 1999, 178)

In the earlier Reinhardt-productions in Germany and later in real Venice, the centre and the heart of the setting was Shylock's house, which was zoomed out of the scenery and made the central site of the play. This, of course, could not have been an accident. Reinhardt as foreigner and a Jew directed a play about a genuine absent other, a wandering Jew and a stranger coming from *elsewhere* and belonging *nowhere*. Just as Shylock in Venice, Reinhardt himself was inclusively excluded within his local society. By turning down the "Aryanship" offered to him by German authorities, a gesture which also echoes the enforced "Christianization" of Shylock, he was deprived of his theatres and became a barbarian and a foreigner in his own country. However, theatre itself and its performative expressions seemed to be more important to him than making any political allusions in his production to Germany of the time.

Staging an imaginary city and using the real locale of Venice, Reinhardt successfully combined the **impossible** of imaginary geography with the **possible** of the real site, mapping the play out on the streets of Venice thus morphing them into imaginary streets. With this gesture, he also [ab] used the real city of Venice, reasserting a myth that the particular story of a Jewish moneylender, indeed, happened in real Venice.

Venice: The Foreign

In what ways, then, is Venice posited as a foreign object? The actors/directors of the nineteenth-century theatre were obsessed to apply real history to imaginary places. In case of imagined locale, the applied history when well researched can help us to reconstruct a new continuum in the mind's eye of the observant spectator, implying a touch of the real necessary to make the incredible fictional world accessible to the observer and credible as real. For example, Charles Kean, whose lavish and historically over-designed Shakespeare productions devoured the visually hungry eyes of mid-nineteenth century spectators, provided them with desired experience. Sir Henry Irving, who did his best to make the visual extravaganza of his productions compatible with the brand-new attractions provided by the emerging film industry, also served the insatiable voyeuristic imagination of the unnamed but numerous 19th century spectators by mounting a motion picture on sixteenth century Venice. As Nicholas Vardac wrote, "such techniques, cinematically conceived and three-dimensionally executed, carried pictorial staging into areas and levels earmarked for the screen" (Vardac 1987, 96)

This kind of stage Shakespeare wrote for and the dramatic technique, which it occasioned, was closer to film than in most periods of dramatic composition. He could use as many scenes as he wanted, could change locales freely, could cover intervals of time. So could film, with its mobility and its flashbacks. (Vardac 1987, 301)

Silent film created an enormous audience, and a potentially large audience for Shakespeare. Those who could not afford to go to theatre went to the cinema. As Vardac has put it, "some of them learned for the first time that Shakespeare was not a far-away figure in the distant past, but a man who wrote good stories about interesting people wrapped in varied atmosphere. The spectators could see Venice, the Forest of Arden, even fairyland, and the sea coast of Bohemia. They could witness the performance of actors and actresses they had only heard about, or see the old familiar faces of the screen smiling and lowering". (Vardac 1987, 302) Despite the fact that silent film, which was not considered an art form or even a good entertainment, often lacking the quality of a theatrical performance, and full of ridiculous moments, movement and gesticulation, it was the necessary preparation for something else. "Shakespeare was to suffer another sea-change, not always rich and sometimes strange, but with infinite possibilities." (Vardac 1987, 302)

In silent film *Der Kaufmann von Venedig* (1923) with Werner Krauss as Mordecai/Shylock, the German version of the play was using a different storyline and different names for the characters, at the same time applying some of the motifs from the original narrative sources Shakespeare had used for his *Merchant*. According to the introduction to the film, "the original Florentine tale by John of Florence (Ser Giovanni Fioretino) had been slightly modified to not offend the modern standard of good taste." The famous casket scenes were cut out entirely and Belmont thus stripped of its magic. On the other hand, the film introduces a sequence of invented scenes, such as the one in which Mordecai's wife dies in a heart attack while trying to persuade the debtors to return their debts. There is a scene in which Rachela/Jessica returns home for her mother's funeral, but is rejected by her father; or the suicide of Eliah, an invented suitor and bridegroom to Rachela.

The film (a copy is kept at the British Film Archive, consisting of six reels) is utterly melodramatic. In *Kaufmann*, both the tragic and the ridiculous are intertwined. The same applies to *The Jew of Mestri*, the British version of the same film, 1923 in which the real Venice is flattened out on the screen and presented to the spectator in a black and white silently expressive mode. Belmont is as real as Venice in this film and seems to be just off-Venice, somewhere on the shores of mainland Italy.

The characters of the film are wearing costumes inspired by paintings of Paolo Veronese, and the palace of Portia with its rows of phallic columns looks like a dark forest of the unconscious in which the decent daughter is trapped and imprisoned by her dead father, otherwise reminding us of any interior of a rich Renaissance household. The film is at pains to depict feasting and revelling. Masked characters carry inventive costumes and create the atmosphere of decadence around them. The chiaroscuro images of real Venice are powerful and close-ups of the suffering faces of the characters are moving in a melodramatic sense. The film is very inventive, but very long. The German actors in the roles of Shylock [Mordecai], Tubal, Jessica [Rachela], her Mother [According to Shakespeare, Shylock's wife Leah was supposed to be dead already!] and other central parts manifest their foreignness in a foreign realm, deepened by black and white imperative frames. This film is conscious of the heritage of Eisenstein and the expressionist movement; the frames are artistically constructed and well balanced; the lack of speech enhances the power of expression through imagery and gesture. What is presented here is the manifestation of the imaginary, the meta-materiality of absence and the uncanny presence of the foreign. Venice as a well-known site is transformed by the simple use of frames and the *noir* quality of the film. The Venice we perceive is not the real one, nor the imaginary, but embraces the magic of *elsewhere*.

In *The Merchant of Venice* (2004), a film with Al Pacino starring as Shylock, the action takes place in fictional Venice as conceived by its authors using a certain visual code, namely, the year 1598. This particular year is suggesting the representation of Venice at a particular point in time. The concept of creating an imaginary continuum [chronotope] of the film by applying a certain year to it, mocks the Real of the reality and very much reminds us of the 19th century obsession to apply the aesthetics of real history to imaginary places. Most of the scenes of the film were shot on location in the real city of Venice at the beginning of the twenty-first century, another continuum hidden underneath the historical one, and thus by layering the imaginary, the imagined, and the real city, a unique universe of the film was created. In doing this, director Michael Radford made a gesture quite similar to Max Reinhardt, but taking it a step further and recording it in a different medium. Visual representation of Venice as a locale in this film is the most impressive and highly artistic one, colour code controlled and well researched. In this case, the film itself is accessible anywhere in the world, the imagined, fictionally created and realistically posited Venice is globally dispensed. On the screen where the visual drama unfolds, the non-presence of the real is replaced by the scandalous presence of irreal, this Venice is compressed and spread out anywhere in the world: thus the *elsewhere* overlaps with the *anywhere*, in this case, the global. To apply a real history to the imaginary one is an attempt to blur the distinction between one and the other, it similarly blurs the boundaries between the *local* and the *foreign*; on one hand it is posited as the 'wonderful' of the neighbourhood, on the other as the 'weird' of a remote otherness. In Radford's *Merchant*, the foreign trade is physically present within the local shores and offered to the spectator with cinematic credibility and visual abundance. The character of Shylock is presented as a genuine other, a stranger, and a ravenous bloodthirsty beast, most dreaded foreigner who raises his whetted knife and holds it high above the bare bosom of the representative of the local Christian 'tribe', who in this case is embodied by Jeremy Irons. With this potential act of violence, Shylock intends to cut out part of the identity of its opponent in order to embrace and appropriate its mirror image. The act of cutting, which does not happen in front of the eyes of the spectator, nor takes place behind the scene, is imagined, dreaded, and fulfilled in the minds of the characters, as well as the audience. The nature of this impotent act is both tragic and utterly ridiculous, which lends a hand to melodrama and the melodramatic tradition. The recent *Merchant of Venice* is another proof that the intrinsic need for melodrama still exists in the minds of the spectators seated in darkness in numerous cinemas of the world. It also demonstrates the unfulfilled desire to be willingly displaced from *here* to *there*, or *elsewhere*. The imaginary is indeed a discrete place into which each one of us can project our desires. The projected desires bounce back to the spectators in the dark cinemas all over the Globe.

Venice: The Global

Shakespeare's *Globe*, positioned in the locality of Southwark, itself already includes the notion of the global in terms of representing the world. The contemporaries of Shakespeare most likely read the Globe Theatre in terms of the *theatrum mundi*, and the analogy between *theatrum* and *mundus* would have worked both ways. As John Gillies in *Shakespeare and the Geography of Difference* has put it, "the world was a theatre in the sense of its delusiveness and emptiness. [...] For its part, the theatre was a world in the sense of the microcosm's epitomisation of the macrocosm. (Gillies 1994, 76)

Theatrum mundi as 'worldly theatre' thus seems to express metaphorically both the theatre seen as the world and the world seen as theatre. The latter is the Renaissance convention of looking at the map of the world as the equivalent of theatre with theatrical description of events accompanying the maps in verbal or visual form. The theatre and its architecture posit themselves as geographic as well as cosmographic entities. *Theatrum* consisted of the spherical (but earthly) auditorium with a celestial audience floating high above looking down at the mundane scene below. According to Gillies, "For all its apparently purely abstract and moral significance, the *theatrum mundi* provides a conceptual mediation between the discourses of Theatre and Geography in Shakespeare's period." (Gillies 1994, 79) The scene, which most likely represented the miseries of human life and bestial wonders of the world was witnessed by God's eye just like the Renaissance maps of the world, which celebrated God as an eternal witness and spectator to fooleries of humankind. The *mundus* would then mean the earth and *theatrum* the whole universe, a hierarchical system topped up with God's eye. Visibility to God was considered essential; it was the eye of God, which cast its glance from *elsewhere*. In *Theatre of the World* Frances Yates has written that,

> "The Globe theatre was a magical theatre, a cosmic theatre, a religious theatre, an actor's theatre, designed to give fullest support to the voices and gestures of the players as they enacted th drama of the life of man within the Theatre of the World... His theatre would have been for Shakespeare the pattern of the universe, the idea of the Macrocosm, the world stage on which the Microcosm acted his parts. All the world's a stage. [...] (Yates 1987, 189, in Gillies 1994, 91)

The concept of the cosmic theatre was thus known to Shakespeare and "was present in the form of the ancient/medieval discourse of the *theatrum mundi*, as well as in the form of a contemporary dialogue with the new geography which, like Elizabethan theatre, was attempting to constitute itself as 'theatre of the world' in the ancient cosmic sense." (Gillies 1994, 90)

In the replica space of Shakespeare's Globe, which had not been around for 350 years, nobody knew exactly how this kind of space actually would work as a performance space. No one really knew how to create the imaginary reality and to act out the truth of the situation between the characters within this highly decorated and coded space, not forgetting the audience seated on the three sides, and up in the galleries. The space has thus been subject to constant experiment through the last ten years.

There is not much evidence left behind to inform us as to how and by what means Shakespeare's Venice as *topos* was re-presented to its audiences. As the recent experiments with new/old performance space at the reconstructed Globe on the South Bank of London have proved, the stage seems to have had at least three hot spots within which the potential (and imaginary) geographical locations were created by merely [re-] positioning the actors. The very centre of the stage is the most important

position in terms of visibility, the other two spots are placed just in front of
the two cheerfully painted columns. The area between the two columns is
known as 'valley of death', a line most weakening the position of the
actors or entirely annulling their efforts. 'Valley of death' could thus mean
positing the actors to *nowhere*. The three spots again could have been
understood as *here* as well as *anywhere*. All possible locales could be
imagined using the knowledge of the space, which has yet to be
rediscovered at the reconstructed space of the Globe. The three openings,
which enact in the space as entrances and exits, become geographical
locales in the mental map of the performance space if necessary. In the
Globe, the 'foreign' as simple *there* thus begins right behind the door;
entering any single opening could mean either a symbolic gesture of
stepping from *here* straight into *nowhere* or *elsewhere* in the fictional
world with its imaginary geography; it could also just mean *next door*. The
use of space at the Globe is as multidimensional as universe itself and the
space embraces the diversity of the audience and the performers into the
one unified whole.

In 1998, *The Merchant of Venice* was staged at the newly reconstructed
Globe theatre for the first time. It was a *commedia dell arte*-production
with the professional clown Marcello Magni in the cast as Lancelot
Gobbo, and Norbert Kentrup, a German actor as Shylock. With this move,
the director Richard Olivier has applied a system of double alienation, the
moneylender as a Jew and a foreigner. Having the cast fully masked from
the very beginning of the play as if for the carnival, the spectators were
deprived of the excitement of the scene where the masked ball otherwise
would have taken place. Instead, what the spectators had in front them was
a group of strangers and thus potential savages whose origin was not clear.
The director Richard Olivier [the son of Laurence Olivier] had turned it
into "a pageant" in which "the masquers and clowns mingle with the
audience, Shylock's daughter eloped with a lover disguised as a giant
Easter Bunny," and the whole piece itself was carnivalized into "a fairly
broad comedy." (Usher 1998, 49) A foreign actor Norbert Kentrup made
his masked presence in a masculine manner but with a strong German
accent. As Martin Spencer put it, "[...] out goes [*sic*] Shylock's hooked
nose, kaftan and red wig and in comes the charismatic German star, [...]
with flat red cap, broken English and big red lips." (Spencer 1998, 26)
Being a double stranger certainly neutralized his otherness as a character
and robbed the spectator of any sympathy towards him. In this particular
production Shylock as an outsider was already posited as a monster, a
solitary and a highly melodramatic character. The director had "taken
pains to show how prejudice and bigotry touch every character in

Shakespeare's play" performed by a multiracial cast. Not only Shylock was "singled out for abuse." The spectators also witnessed "the disdain with which Portia treated her Moroccan suitor, or how Jessica traded her Jewish father for Christian bean." What else was left there, was a "grim entertainment and a larger-than-life style of performance," and the outcome was considered as utterly "indescent." The audience was thought to have "responded to this straightforward account of an anti-Semitic play with a troubling enthusiasm," (Julius 1998, 48) which kept the spectator relatively unaware of the natural distractions of the site, such as the ringing of mobiles, the aeroplanes, and the ushers busy among groundlings. With random incoming mobile calls from abroad, and planes flying from other continents, the local of the *here*, the foreign of the *there*, the global of the *anywhere* and the imaginary *elsewhere* all became merged for the spectator in a most confusing manner. The Globe theatre thus not only embraced the imaginary universe, but also the whole world, the microcosm holding the macrocosm in a nutshell.

Venice in Between: Elsewhere

It is a common understanding that Shakespeare's scenes usually nest inside the civilized world and the Christian Europe known to geographers. This is how Shakespeare is thought to have generally mapped the geography of his plays. However, it seems to have been the local scenery, which he actually posited as both familiar and strange. It is thought, that behind the sophisticated geographic imagination of strange characters and foreign places, which emerge "half within and half without his intellectual horizon," images of a local gentleman and of Renaissance England are hidden. It is believed that "beyond these European limits lay the unknown, or hardly known, wonderland of discovery and romance, where monsters dwelt and miracles were common, [...]" (Gillies 1994, 1) Yet, as Gillies has put it, "the poetic dimension of Shakespeare's geographic imagination is not to be understood *sui generis*."

> Shakespeare's geographic imagination is informed by a rich geographic tradition which is already moralised, already inherently poetic in the sense of being alive with human and dramaturgic meaning: specifically with the human difference. (Gillies 1994, 4)

Within the notion of the 'foreign' the concept of a difference is already implicitly inscribed. To imagine 'foreign', means to think of something wild, dangerous, and daunting. While the 'local' appears to us in full dimension, the 'foreign' still tends to be somewhat two-dimensional and is thus open ended. The concept of the 'foreign' is deprived of an important dimension; it becomes timeless, and somewhat eternal. Foreign becomes local when the borders are crossed and the time-gap between the two is conquered. Just as the 'local' is always closer to our hearts and understanding of the real, the imaginary is always already included to the 'foreign.' [While the Newtonian term of a *continuum/continua* as a three-dimensional unity of time and space is best to describe our world and thus the real Venice, the Bakhtinian concept of a *chronotope* seems to suit best to describe the imaginary world of Venice in which the characters of *The Merchant of Venice* move.] To create an imaginary 'foreign' in one's imagination is a tricky task and allows an infinite number of possibilities. It could be any country, both imaginary and real. An imager can imagine an imaginary place by screening it in his or her mind. The imaginary place then appears on the mind/screen in a film-like mode and depth, yet it lacks all the parameters of a three-dimensional world. Only in theatre, can an imaginary place become spatially constructed and materialized,, allowing us to cut out the slice of a fantasy world and experience it in full dimension.

To some extent, the notion of the 'global' also seems to be linked to the Greek term *oikumene,* [οικω means "I inhabit"], originally combining the idea of a 'home/world', a concept which made a difference between the lands inhabited by Greeks and the ones inhabited by barbarians. While *oikumene* originally would have meant *here* or *there*, the contemporary notion of the 'global' simply means that anything different could be present right *here*, *there*, or *anywhere*, and it would make no difference, since the differences are either already blurred or completely erased. The 'home' could be the 'world' just as the 'world' can become a 'home'. This concept seems to suit very well to the imagined fictional worlds of theatre and the Shakespeare-plays in particular.

The notion of the 'global' as a referent to the planet Earth [the Globe] always already contains a definite number of localities, each of these having a unique entity of its own. These places we can visit in reality as well as in dream. In the realm of the imaginary, global could mean anything that an imager can imagine to happen. The imagined planet is something distant, remote, and different, as something which has no name or even yet a figure, a place yet to come; the nature of imaginary universe is not a *being* but more of an endless *becoming*. The global, the foreign and the local of the imagined world are both infinite and infantile, and remind us of an idle daydreaming of a child. Within the concept of Shakespeare's Venice, the notions of the 'real' and the 'imaginary' are present in all three discussed modalities. However, as demonstrated through the performative examples, the imagined city seems to keep its position *in between* and can only be [re]visited as *elsewhere*. This is the *terra incognita* of theatre and scenography in particular which allows us to act out these imaginary moments.

Bibliography

Fischer-Lichte, Erika. 1999. Theatre as festive play: Max Reinhardt's production of "The Merchant of Venice". In *Venetian views, Venetian blinds: English fantasies of Venice*. Ed. Manfred Pfister and Barbara Schaff. Amsterdam/Atlanta: GA.

Gillies, John. 1994. *Shakespeare and the geography of the difference*. Cambridge: CUP.

Julius, A.1998. To do a little right do a great wrong? *New Statesman & Society*, June 5; *Plays International*, August: 48.

Sartre, Jean Paul. 2004. *The Imaginary*. Routledge.

Shakespeare, William. 2003. *The Merchant of Venice*. Ed. M. M. Mahood. Cambridge: CUP, The New Cambridge Shakespeare.

Spencer, Martin. 1998. The Merchant of Venice. *Midweek Magazine*, June 8.

Tollini, Frederick. 2004. *The Shakespeare productions of Max Reinhardt*. USA/Canada/UK: Mellen Press.

Usher, Shaun. 1998. *Daily Mail*. June 5, 49.

Vardac, Nicholas. 1987. *Theatrical origins of early film: David Garrick to E.W. Griffith*. Da Capo Press.

The Jew of Mestri [original: *Der Kaufmann von Venedig*]. 1923. Directed by Peter Paul Felner. BFI, 6 reels.

William Shakespeare's The Merchant of Venice. 2004. Directed by Michael Radford. USA,138 minutes.

CHAPTER FOUR

ELPIDA-SOPHIA CHRISTIANAKI

THE PIPE AND THE LYRE'S SOUND
CONTRA SOCRATES' TEACHING:
A RE-APPROXIMATION OF NIETZSCHE

i) How the contrast between Nietzsche and Socrates reflects Nietzsche's different interpretations of tragedy

As Stefan Lorenz Sorgner observes in his article "Who is the 'music-making Socrates'?" Socrates is depicted in Nietzsche's *Birth of Tragedy* as "a figure who is very different to Dionysus" (Sorgner 2004, 7). This is because Socrates is here portrayed as not practicing the art of music and poetry. Knowledge is of primordial importance in the teachings of Socrates since to have knowledge is to be virtuous. In extension, virtue is in effect linked directly with happiness. As Sorgner eloquently puts it: "according to Socrates, knowledge of the truth leads to happiness" (Sorgner 2004, 9). Nietzsche, Sorgner explains, takes a Dionysian approach whereby the world is viewed as being full of change. This world is portrayed as being self-contradictory and unified at the same time and most importantly as "unbearable for men" (Sorgner 2004, 12). Isn't it peculiar that the basic Dionysian truth as explained in "The Argument" of the *Birth of Tragedy* is presented as "the underlying reality of existence in unchanging contradiction, pain and excess" (Nietzsche 1956, 65)? Nietzsche, as explained by Sorgner, is, in essence, against the Socratic idea that 'by using reason one becomes virtuous' (Nietzsche 1956, 15).

We should be aware that we have different representations of Socrates coming from different sources. Xenophon's Socrates is less lively than the Platonic Socrates and different from Aristotle's Socrates. Aristotle presents Socrates as preoccupied with practical moral behaviour. Aristotle emphasizes the Socratic ability of establishing general definitions in determining what is morally right. The Aristotelian Socrates is praising the continuous search for self awareness. It seems to me that there are many similarities between the function of tragedy and the Socratic preaching on knowledge. Norman Gulley argues in *The Philosophy of Socrates* that the philosopher can be characterised by his "readiness to refute the opinion of others and his reluctance to offer any opinion of his own" (Gulley 1968, 63). These are the words employed by Gulley to sum up the Socratic irony. This approach towards knowledge seems to be very familiar with the route adopted the Greek tragedian who aspired, through their tragedies, to enable the audience to "excavate" their deeply seated fears and unexpressed cries of agony and hope.

A good paradigm of the Platonic Socrates' idea of self knowledge is explained in contrast to the word illusionary. We can draw on the *Symposium* for an explanation of this approach towards self-knowledge. Nalin Ranasinghe states in *The Soul of Socrates* that Socrates dismisses the Trojan Helen in Plato's *Symposium* as having no real identity. Plato's Socrates believed that the beautiful Helen was nothing without the erotic recollections of her victims. To explain more accurately Socrates' opinion of the great beauty as expressed via Plato, Helen is presented as endowed with the ability to charm her victims by projecting on them their erotic recollections. We can assume from this that Helen could use her body as an empty vessel. This vessel took form and shape from the desires of the other. For this reason Helen is portrayed as not having any identity of her own. Socrates praises love in the form of erotic recollection of an idea. This can be deduced in *Phaedo*. Socrates tries to transform erotic youth love into the union of the physical and the spiritual. Socrates views the undiluted physical love as incomplete. By equipping himself with Perseus' shield, Socrates believed that the lover can be protected from being maddened by his love object and all its monstrous beauty. The realm of true beauty is equated with the Apollonian realm that is also an abstract impersonal love while Dionysian love is related to desire.

Socrates tried to draw attention to mistaking the sign with the signified. In other words true love is a state when the lover is self-aware and is in a state of intellectual awe between *eros* and *logos*. But isn't this exactly what tragedy aims to do? Doesn't it function as Perseus' shield for it displays the pain and struggle of humanity in a medium that renders the performance endurable and didactic for the audience? Terry Eagleton catches brilliantly the taste of tragedy in his *Sweet Violence* since it presents disturbing matters in a tempting and almost addictive way.

The Greek tragedians did not directly give their opinion on different matters but let the audience's reaction to the performance do the talking by employing the actors/characters as the vehicles, the empty Helen vessel upon which the tortures and pains of the audience were reflected upon with the shield of make-believe. Socrates' general definitions and universal characterizations match well with the universal and classical messages of myth-inspired tragedies. For what else are myths than the condensed expression of mankind's feeling of awe before meaning and existence?

We can borrow Schopenhauer's words to link philosophy with tragedy. Nietzsche quotes Schopenhauer in *The Birth of Tragedy* when he is reflecting on the link between philosophy and theatre. For Nietzsche, Socrates identifies a person's capacity for philosophy with their capacity for imagining the possibility that all they have come to believe could be nothing more than a dream. Nietzsche stresses the connection between the artistic sensibility and the philosophical awareness of existence. Wouldn't it be possible to turn that on its head and state that theatre functions both as a dream world that bears unmistakable signs of our everyday existence, while on the other hand theatre retains the possibility of providing such an intense stimulus to the audience that it functions as a catalyst for philosophical pondering? To be more precise, what seems to connect tragedy and philosophy is their passionate love affair with knowledge. What changes from the theatrical to the philosophical realm is the manner through which this affair is approached, nourished and through which it reaches its climax. Tragedy occurs through projecting on the stage the audience's secret desires and untold horrors. With philosophy, on the other hand, it operates through the abstract attempt to reason deductively from one premise to another. For theatre we observe the route from the apparently mundane to the truly philosophical, while for philosophy we witness the path from abstract philosophical ponderings to specific questions that can be applied in our everyday life. It seems to me that what the first one calls dream and entrancement the second one identifies as higher truth.

ii) What the audience knows: The issue of knowledge and behaviour in the reception of performance

Once upon a time Nietzsche started wondering about the inspirational moment that created and nourished tragedy. He started considering the bravery and madness of the nation that was in need of art. He considered that tragedy can be pessimism and the latter can be equated with signs of decline, of tired instincts. Nietzsche had started wondering about the pessimism of strength and the link between performance and knowledge. For Nietzsche tragedy came into existence from the marriage of the

Apollonian with the Dionysian or the god of science with the god of nature. The centre of Dionysian religion is the evocation of nature's unity concealed by our dismemberment as individuals. The dithyramb, the song of tragedy helps us to become reconciled with the agony and pain of this aspiration. Tragedy seems to have come into existence when Thespis delivered the first line to the chorus and, in doing so, established a barrier between self and others.

Nietzsche writes in *The Birth of Tragedy* that tragedy's function is to perpetuate conflict. What is this conflict? The conflict between self and other, knowledge and ignorance, truth and illusion and may I add, the resourcefulness of using tragedy as the medium to bridge apparent polarities. The one polarity is the pipe and the other is the lyre, or Dionysus and Apollo, or Nietzsche and Socrates. Theatre sprang in Greece when dreams and intoxication became fused into a performance that reflected deeper reality. In the state of intoxication the individual loses oneself and we witness the collapse of individuation through the process of an ecstatic experience with mystical implications. We are talking about the rapturous and terrifying attempt to cross the barriers between self and others. Dionysian religion is centred on the evocation of nature's awesome unity concealed by our dismemberment as individuals. While praising Dionysus through participating in performance we progressively become the worshippers of our pain and joy. It is through theatre that we recognise that we are essentially alone and this recognition and the acknowledgement of this state produce an orgiastic cry of relief from the illusory, everyday pursuit of ephemeral happiness. Knowledge of our true situation tears us apart and makes us whole for the very first time. Socrates pondered about the dynamics of knowledge provided that it was placed in good hands.

iii) Plato and Socrates

We know that Plato was an artist who destroyed his works after meeting Socrates. Plato stopped writing short tragedies and, being won over by the preaching of Socrates, which emphasised the mal-habits that originate from the glorification of illusion, immersed himself in philosophy. Interestingly enough, after Socrates death, he was inspired by the same person who influenced him to destroy all his previous work to embark on writing his philosophical dialogues. Set against Nietzsche's claims about Socrates it surely comes as a surprising fact that for many Plato is considered the father of the novel, giving a story with characters embroidered with dialogue that aims to instruct by giving a moral conclusion. It is stated that the only artist Socrates praised was Aesop, who wrote sort stories with simple plots that culminated with a simple but witty moral maxim. Socrates praised knowledge for its beneficial influences to the individual's life and condemned theatre on the basis of being misleading.

My approach in this essay is that Socrates had a misleading understanding of the nature of performance that did not, as Nietzsche claims, have a detrimental role on the evolution of tragedy. What I do accept is the possibility that Sophocles influenced the extension of choral odes in performance. One might stop me at this point to remind me that the first component of tragedy was the dithyramb, a song. If Nietzsche challenges the evolution of the role of music in performance then I am a hundred per cent on his side. Even though his long treatise on tragedy includes the word "music" in *The Birth of Tragedy*, Nietzsche states clearly that he holds Socrates as the main agent not of the restriction of the chorus but of the death of tragedy.

My argument is that even though the chorus was essential in the first steps of theatrical performance, Socrates, with his ironic sense of knowledge gave, unwillingly, a mature approach towards the projection of the audience's recollections. What was before conveyed with the anonymity and universality of music was now operating through the issues of knowledge in the forms of tragic irony, tragic awareness, fate, moral preaching, the curse of knowledge and the destructive impact to the individual of shutting ears and mind to his surroundings. With such a Socratic knowledge, theatre conveyed values; objectifications of seeing (eye). What Socrates brought to the picture was intensified attention to self-awareness. The will could be paired with consciousness in the same way that music could before be linked with objectification.

iv) Socrates' objection to tragedy

What Socrates teaches is that man attains happiness by having *phronesis* (prudence), which is nothing other than a correct understanding of how things are. Who can say that Oedipus was in fact knowledgeable or even wise when he, of all people, was able to solve the riddle of the Sphinx, the answer of which was surprisingly "man". How interesting is the fact that Oedipus displays brilliant signs of wisdom through glorious acts of stupidity. Having been told by the Delphi Oracle that if he went away he was to kill his father and marry his mother, he still killed a person old enough to be his father and married a woman old enough to be his mother. Oedipus reaches knowledge after blinding himself so as not to see his mother/wife or his children/brothers after he manages with the help of the prophet to piece together the gruesome puzzle of his life. How well does this story fit with Socrates' teachings of the happiness attained by *phronesis*? If Oedipus had had a choice, he would have chosen another route of action. But as things stand he is a glorious example of the men that Socrates questioned in the Agora. Such men immersed themselves into dialogue with Socrates feeling confident about their values and sense of self but came out of the dialogue realising their ignorance. However, just the fact that they realise their ignorance renders them as more knowledgeable than they were when they entered into the conversation with Socrates.

Socrates' basic objection to tragedy was that he didn't perceive it as portraying reality since genuinely good men appeared to suffer, something that he considered an impossibility that led the audience draw incorrect conclusions that they later applied in their lives. But no genuinely good men suffer in tragedies. What we witness is people of high or heroic status burdened by dilemmas and making wrong decisions that reflect their limited awareness both of their situation and of the greater picture. What causes waves of shivers on the audience's bodies is the fact that these characters cannot be dismissed as villains. The beauty of the whole situation is that the characters are painfully and truly vulnerable to false readings that culminate in destructive endings through much too late a resurfacing of knowledge. This occurs because even though they have many good qualities they allow one of their most dangerous flaws to govern them and launch them into a frenzied self-destruction. I think that the audience is more able to empathise with characters whose personality retains the average amalgam of virtue and conceit. The fact that the characters are hold positions of high influence that arouse a sense of respect when they are, no doubt, shaken and torn apart by their own weaknesses renders the performance as all the more realistic and didactic to the audience while retaining the fake illusion of mere art when in fact performance plunges her teeth deeply into the audience's anxieties, anaesthetising them from themselves and allowing them to perceive the tragic message only through empathy.

Bibliography

Allison, David. 2001. Reading the New Nietzsche: The Birth of Tragedy, The Gay Science, *Thus Spoke Zarathustra, and On the Genealogy of Morals*. Boston: Rowman & Littlefield.

Ansell-Pearson, Keith. 1994. *An Introduction to Nietzsche as Political Thinker.* Cambridge: Cambridge University Press.

Eagleton, Terry. 2003. *Sweet Violence.* Oxford: Blackwell Publishing.

Gulley, Norman. 1968. *The Philosophy of Socrates.* Basingstoke: MacMillan.

Nietzsche, Friedrich. (Golffing, Francis trans.) 1956. *The Birth of Tragedy and The Genealogy of Morals.* New York: Doubleday Anchor Books.

Sophocles, 2002. (Fitts, Dudley & Fitzgerald, Robert trans.) *The Oedipus Cycle: Oedipus Rex, Oedipus at Colonus, Antigone.* Washington: Harvest Books.

Plato. (Gallop, David trans.) 1999. *Phaedo.* Oxford: Oxford University Press.

—. (Gill, Christopher trans.) 2003. *Symposium.* London: Penguin Classics.

Ranasinghe, Nalin. 2000. *The Soul of Socrates.* New York: Cornwell University Press.

Sorgner, Stefan-Lorenz. 2004. Who Is The "Music-Making Socrates"? *An Internet Journal of Philosophy.* 8: 91-113.

CHAPTER FIVE

LAURA CULL AND MATTHEW GOULISH

A DIALOGUE ON BECOMING

Presence as Becoming
Laura Cull

1.

March 1954: *Creature from the Black Lagoon* is released. In the film a palaeontology expedition along the Amazon River discovers the infamous Black Lagoon and its prehistoric resident, a fish-human hybrid. The team of scientists manage to capture the creature after it fatally attacks their local guides, but it soon escapes. Returning to kidnap the female research assistant (played by Julia Adams), the creature carries her away to its cave where the others try to rescue her.

2.

March 1991: an audience gather together to discuss their encounter with a work-in-progress showing by the Chicago-based performance company, Goat Island. Given the opportunity to direct questions to the company members, one person in the audience asks Karen Christopher, who joined the group in 1990, how she feels about being "the only woman in a company with three male performers"(Goulish 2000, 77). At this time, the company are Christopher plus the founding members: brothers Timothy and Greg McCain, Matthew Goulish, and director Lin Hixson. Joan Dickinson, who is accredited on the company website as a co-creator of the performance in question - *Can't Take Johnny to the Funeral* - left the group before its first public presentation. What happens when Christopher is left as the only woman on stage? A question. "I do not consider myself a male performer. I consider myself The Creature from the Black Lagoon"(Goulish 2000, 77). An answer. Or, rather a response. Not from Christopher, but from Goulish who re-presents this exchange in his book, *39 microlectures: in proximity of performance*(2000). To a question framed in terms of a fixed binary distinction between male and female performers, Goulish replies with an affirmation of performance as becoming; performance as a process in which the performer experiences him/her 'self' as a series of transitions:

> "Myself BECOMING an illustration in a figure skating manual
> Myself BECOMING The Creature from the Black Lagoon
> (...) Myself BECOMING a microphone stand."(Goulish 2000, 79)

Performance, Goulish says, is like dreaming, because it "presents us with intersections. In a performance, a performer is not a single entity. Instead of a unit, a performer is an identity in motion in a particular direction. A performer is a becoming." (Goulish 2000, 79)

3.

For Gilles Deleuze, as for his predecessor Henri Bergson, there is no being beyond becoming. All the different beings, identities and entities we conceive in conscious experience are but the effects of a primary, universal becoming. For too long, Deleuze argues, philosophy has misconceived the nature of the relation between time and life. Time is not a discrete 'now' that beings occupy or are contained by; time is immanent to what lives and as such what lives is ceaselessly becoming, self-differentiating, creative. For Deleuze, there is no essential being of the thing that grounds or limits these creative processes - only dogmatic ways of thinking and acting that attempt to block or control becoming which his thought encourages us to abandon.

As Goulish's text echoes, Deleuze speaks of specific *becomings* as well as of universal becoming as the ontological real, particularly in the later collaborations with Felix Guattari. A becoming is what Deleuze & Guattari call a 'molecular' form of subjectivity - constantly transforming, the molecular subject is not a thing or a being but a discontinuous series of flows and processes seeking new modes of connection or relation to other becomings. A becoming is contrasted with what Deleuze & Guattari call 'molar' subjectivity. Becoming the *Creature from the Black Lagoon* Goulish flies from his 'molar' identity: his definition as a male performer, as adult, as human. He makes a bid to escape the perceptual and behavioural habits imposed upon him by the regulating power of a fixed subjectivity. In telling us what we are, identity limits creativity; entering into becomings we create ourselves as always more than we are.

Deleuze's corpus has been largely ignored by performance studies in favour of his contemporary Jacques Derrida[1]. But through Deleuze performance can be reconceived as the challenge of finding ways for both performer and audience to access presence conceived as this universal becoming. Presence is the meeting with new ways of speaking and moving that resist recognition; a connection to new ways of seeing and feeling beyond identification and naming.

Often, Deleuze & Guattari's examples of these becomings come from literature: the becomings-animal of Kafka and Melville, but surely they are also to be found in performance - in Una Chaudhuri's recent work, *The Animal Project*[2], or in the work of Goat Island. To enter into a becoming, as a performer, is to approach new ideas and affects by dismantling the conventional separation between oneself and what is not oneself. Becoming is not mimetic or metaphorical, Deleuze & Guattari insist; it is to *really* see, think and feel differently by participating in or making a connection to the ways of living of animals, children, even of the so-called 'inanimate'.

Becomings, for Deleuze & Guattari, take place in a specific order: starting with the most accessible and moving towards the most radical; starting with a destabilization of one identity and moving towards the total dissolution of identities per se. Problematically for many feminists, Deleuze & Guattari chose to call the first step of this order: 'becoming-woman'. All becomings, they say, must begin with or pass through 'becoming-woman' and women must become-woman first in order to lead the way for men. Becoming-woman then has nothing to do with the imitation of feminine identity, rather it is a process that involves the breakdown of what Deleuze & Guattari call one of 'the great binary aggregates': the division of the sexes into man and woman. Becoming-woman is a movement traversing this division that releases sexuality from molar identity; from its repression in an organized and sexed body.

Even feminists who have gradually become sympathetic to Deleuze, like Elizabeth Grosz, remain suspicious of the concept of becoming-woman. In 1993, while Goat Island were touring *Can't Take Johnny to the Funeral*, Grosz published an article detailing these lingering doubts. One major concern was with the idea that women needed to 'go first' in this embrace of becoming over being; that they had to lose their molar identity as 'women' before 'men' lost theirs. With its references to escape - from territories, from organs, from Oedipus - the celebration of becoming is based on the notion of a prior state of identification or organisation from which the body is then released. In 1954, when *Creature from the Black Lagoon* was released, the Convention on the Political Rights of Women had only just come into effect - expressing a commitment to securing equal rights to participate in governance for women and men. Such commitments were not secured without a fight; fights which Deleuze and Guattari refer to as molar politics on account of their dependency on a fixed category or subject position called 'woman'.

While they graciously acknowledge the strategic necessity of such a molar identity for the women's movement, Deleuze & Guattari also warned against any long-term determination of action by the category of 'woman' as ground or foundation. The struggle for the liberation of something called 'woman' should eventually be superseded by the broader struggle to liberate becoming from all molar identities. For Grosz, this is a formula with all too familiar implications. As when Marxism insisted on the subordination of women's struggle to the class struggle, women will find themselves bound to struggles which represent men's interests while claiming or perceiving themselves to be concerned with universal interests (Grosz 2001, 1461). But as Claire Colebrook asked in 2001: "Should the women's movement really be told that it must be 'molar' or concerned with identity only for a moment on the way to a 'molecular' becoming?" (Colebrook in Colebrook and Buchanan 2001, 2)

4.

"How does it feel to be the only woman in a company with three male performers?" It's not hard to imagine what Matthew found "dissatisfying" about the audience member's question. It implies the reality of an unquestionable ground or foundation for living and working; a division between male and female which thought, as philosophy or performance, cannot escape or reinvent. It suggests that no matter what becomings he or Karen Christopher participate in, their presence in performance is recognised, first and foremost, as female as opposed to male or vice versa and, critically, as at least partially fixed. But just as Grosz remains suspicious of Deleuze & Guattari's becoming-woman, there are reasons for us to question Goulish's affirmation of the concept of becoming over being in this particular context. For instance, in his document of the event he effectively edits out Christopher's own contribution to the discussion, saying: "I don't remember her [Karen's] response as much as my own reaction" (Goulish 2000, 77). No big deal, perhaps - but a micro-repetition nevertheless of a gesture of erasure that history has performed on so many women's contributions to culture[3]. Secondly, though, we might ask whether the question of sexual difference is as easily overcome as Goulish's response or indeed as Deleuze & Guattari's writings suggest. Indeed we might ask ourselves if we want to overcome at all what Claire Colebrook calls "the question of our epoch - as the opening of a possibility for thinking beyond subjectivity and identity" (Colebrook in Colebrook and Buchanan 2001, 3).

As Deleuze's ideas filter through into the fields of art history and film studies (and gradually, into performance studies too), we are increasingly invited to think the art work in terms of what it does rather than what it means; we are encouraged to feel film as that which operates directly on the nervous system not as a signifying narrative. But are these affective encounters privileged at all costs? What happens to the critique of representation when we, as audience, are being invited to see past identity to becoming? Might there be reasons for wanting to consider oneself a female performer rather than as a becoming? Or even, regardless of desire, are there not limits on the freedom to become of those identified as female performers?

Watching *Creature from the Black Lagoon*, Matthew Goulish saw a way to move differently. However, I expect he also saw a reproduction of the stereotype of woman as defenceless object of desire - Julia Adams in the white swimsuit - in all her 'molarity'. In their workshops, the company encourage students to look out for the miraculous and memorable, whether on a walk, or watching a performance. We proliferate whatever we look for, they say, so why not become someone who proliferates miracles rather than problems. These miracles can then form the basis of our critical response to the world. The company resist the opposition of the creative and the critical, and particularly the association of the critical with the negative. Rather, they insist, to be critical is to be discerning; to have the capacity to separate something into parts[4]. It would be hard to overstate the productivity of this insight for practitioners - and yet, I hesitate. Surely in performance, as in life, there are problems as well as miracles; there are things which would justify a negative response? This seems indisputable, but the politics of Goat Island's practice is (more often than not) based on a strategy of affirmation rather than critique or ironic repetition. While they continue to experience contemporary America as a cultural space in which the imagination is under attack, the company respond by prioritising the freedom of the imagination in their own process.

Useful Memory
A Response for Laura Cull
Matthew Goulish

To escape the question has been my intention since I began to understand, or, as the poet Robert Creeley wrote, *even if I was still too dumb to know anything*. It strikes me as jumping to a conclusion to claim I enacted an erasure of the words of my colleague when I wrote my alternate answer (i.e. escape) to a question; when I wrote that I could not remember my colleague's answer. Is faulty memory erasure? After all, my own answer, with respect to the moment of the question, remained unspoken (despite my outburst, no doubt considered bizarre at the time, asserting my identity as *the creature*). I wrote it because of its silence, wrote it in a sense to maintain its silence, its unspokenness. Of my colleague's answer I wrote that there had been one. I indicate the presence of her voice without quoting her. Certainly I would have liked to have quoted her. But my memory lapsed. Is it not peculiar to attribute a motive to my lapse, by equating it with erasure? Might we not ask instead what all such memory lapses have in common? There we encounter the criteria of usefulness, the presence of the useful memory, Bergson's term, and also the imperative of escaping the question. In those days I had read, somewhat obsessively, the first two and one-half pages of *Dialogues* by Gilles Deleuze and Claire Parnet, its opening contemplation of the question. *Questions are invented, like anything else. If you aren't allowed to invent your questions, with elements from all over the place, from never mind where, if people 'pose' them to you, you haven't much to say. ... The aim is not to answer questions, it's to get out, to get out of it. Many people think that it is only by going back over the question that it's possible to get out of it. ... But getting out never happens like that. Movement always happens behind the thinker's back, or in the moment when he blinks. Getting out is already achieved, or else it never will be.* This imperative of escape reveals itself: it is always the question that erases the answer. It does so by demarcating in advance a region of usefulness. The escape replaces the answer, replaces the question, maybe proposes a different set of questions altogether, but not before it challenges the usefulness of all questions and all answers. What was the question?

How does it feel to be the only woman in a company with three male performers? Let us consider the question's territory. 1) Performers are particles. They are separable from non-performing members of the company, such as the director, who, in our case, has always been a woman. (I should note the generous interpretation of the question here, since it could be considered demonstrably false – my colleague was never *the only woman in the company*, only the only woman performer.) 2) Performers are separable as individuals from one another according to the criteria of gender. 3) It is fair to ask the woman performer to respond to her presence as a woman in the vocabulary of *feeling*. Certainly we can consider each of these points, to some extent, true. But rather than debating their trueness, let us ask instead, according to these three points, what answers did the question erase in advance? Perhaps, most apparently, it erased the opposite of each of the three points. 1) Performers are not distinct particles, but facets of a whole, inseparable from one another and from non-performing company members. 2) Performers may not be separated as individuals according to the criteria of gender. 3) It is not fair to ask the woman performer to respond to her presence as a woman in the vocabulary of *feeling*. These three points are as clearly not true as the previous points are true. Our interest lies somewhere between the three proposals of the question and their three parallel negations. But if we leave trueness aside for a moment, what happens if we ask instead what each discourse allows? What does it allow us to think? How does it allow us to live? What does it make possible?

Let us say the question's erasure, if we may adopt that term, happens through a reading of the past. As Bergson wrote in *Matter and Memory* (which I did not understand then, but am starting to understand now) memories arise out of perceptions according to criteria of usefulness. The criteria fall into categories of similarity or contiguity. I remember x because it resembles x´, or I remember x because it follows x´´, either similarity or contiguity investing it with its usefulness. The notion of identity as becoming, it seems to me now, comes to us via this understanding of perception and memory. Memory exists in each perception, because each moment, however small, has duration. A change transpires in each moment. Memory in a sense coheres a moment as a moment, as we might remember its start a certain way at its end, in order to make it one thing, a moment. We perceive duration through change; we perceive change through movement. A moment, then, is moving. Because it is moving, it is always becoming. It will never become what it is becoming. It will only move in that particular way, according to the mode of its model of becoming, not an act of imitation, but one of determining usefulness, according to a sort of *mutual mistaken identity*. As the wasp thinks the orchid is a wasp, and the orchid thinks the wasp is an orchid. Here again, a moment of text from the first two and one-half pages of Deleuze and Parnet exploded in my memory then like a hopeful firework. *The wasp-becoming of the orchid, an orchid-becoming of the wasp, a*

double capture since 'what' each becomes changes no less than 'that
which' becomes ... an 'a-parallel evolution of two beings who have
nothing whatsoever to do with one another'. Some years later I would
discover the source of the imagery at the midpoint of Proust's seven
volumes, but for now, for then, the becoming was the energy and the
engine of the choreography. We had photographs clipped and assembled
in rows on paper by our director, composed for each of us individually,
given for us to interpret as scores. As we devised those dances, those
simple acts and movements *of beings who had nothing whatsoever to do*
with us it felt to me like becoming human again – to make oneself from the
outside. By that I mean the movement of a moment, the criteria by which
we transform our perceptions into useful memories, had been given to us
from the outside, not discovered from the inside. There was in this a
suggestion of a future for performance – not a future in the traditional
sense of what performance will become someday, but a future in the
momentary sense, that performance will remain alive and lively because it
has a future edge of a moment to become now, and that future edge has
everything to do with who and what we become as we dance, which must
be a who or a what that has nothing whatsoever to do with us. Maybe we
consider the rupture of this other a product of similarity rather than of
contiguity. By this I mean I am a gender by contiguity, but a creature by
similarity. It is a mistaken similarity, perhaps, but in this mistake we find
the force of the ordinary: the example of wasp and orchid, the case study
of children playing at creatureness. What movement does the mistake
allow? If when we say movement we mean dance, let us understand this
not only as a transit of the body in space, but also as a transit of the mind
from one state to another. What is the motor of the movement? If gender,
perhaps it is a motor of contiguity usefulness, of identity mathematically
determined from the previous moment. If creature, perhaps it is a motor of
similarity usefulness, one of style, rhythm, intensity, held together by a
delicate tension facilitated by memory and imagination, by an act of
intuition, reforming me in the direction of an impossible whole for the
duration of the dance.

Any question that erases these possibilities, such as the question under
discussion, dismisses the exteriority of the becoming, perhaps dismisses it
because of its unlikeliness, its absurdity. Such a question throws us back
on our contiguity, or to put it in more everyday terms, on habit. *How does*
it feel etc. This is a question that erases all answers that stray from its
territory of the habitual – as thinking of self in terms of gender, of thinking
of self in terms of feeling. Certainly we must do that in order to make a
coherent and functioning self-image. But we were not talking about that,

were we? Nor were we discussing political strategy. As I recall, the topic of conversation was dance. And for dance to have a future, the question must have an escape.

Notes

1 There are, of course, a number of exceptions to this rule. For instance, see: Kowsar, Mohammed. 1986. Deleuze on Theatre: A Case Study of Carmelo Bene's "Richard III". *Theatre Journal* 38 (1): 19-33. Of particular relevance to this paper is also: Bottoms, Stephen J. 1998. The Tangled Flora and Fauna of Goat Island: Rhizome, Repetition, Reality. *Theatre Journal* 50 (4): 421-446.
2 For more information on Una Chaudhuri's work, see Chaudhuri, Una. 2006. Animalizing Performance, Becoming-Theatre: Inside Zooesis with The Animal Project at NYU. *Theatre Topics* 16 (1):1-17.
3 One such erasure is the contribution of make-up artist, Milicent Patrick. Although Patrick is confirmed by a number of sources to have been the creator of the original design for the *Creature from the Black Lagoon*, it tends to be her supervisor, Bud Westmore, who is given accreditation.
4 For a fuller articulation of Goat Island's notion of 'creative response', see the text on the company's website: www.goatislandperformance.org/creativeResponse.htm

Bibliography

Bergson, Henri. Trans. N.M. Paul and W.S. Palmer. 1998.*Matter and Memory*. New York: Zone Books
Bottoms, Stephen J. 1998. The Tangled Flora and Fauna of Goat Island: Rhizome, Repetition, Reality. *Theatre Journal* 50 (4): 421-446.
Chaudhuri, Una. 2006. Animalizing Performance, Becoming-Theatre: Inside Zooesis with The Animal Project at NYU. *Theatre Topics* 16 (1):1-17.
Colebrook, Claire and Ian Buchanan, ed. 2001. *Deleuze and Feminist Theory*. Edinburgh: Edinburgh University Press.
Creeley, Robert. 2006. *On Earth - Last Poems and an Essay by Robert Creeley*, Berkeley, Los Angeles, London: University of California Press.
Deleuze, Gilles and Felix Guattari. Trans. Brian Massumi. 1987. *A Thousand Plateaus: Capitalism and Schizophrenia*. Minneapolis: University of Minnesota Press
Deleuze, Gilles and Claire Parnet. *Dialogues*. Trans. Hugh Tomlinson and Barbera Habberjam. 1987. London: Athlone Press.
Goat Island. http://www.goatislandperformance.org/ (accessed 17 December 2006)

Goulish, Matthew. 2000. *39 microlectures: in proximity of performance.* London and New York: Routledge.
Grosz, Elizabeth. 2001. A Thousand Tiny Sexes. Feminism and Rhizomatics. In Genosko, Gary (Editor). *Deleuze and Guattari : Critical Assessments of Leading Philosophers.* Volume 3. Florence, KY, USA: Routledge. 1440-1461.
Originally published in *Topoi. An International Review of Philosophy* 12 (2): 167-179.
Jardine, Alice. 1984. Woman in Limbo: Deleuze and his Br(others). *SubStance* 13 (3-4): 46-60.

CHAPTER SIX

DONGNING FENG

AESTHETICS AFTER PROPAGANDA: THE SECOND COMING OF THE CULTURAL REVOLUTION PERFORMING ARTS

Introduction

In the midst of emergence of pluralistic cultural and socio-economic landscape in contemporary China, many works of the "Cultural Revolution arts", most notably among them the so-called model Beijing operas [Yangbanxi], have re-entered the Chinese cultural spectacle. The audiences have come to embrace for a second time and re-appreciate this particular form of art and many other films, songs, paintings and the literary writings produced and promoted in the Cultural Revolution (1966–1976), the most turbulent time of the recent Chinese history, but not out of political manipulation and dispensation this time around. The revival of the Cultural Revolution arts has baffled many critics and political commentators in China. Some critics applied a socio-political interpretation and saw it as political nostalgia on the part of the hard-line radical leftists. Some read it as a sign of dissatisfaction of the disfranchised passed over by China's current development. A close examination of the demographic makeup of audiences and readership disproves either argument. The truth goes beyond a simple and straightforward answer, and to address this question will shed light on recent Chinese history and development and understanding of China "as a modern sovereignty engaged in its own trajectories, articulated in its own circumstances – a political and economic entity that is radically different from the fetishized images of the Tang or Ming dynasty", or a neoliberal vision of China on a racetrack to become part of the global modernity, or even the transfixed view of "a 'Red China' with demonic intents of the enemy", (Wang 2002) largely nurtured by the Western bestseller on China

such as *Red Azalea, Wild Swan, Red Flower of China*, and more recently
Mao, The Unknown Story. It has been three decades since the Cultural
Revolution (1966-1976) ended and yet for many Chinese it still is a living
memory. The subject continues to be an epic theme in films and literary
writings in the post-Cultural Revolution years to the present day. It is an
inexhaustible source of inspiration for artists, writers and filmmakers. It can
be said that the best testimony and representation of the Cultural Revolution
can only be found in Chinese cinema and literature. Many of the films and
literature with the theme of the Cultural Revolution have drawn extensive
critical interests from academics, journalists and cultural and socio-political
commentators in and outside China, especially the more recent films such as
Blue Kite (1993), *In the Heat of the Sun* (1994), *Balzac and the Little
Chinese Seamstress* (2005), to name a few. However, critiques on arts
produced in the Cultural Revolution era are surprisingly few given the fact
that this period lasted over a decade and continues to provoke debates and
shape China's future and identity in the new circumstances. Moreover, most
of the analyses and investigations, which appeared during the immediate
post-Cultural Revolution years, are disappointingly lacking in depth. They
tend to be overly descriptive and exclusively politically predisposed in the
way in which they deal with these works of art characteristic of this particular
time in Chinese history. They overlook either a comparative, developmental
perspective or one of distinctly Chinese aesthetics and necessary references to
its society, culture and tradition. Thus, these criticisms somehow are unable
to explain why Chinese people have come to re-embrace such once labelled
"propaganda arts", which was seen to play a part in the most tragic period in
recent Chinese history. The revival of the Cultural Revolution arts has
caused trepidation amongst academics and official gurus in China. For
academics, who were considered to have suffered the most during the
Cultural Revolution, anything associated with it should be condemned to
purgatory. For official gurus, renaissance of such arts would serve as an aide
mémoire of an irredeemable past, undermine the legitimacy of the current
authorities and spill over to a discontent with the present. By default, both
views are in accordance of the official line of repudiation of all things
engendered in the period. This paradigm also invariably predominates the
West-based academic circles, particularly in the US. Brown's article
succinctly sums up this situation by pointing out that such a "dominant
paradigm limits our understanding of the 1966-1976 years" (Brown 2003)
and more importantly, of China as a modern sovereign nation that has a past
and future of its own. Recently there have emerged some works that "reveal
the cultural complexity and diversity of China during the Cultural
Revolution." (Brown 2003) However, without effective analytical tools,

these efforts, though reflecting "the multiplicity of ways in which Chinese people experienced" during the era to some degree (Brown 2003), either focus on contents (which are very often analysed independent of the form, or even the context), or on anecdotal personality conflicts and power struggles, or are on the lookout for archaeological traces of marginalised artistic products and treat them as the norm. In his article, "Putting culture back into the Cultural Revolution: Shifting scholarly views of Chinese art and culture, 1977-2002", Brown argues

> if we limit our analytical toolbox to gossip, personality, and cynical power struggles (not that these implements should be left out of the box altogether), we further marginalize China in Western eyes as a strange, impenetrable, immoral place. In order to better understand the full complexity of the sometimes violent, sometimes triumphant, sometimes lethargic "ten years of chaos," scholars must not only cast a wide net for official and unofficial sources and formulate analytical frameworks with more explanatory potential than "power struggle" or "personality," but they must also pay careful attention to how non-elites in China responded to – and themselves affected – official cultural policy. (Brown 2003)

Brown's argument opens up possible avenues to reassess the true impact of these forms of arts. He outlines a plausible interpretation why these forms of arts are eschewed by the liberal academics, but more importantly points out that it is equally ironic that the very same "liberal" position restricts what scholars can say about the period and its culture. (Brown 2003) It is important to realise what these forms of arts and cultural representation say about the era, and also about the modern China. Although there have recently published some refreshing and informative studies on the Cultural Revolution arts (Andrews, 1994; Chen, 2002; Brown, 2003; Wu, 2004), few have linked their investigation to the recurrence of the Cultural Revolution arts, despite the fact that this phenomenon offers a constructive locus for critical enquiry. Recently the Cultural Revolution arts in China have been drawing more serious academic attention (Gu 2005; Dong 2005; Wang 1999; Yang 1997) evidently as a reaction to the revival of this form of art, though the majority of them very much replicate the earlier line of argument, for this phenomenon was seen as an unwelcome poltergeist by most of the academia in and outside China. This paper examines the phenomenon of the revival of the Cultural Revolution arts with reference to aesthetics and philosophical hermeneutics in its cultural contexts, first in its original context, and then in the contemporary circumstances.

New Beijing Opera: Building the Superstructure

Mao's theory of literature and arts was derived from his understanding of the Marxist concepts of subjectivity and objectivity, especially Lenin's argument of "base and superstructure". Mao himself was an accomplished poet and always took great interest in literary and cultural matters, i.e. components of superstructure. His involvement in literary and artistic matters can be traced back to the Yan'an years (1936-1947), which witnessed formation and maturity of his political philosophy and beliefs and produced most of his philosophical writings.

He believed that culture and arts were something belonging to the consciousness and superstructure which reacted upon people's actions, thus revolutionary ideas should be advocated and disseminated through various means including artistic representations, which, in turn, he hoped, would strengthen and improve the socialist economic base. He noted unequivocally that literature and art should be subordinate to politics so that it could exert a "positive" influence on politics. Paradoxically, he came to believe that literature and art were playing a decisive role in the revolutionary movement. He continued to assert that they are indispensable cogs and wheels in the whole machine, an indispensable part of the entire revolutionary cause. If there was no literature and art even in the broadest and most ordinary sense, the Chinese people could not carry on the revolutionary movement and win victory. (Mao 1967, 86)

Mao's concern about the superstructure and determination to bring it up to speed with the socialist economic construction can thus be said to have been the primary motive for him to launch the Cultural Revolution, which, he had hoped, would lead to a more equal society. Mao manifested his concern that China was sleep-walking back into an inegalitarian direction and a new elite was taking over the Party and subverted the ideal of the 1949 revolution. However, some scholars came to arrive at an argument of a more personal nature, which speculates that Mao's position in the Party by early 1960s was seriously undermined by the failure of his Great Leap Forward drive (1958). His paranoia of losing control of the Party might lie behind his call for the Cultural Revolution, though the link of these two events cannot be substantiated by sufficient historical documents. Admittedly, what exact aims Mao had in mind when he started the revolution remain a contentious subject. However, many serious scholars hold the view that the fundamental aim was to transform people and remould the soul (Karnow 1990, 182) and specifically to revolutionise Chinese society in terms of arts and literature, culture in general, ideology and politics. This view can be evidenced by an analysis of the actual progress and the management of the revolution.

Mao believed that through the creative labour of revolutionary artists and writers, the raw materials found in people's lives could be shaped into the ideological form of literature and arts to serve the masses. (Mao 1967, 81) However, far from being a literary and aesthetic theorist, Mao's concept of the relationship between arts and politics appeared to be muddled and driven by political utilitarianism.

With such a staunch belief, Mao repeatedly called for reforms of arts and literature. The Cultural Revolution provided a hotbed for Mao to implement this concept. Mao reiterated that literature and arts should "serve the interests of the masses" in the new socialist context. Anything else was written off as "revisionist" and thus must not have any place in the new socialist society.

It was under such circumstances that the Cultural Revolution arts, the model Beijing Operas in particular, were shaped, crafted and (re)produced. This was a time that "steadfast political correctness" completely dominated the cultural activities and intellectual thinking. According to Mao and other Party ideologues, literary works and cultural and artistic presentations should reflect achievements of the socialist state and the struggle of the labouring masses against the old ruling classes. They also repudiated the complexities and ambiguities of aesthetic modernism and any obscure western forms of arts in favour of an uplifting clarity, simplicity and directness in artistic expression, literary writing and performing arts.

This era produced some highly politicised artistic and literary works including songs, films, paintings and other forms of literary works, with the so-called eight revolutionary model operas and ballets at its pinnacle, which were further made into films and adapted into other forms of plays and regional operas. Hence the decade was known as the "era of the eight model operas" in terms of artistic and cultural creativity.

The 1949 revolution, for the first time in history, established the unified modern nation state. The political unity of the new nation gave rise to Marxism as an official ideology that became an overarching grand narrative, which sanctioned legitimation to other forms of languages and discourses. The Cultural Revolution arts arose to the calls of such a grand narrative. It posited a different language unprecedented in Chinese society. However the marriage between this traditional form of art (Beijing opera) and the new language under the grand narrative is a subtle and complex one.

It was not just a coincidence that Beijing opera became the medium for such a purpose. The conventions of the traditional Beijing opera [Jingju] with their moral didacticism, clarity of characterisation, highly emotive conventional melodic tunes, and emphasis on perfection of performing technique complemented in a subtle way the new ideology that the Party wanted to procreate and disseminate. They represented a concurrent of the Chinese cultural heritage and that of the new socialist meta-narrative.

Initially, the fundamental raison d'être for the birth and growth of revolutionary arts was partly due to an "irresistible impulse" to create a language and culture in the context of the grand narrative that took upon itself a new language of "emancipation of humankind", with heroic workers, peasants and soldiers at the heart of artistic and literary works, which represents a revolutionary departure from the conventional artistic and literary representations of characters in this form of art.

However, there new type of Beijing operas was not created by Mao's wife, Jiang Qing and her cronies in the first place. In fact, these modern operas were created by some enthusiastic traditional opera writers. They were originally *a* form of art among many others and thus contributed to a cultural diversity and development. Jiang Qing merely selected a number of existing new Beijing operas[1], or revolutionary modern operas, and revamped them into "model operas" to serve a purpose. The transformation from traditional Beijing opera to model opera was itself an interesting political cultural phenomenon, which was linked to many cultural and political dynamics of Chinese society and history.

These model operas were initially genuinely received and widely applauded. Some scholars argue that external reasons could be accounted for this initial enthusiasm, such as lack of other form of entertainment, political pressure to embrace them, and simply curiosity for such innovative artistic representations. However, a close analysis will inform that that there exist some intrinsic qualities as well as contextualities that attracted its spectatorship, not only for the first time, but also for the second time around.

On the surface, it was regarded at the time as a totally revolutionary renovation breaking down the conventions that Beijing opera should only portray the historical. The official slogan that legitimated such a transformation was "to inherit critically". However, artistically and culturally, the earlier modern operas, especially the five original ones[2], were already in existence and had been well received by the viewing public. These are the results of a successful reform of the conventional theatre. The new operas maintained the conventional performing protocols, leitmotifs and musicality that were deeply rooted in Chinese culture and psyche. It did away with the facial painting or face masks [lianpu] and employed the modern standard vernacular [putonghua] for spoken parts instead of the conventional classical articulation. The following analysis proves that the appeal of Beijing opera was deeply rooted in Chinese consciousness.

First of all, the modern operas, though telling stories of the contemporary rather than the historical, basically follow the conventions of two sub-genres of the opera, the martial [wuxi] and the civil [wenxi]. Martial plays mainly portray historical events with a particular spectacle of battle scenes by employing acrobatic martial arts performance. The protagonists are normally heroic historical figures. The stories of more recent warfare of the anti-Japanese war and civil wars led by the Communist Party can be suitably adapted to this genre. Civil plays (wenxi) are traditionally love stories, or portrayals of events of a social nature. This genre in the new context was reworked to portray the political struggle of the time to a great effect.

Secondly, a Chinese Beijing opera theatre can be said to symbolise a minimalism. With a particular emphasis on highly stylised artistic performance, the mise-en-scène or stage setting is more imaginary than realistic. The props and setting are kept at a minimal necessity, except for occasionally a lavishly embroidered silk backdrop. Even for the very few props that are placed on stage, they are very often highly symbolic dependent on the context of the play and generally not for realistic usage[3]. This imaginary and symbolic quality of the stage setting appeal to audience's imaginative faculty and creativity and prompt them to rationalise the events and concepts by applying their imagination. This routine also requires impeccable skills from the performing artists and makes the audience focus on the actual dialogue and performance. On a level of *realpolitik*, the gap between the real and idealised world can be filled by the audience's imagination. On a practical level, the minimal requirement of settings and props proves to be advantageous in production, a contributory factor for the popularity of this form of artistic representation.

Thirdly, the musicality is another unique feature which adds to its artistic complexity of Beijing opera. The music is highly rhythmic and percussion is at the times exceptionally intense with the loud clanging of gongs and cymbals, sharp clatter of the drum, clapping of the wooden castanets, and piercing sound of the Beijing violin [jinghu], together with the traditional melodic tunes, all of which adds to an uplifting sensation and suspense at times. Beijing opera can be said to contain a wealth of unique Chinese musical genomes, to form a unique symphonic composition, which strikes a poignant chord of a Chinese psyche.

Fourthly, highly stylised and crafted and strictly structured performance is another dimension that accentuates the artistic and the abstract. The body movements are crafted to be symbolic rather than realistic. The actions on stage are *sculptured* to be different from the real, presenting a series of sculpture-like movements, which very often signify a physical or an inner world beyond the character. The interpretation is highly dependent upon the viewer's imagination. The performance follows an extremely stringent set of rules and criteria.

Finally in contrast to the minimalism of mise-en-scène and props, the costumes of Beijing opera are remarkably elaborate, bright in colour, using reflective fabric materials, and often decorated with metal ornaments. Furthermore in traditional Beijing operas, faces are painted with a variety of colours to indicate the persona of the characters. In the model Beijing operas, the traditional costumes obviously became anachronism and the facial painting became redundant because of the emphasis of a much-vaunted clarity and simplicity of characters by the new artistic initiative. However, in this context its clarity, simplicity and directness in artistic expression are complemented by the traditional signatures of musical forms and exigency of performing techniques.

Artistically speaking, the cultural legacy of this new form of opera is clearly recognisable. The principle of "inheriting critically" mainly applied to the content of the operas and the integrity of this artistic form and the cultural representation was very much intact. This reflects Mao's literary initiative to "strife for the unity of revolutionary content with the highest possible artistic form". (Mao, 1967) This implementation of this initiative was made possible by reinventing this traditional form of art. In so doing, though such a practice bears a utilitarian badge, it recognises the quintessence of the Chinese history and culture and the process cannot be said to be totally arbitrary.

However, the crisis occurred when the Gang of Four made them into the *only* form, and the meaning of these plays metamorphosed, because art as Form means not the beautification of the given but the construction of an entirely different and opposed reality. The aesthetic view is part of the revolution". (Marcuse 1972, 51) Mao's policy in literature and arts led to a state-managed culture which assumed hitherto unimagined proportions in the Cultural Revolution, during which a reconstruct of political system and the creation of a revolutionary culture took place in a parallel manner, one complemented and reinforced the other. The playwrights were constantly told by Jiang Qing and political authorities to mend and patch their works in order to produce revolutionary artistic works of perfection. Consequently, they were torn between their artistic instinct and professionalism as an artist, and the overriding political correctness and more tragically the consequent fear of being accused of political incorrectness. Thus in such a context these model operas became an instrument to cultural hegemony and political deprivation all in the name of the Cultural Revolution. Once it was upheld as the only and highest form of artistic expression, other forms were either neglected or condemned to history. Eventually this form of art only reinforced an increasingly monolithic social and political discourse which left the nation without a real denominator and designator to analyse the meaning of the events and affairs. Moreover, the one-dimensional political discourse – regarded as instrumental to the Cultural Revolution conducted in the name of cultural and political revolutions – resulted in society of a subservient mass mentality and little individuality. It is not surprising that the Cultural Revolution turned into cultural vandalism. Most culture-creators were banished from society. Many of their talents and resources were squandered by the regime's leaders in the pursuit of a flawed political ideal. This political ideal created a one-dimensional society and these operas were canonised into the only form of art which did nothing but to reinforce a received political wisdom in society.

Arts and Contexts: Aesthetics after Propaganda

The death of Mao Zedong (1976) gave the more liberal-minded leaders in the Party an opportunity to take control of power and they swiftly put a stop to the Cultural Revolution, which was implicitly and officially denounced and liquidated. The model operas were invariably criticised and ridiculed because of its close association with the Gang of Four and the radical leftist ideology. Some classic Marxist doctrines were questioned. Under such circumstances, the Cultural Revolution arts were conveniently "forgotten". They disappeared altogether from the Chinese cultural landscape for a number of years. Extraordinarily enough, the main criticism, from official media and academic publications alike, mainly focused on their association with the Gang of Four and their ultra-leftist thinking rather than the works themselves. This tendency, not surprisingly, reflected the public's repulsion about these works as a result of imposition upon them by the authority and more importantly their destitute brought about by the ultra-leftist ideology and policies.

The new leadership pursued a more open and pragmatic political policy. China has since embarked on a programme of economic reforms aimed at liberalising the planned economy by a gradual implementation of the market mechanism. The reform and social transformation was unprecedented in recent Chinese history and required a new cultural and socio-political discourse, images of the time, and new ways of thinking. These model Beijing operas and ballets were seen in contradiction to the spirit of the reform and thus they were shunned by the authorities and the generally public alike. Meanwhile, other forms of arts and literature mushroomed, most notably novels, plays and films and many pre-Cultural Revolution works also made a momentous comeback. All these drew the public's attention from the Cultural Revolution arts. It was not until years later that when the economic reform was firmly on the way, the model Beijing operas and other forms of the Cultural Revolution literature and arts gradually resurfaced. In 1985, to mark the occasion of the 40th anniversary of the victory over Japan and the end of World War II, a compilation of original model operas was broadcasted for the first time on a national television network, which signalled the second coming of this particular form of arts, though previous acts of the model Beijing operas were on occasion performed in public arenas and arias were broadcasted on regional radio and television channels. Later on, Tianjin Opera Troupe made a tour to Guangzhou and Hong Kong with some of the model operas, among them an earlier version of *Capture of the Tiger Mountain* [*Zhiqu Weihushan*] (before Jiang Qing got involved in taking charge of supervising the production). A new production of the model version of *The Red Lantern* [*Hongdeng Ji*] was televised on the Chinese Central Television with most of its original cast. Into the 1990s and the new century, with the advent of the new technology, a large quantity of CDs and DVDs of the model Beijing operas, ballets and songs were sold for more personal consumptions this time. Online sites devoted to model Beijing operas are thriving rapidly. Soon the revival of the model Beijing operas have formed part of the campaign for conservation of the cultural heritage of Beijing opera as a whole in recent years. Presently Shajiabang is being made into a 30-episode television drama series with a strong cast, some of whom are internationally renowned film actors. These Cultural Revolution arts have now become regular programmes on national and regional radios and television channels.

This phenomenon not only affords refreshing insight into Chinese society and culture, and raises serious theoretical questions about literature and arts, but also opens up cultural and socio-political spaces for both Chinese and Western scholars to rethink the politics of Chineseness and to debate the promises and perils of the socialist revolution as well as global capitalism and its implication to China. This paper tries to link this phenomenon on two levels: pragmatic and theoretical. The revival of the Cultural Revolution arts is first determined by the intrinsic nature of this form of art itself, and equally importantly by the historical context when the works are being read or seen.

The first element has been partly analysed in the last part. To further the previous argument, I quote Gadamer, who notes in his edifying book, *Truth and Method*,

> Temporal distance has obviously another meaning than that of the quenching of our interest in the object. It lets the true meaning of the object emerge fully. But the discovery of the true meaning of a text or a work of art is never finished; it is in fact an infinite process. Not only are fresh sources of error constantly excluded, so that the true meaning has filtered out of it all kinds of things that obscure it, but there emerge continually new sources of understanding, which reveal unsuspected elements of meaning. (Gadamer 1975, 265–6)

As the economic reform was deepening, a feeling of ambiguities, contradictions and uncertain trajectories of development started to unsettle Chinese society. The social price and pain of the transformation cast a long shadow over the direction of development and future in store for China. Politically, a theoretical conceptualisation of the meaning of Chinese socialism or post-socialism in the context of global capitalist modernity was imperative in order to explain China's direction. As some commentators observed at the time, "economic progress has exacted a fearful social price". (Meisner 1999, 478–9) In addition, against such an international background, in which the anti-capitalist emancipation was widely discredited and globalisation became the world's only currency, the poor and the disfranchised seemed to be further marginalised and have much to lose and little to gain. Though the reform was regarded as a panacea to China's existing problems, it came with the plights of emergent capitalism and the European ideology of modernity. Whilst the 1990s was characterised by a binary position amongst Chinese intellectuals; the continuing sense of the euphoric New Era sustained by a longest economic growth in history and the feeling of disorientation, a "depressingly bleak, disoriented period," (Zhang 1998, 1–8) it was seen by many Western scholars through "the language of lack."

This second coming of the past propaganda literature can be explained by Gadamer's concept of temporal distance. Fundamentally, arts and literature are forms of representation. Hence there exists an irreducible difference between representation and what it represents. Social and political developments add new elements and dimensions to the representation, which makes the reading of literature a perpetual liberating process. Once the reader is freed from all the subjections and captivities, as Gadamer also argues, "not occasionally only, but always, the meaning of a text goes beyond its author. That is why understanding is not merely a reproductive, but always a productive attitude as well". (Gadamer 1975, 264) The truth artistic works try to communicate is always a referential one, not a predetermined one. To bridge the representation and the represented is a contingent engagement, which created a space to draw the viewer, the reader and the spectator into an open critical dialogue rather than being guided by an established genre of discourse that has particular ends in mind from the beginning.

Thus consequently a re-visit to such arts in the reform years in China has created a new critical language and improve critical literacy among the general public. Because the texts of the past have now become objects in our present-day world, they can be scrutinised by our present-day notions and concepts. Thus we are able to see similarities and differences, and continuities and discontinuities. Only by way of employing our new understanding to these artistic expressions can we construct their historical meaning in the present day, and their relevance and insight to our current existence.

On the other hand, due to the process of reforms in many aspects of the Chinese life, it has acquired a new critical language that is able to reconstruct new meanings of such forms of arts.

Moreover, because some propaganda literature and arts were created to compensate for the shortcomings of the system, it also bears witnesses to these shortcomings. Inferentially they represented irony to the contemporary reader. The new historical environment translated these works into a new autonomy and broadened their literariness and poetic quality so that they were to release new meanings into society and politics. These works of art (admittedly some are of high artistic quality) have regained qualities that opposed the given reality in the new context. They made *us* uncomfortable, and quasi-pessimistic. However, a pleasure will arise from the viewing and reading, a pleasure of a better understanding of *ourselves* and the world around us. Thus to revisit such forms of arts not only remind us of our past, but also inform on the present and the future.

It can be argued that new historical circumstances impose new meanings on artistic representations, even those once-inanimate artistic works. Levinson, whilst assessing Budd's recent publication *Values of Art: Pictures, Poetry and Music* in his article "Art, Value, and Philosophy" argues:

> Since actual influence on the history of art depends ... not only on the nature of the work and the relations it bears to its antecedents, but on a contingent degree of receptivity to and uptake of what it offers, this means we may need to recognize a measure of artistic luck in how much artistic value attaches to a work – for that is what actual as opposed to merely

potential, groundbreakingness, seminality, and so on, require. We should in addition be prepared to accept the consequence that the full artistic value of a work in effect accumulates over time, and is thus not definitively assessable at a work's point of origin. (Levinson 1996, 672)

After all, like literature, arts are "like an ear that can hear things beyond the understanding of the language of politics; it is like an eye that can see beyond the color spectrum perceived by politics", (Calvino 1987, 97) because literature and arts can "make discoveries that sooner or later turn out to be vital areas of collective awareness". (Calvino 1987, 97) In today's world, it is still artistic and literary works that travel the farthest and echoes mostly loudly.

Against the new socio-political circumstances, the propaganda literature and art is to release a profound social and political consciousness into the mind of the readership and audience. It makes the reader and the viewer to question their own thought systems, the history and the given. By doing so, the reader enter a new engagement with the political world, which eventually is to translate into actions to chart the future of their destiny. Thus this forms of art, viewed in the new circumstances, offer both symbolic and metaphorical meaning which depends on the notion that they not only form part of our consciousness, but also provide a space to relive the conflicts and contradictions. Only this time around the audience are repositioned to seek their own subjective reality, rewrite their own individual history from the visual spectacle of a historical China. "To be 'ill' brings hope; for every sickness there is a painkiller, a therapy or a medicine". (Schuster 1992, 595) Thanks to the philosophical power of arts to oppose the given reality, it is not only able to diagnose the noxious symptoms in society, but also to start a healing process. To go back to Aristotle, literature contributes to the elevation of mankind, to *paideia*. By showing us that which is possible, and by involving us in the inescapable passage of tragic events, readers and spectators are drawn into emotions of fear and compassion, emotions that lead to *katharsis*, a process that purifies us of megalomania (*hubris*), protecting us from unrestrained tyranny from either a totalitarian rule, fundamentalist religion, or dehumanising globalisation of capitalism.

In conclusion, these arts bear a sensitivity of the time and represent a vision, which, though largely discredited due to destruction in the Cultural Revolution, but is nonetheless a vision that contains sensibilities of Chineseness. The revival of these forms of arts recognised the uniqueness of the Chinese revolution and history and serves as an antidote to the sweeping globalisation that is going under way in China. The revival of these particular forms of performing arts is conducive to accommodating diversified political values and to recognise China's historical and cultural tenets. In theoretical terms, they add a new dimensional to the development of political concepts and prospects in society. It precipitates the economic and political reforms and developments by way of interpolating new ideas and visions and concocting all parameters such as politics, economics, philosophy, psychology and language in society into an extensive cultural and intellectual development. This also proves what Connery pointed out previously, the phenomenon helps Chinese people recognise their history and the 1949 revolution, which, according to Connery, "was not just a marking of the China difference", but "also the hope of a global possibility". (Connery 1992)

Notes

1 Traditionally, all Beijing operas carried the theme of a historical event. Therefore, Beijing operas that portray contemporary or modern events are called new Beijing operas [Xin jingju].
2 They are *Capture of the Tiger Mountain* [*Zhiqu Weihushan*], *On the Docks* [*Haigang*], *Raid on the White Tiger Regiment* [*Qixi Baihutuan*], *Shajiabang* [originally entitled *Sparks Amid the Reeds* [*Ludang Huozhong*], and *The Red Lantern* [*Hongdeng Ji*], plus two modern ballets, *The Red Women Brigade* [*Hongse Niangzijun*] and *The White-Haired Girl* [*Bai Maonü*] and a symphony version of *Shajiabang*. Other later model operas include *Song of the Dragon River* [*Longjiang Song*], *The Azalea Mountain* [*Dujuan Shan*], *Ode to the Yimeng Mountain* [*Yimeng Song*], *Battle on the Plains* [*Pingyuan Zuozhan*], and *Sons and Daughters of the Grassland* [*Caoyuan Ernü*].
3 For instances, the table and chairs covered with colourful fabrics can symbolise a throne, or a wall, a well, a mountain, or other locale. A bridge is signified by a table with a chair facing outwards on each side; a tower or throne is represented by a table with a chair atop clad in embroidered fabrics.

Bibliography

Andrews, Julia. 1994 *Painters and politics in the People's Republic of China, 1949-1979*. Berkeley: University of California Press.
Brown, Jeremy. 2003 Putting culture back into the Cultural Revolution: Shifting scholarly views of Chinese art and culture, 1977-2002, http://orpheus.ucsd.edu/chinesehistory/cr/jeremy.htm (accessed October 18, 2005).
Calvino, Italo (1987) *The literature machine: Essays*, (trans. Creagh, Patrick) London: Secker & Warburg.
Chen, Xiaomei. 2002 *Acting the right part: Political theater and popular drama in contemporary China*. Honolulu: University of Hawai'i Press.

Connery, Chris. 1992. The China difference. *Postmodern Culture.* 2 (2) (January 1992).

Dong, Jianhui. 2005. Political culture and the public literary creation of the Cultural Revolution. *Journal of Shandong Normal University (Humanities and Social Sciences).* 50 (1): 82–86.

Gadamer, Hans-Georg. 1975. *Truth and method.* London: Sheed & Ward.

Gu, Yuanqing. 2005. Review on literature of the Culture Radical Party During the Period of Cultural Revolution (sic). *Journal of Hubei Institute of Education.* 22 (1): 6–13.

Karnow, Stanley. 1990 *Mao and China: A legacy of turmoil.* London: Penguin.

Levinson, Jerrold. 1996 Art, value, and philosophy. *Mind,* 105 (October 1996).

Mao, Zedong, 1967 *Selected works of Mao Zedong vol. iii,* Beijing: Foreign Languages Press.

Marcuse, Herbert. 1972 Art as form of reality. *New Left Review,* 1972 (74).

Meisner, M. 1999. *Mao's China and after: A history of the People's Republic.* New York: Free Press.

Schuster, Shlomit C. 1992. Philosophy as if it matters: The practice of philosophical Counselling, *Critical Review.* 6 (4)

Wang, Ban. 2002 The Cold War, imperial aesthetics, and area studies. *Social Text 72,* 20 (3): 45–65.

Wang, Yao. 1999. Constitution and operation of the mainstream thought of literature and art during Cultural Revolution (sic): The first study of the literature during Cultural Revolution. *Journal of Huaqiao University (Philosophy & Social Science).* 1999 (2): 56–62.

Wu, Shanzeng. 2004 The origin of modernity in the mainstream Cultural Revolution literature. [Original translation of the title: The deep-going source of modernity in the mainstream literature of 'Cultural Revolution']. *Journal of Qinghai Normal University (Philosophy and Social Sciences)* 2004 (4): 75–9.

Xu, Xun. 1998. *Nationalism and the Nation State [Minzuzhuyi].* Beijing: Chinese Social Sciences Press, 144.

Yang, Dingchuan. 1997. The literature in the Cultural Revolution: A distorted literature. *Journal of Foshan University.* 15 (3): 67–72.

Zhang, Xudong. 1997 *Chinese modernism: In the era of reform; cultural fever, avante garde fiction and the new Chinese cinema.* London: Duke University Press.

CHAPTER SEVEN

ELIZABETH JACOBS

CHERRÍE MORAGA AND THE DISRUPTION OF PSYCHOANALYSIS

Recent theorising by Chicana feminists attempts to construct a specific linking of literary practice with the historical, political and cultural particularity of Chicana experiences. Some of the most exciting interdisciplinary developments in Chicana/o criticism in recent years has been the creation of a diverse range of theoretical approaches with which to think seriously about the perspectives of politically and culturally marginalised Chicana women and their literature. Their texts resonate with the tensions of political and economic disenfranchisement, with gender stratification, with the Chicano ideology of sexual orientation and machismo that historically defined and delimited Chicana subjectivity; with the conflicted trajectories of racial identification, but also with the diverse forms of self-empowerment they have employed to carve out some resistant cultural practice. Their theoretical practice while emerging from a generic "U.S. Feminism", is thus at the same time deeply rooted in the material conditions of Chicanas in the United States.

While this method enables Chicana women to create their own viable models for literary analysis, much contemporary writing by Chicanas or Mexican American women also resonates with the issues articulated by the French feminists in the late 1970s and early 1980s. Among Chicana critics Norma Alarcón is perhaps the most purely theoretically based, constructing her theoretical and analytical framework from French and American feminist writing. She states that Chicanas who define themselves primarily as creative writers also readily incorporate a critical engagement in their writing suggesting "a complicity with, a resistance to, and a disruption of Western psychoanalysis" (Lavie and Swedenbourg 1996, 52). For Alarcón this strategy is uppermost in Gloria Anzaldúa's highly influential text, *Borderlands/la frontera* (1987) which records "frequent shifts of the subject from one fixed position to another in a kind of optional multiplicity of insertions of the subject into a relatively fixed Symbolic Order":

> She cuts across Eurohegemonic representations of Woman, now Freudian/Lacanian psychoanalysis ("I know things older than Freud" 1987, 26) through Jungian psychoanthropology, and the rationality of the sovereign subject as she, in non-linear and nondevelopmental ways, shifts the names of her resistant subject positions: Snake Woman, La Chingada, Tlazolteotl, Coatlicue, Cihuacoatl, Tonantsi, Gaudalupe, La Llorona.... (Alarcón 1996, 47-8)

The polyvalent name insertions are, in Alarcón words, a "rewriting of the feminine, 'a reinscription of gynetics' an attempt to rediscover what Freud's system and in Lacanian terms the 'patronymic' legal system displaces." (1996)

Cherrie Moraga's *Giving Up The Ghost* (1986) and *Loving in the War Years/ lo nunca pasó por sus labios,* (1983) also epitomise this tendency. They articulate a blurring of the creative and critical that mixes theoretical discourse with literary texts. Their perspective is political, ideological, and critical, incorporating many of the principal ideas of feminist thinkers, at the same time as Alarcón (1990b) points out, they also problematise the theoretical subject of their discourse (Anzaldúa 1990, 356-369). Most obviously concurring with mainstream feminist approaches in the sense that they address the political motives behind male constructions of female sexuality, Chicana writers reveal the binary oppositions and stereotypes that have served to alienate and disempower them. They often critique binary logic, particularly the subject-object dichotomy, in a way that has resonance with the theoretical work of Hélène Cixous. Like Chicana writers, Cixous argues that a patriarchal western philosophical tradition has consistently organised conceptions of the world into binary oppositions, such as light and dark, man and woman, logos and body (Marks and de Courtivron 1980, 366-71). Within this system these terms are never equal but are "hierarchised" within patriarchal culture, resulting in the privileging of one side of the opposition (male) at the expense of the other (female). Cixous (1980) goes on to argue that the underlying structure of a phallocentric symbolic order is therefore geared towards securing meaning through the repression of the feminine. The patriarchal imaginary and its symbolic register is organised around the privileging of the phallus and so implicitly inscribes the female as an absent and passive second term. In this structure of differences the female is only present in such a way as to confirm the primacy of the male (Marks and de Courtivron 1980, 366-71).

Chicana writing often questions this hierarchical ordering, and ultimately seeks to subvert its assumptions. Chicana works both reveal and deconstruct cultural constructions of female identity particularly the restricted gender roles defined through the binary logic of masculine/feminine, active/passive, and subject/object. As I go on to discuss, in the Chicano context this logic is expressed more specifically through the virgen/puta (virgin/whore) and chingón/chingada polarity. These opposed pairs were basic to gender distinction in Chicano culture and served to reinforce a general sense of the masculine as that which always desires to dominate, to categorise, and to limit with set terms. Cixous (1980) suggests that something in the dominated side of the couple could escape from this hierarchisation. She states, "either the woman is passive or she doesn't exist. What is left is unthinkable, unthought of." (Marks and de Courtivron 1980, 366-71) Here the first sentence refers to the logic of patriarchy, in the sense that Chicana subjectivity has been traditionally confined to passive stereotypes. The second sentence suggests that there may be something in the feminine that is not passive; an argument that in turn has resonance with contemporary Chicana feminism. According to patriarchal logic, this could not exist, it is left "unthinkable, unthought of." Cixous (1980) however goes on to argue that this logic is threatened by the "bringing forth" of possibilities within the term of femininity itself. Any discrepancy in the circularity of this logic (the masculine is always superior because the feminine is always inferior) will bring about its collapse (Marks and de Courtivron 1980, 366-71).

At the level of representation Chicana writing initiates an unsettling and a reconfiguration of patriarchal ideology in terms of the "violent hierarchy of the man-woman" dyad outlined above. In many Chicana literary works representations of sexuality are played out against normative models of sex, gender and associated social roles and qualities. In *Giving up the Ghost* Moraga's representation of the lesbian subject involves a radical challenge to the traditional construction of gender in psychoanalytic terms, which is usually constituted through ideas of contrasting male and female imaginaries. In the Freudian paradigm female sexuality is viewed and defined in relation to or in opposition to male sexuality, and coded in terms of reproduction that are linked to male pleasure and desire. In contrast, lesbian sexuality exposes the contradictions in heterosexual models of femininity and reveals the control that phallocentric systems of thought exert upon women. Moraga refuses to align lesbian sexuality with either masculinity or femininity, but employs it to expose the artifice of the division between the two. Thus the introduction of lesbian sexuality into modes of representation reserved traditionally as the arena for male desire also destabilise the gender constructs entrenched within Chicano culture. One of the main tools for the transmission and maintenance of the hierarchies within Chicano culture has traditionally been the family, a model that replicated Freud's Oedipal economy shaped by the father as transcendental signifier. Chicana writing and interpretation disrupts this model by subversively exposing the gaps and contradictions in heterosexual structures and systems of thought in ways that have recast the form and function of *la familia*. The primacy of the nuclear family characterisable as a patriarchal site with rigidly delineated boundaries and an exclusively heterosexual orientation is contested in much contemporary writing. I explore this tendency with particular reference to *Giving Up The Ghost*, which articulates a controversial use of the Freudian Oedipal complex to yield an image of family pathology as the following quotations from the play illustrate:

> My sister was in love with my brother
> My mother loved her father.
> My first woman, the man who put her away. (Moraga 1986, 16)

The main protagonists are also said to have "gone against the code de pueblo" in forming their same sex relationship as it contests the terms of "the law":

> I was not afraid the gods would enact their wrath
> against our pueblo for breaking the taboo.
>
> it was merely...that the taboo...could be broken.
> and if this law nearly transcribed in blood
> could go...
> then, what else?
>
> what was there to hold to?
> what immovable truths were left? (Moraga 1986, 52)

Violating the laws and taboos surrounding gender roles and sexuality their relationship functions to define their subject positions as transgressors of the Freudian economy as well as conventional theatrical space, as the opening speaker tells us, the play mainly revolves around the question of "prison, politics and sex" (Moraga 1986, 1). The prison to which the speaker refers designates the repressive coding given to women, Moraga's stage directions emphasise this as the play centres on limited locations within which the female characters move. These locations, which are described as "the street, a bed, a kitchen", reflect the three main spaces offered to Mexican American women within their culture, and indicates a prescriptive and rigidly defined conception of female identity. As Anzaldúa (1987) states, "for a woman of my culture there used to be only three directions she could turn: to the church as a nun, to the streets as a prostitute, or to the home as a mother." (Anzaldúa 1986, 17)

The action of *Giving Up The Ghost* centres on these spaces as much as the three female characters and the relationships between them. Two of the characters are one and the same person; Marisa is a Chicana in her late twenties, Corky, her "other" pubescent and adolescent self, is a pachuca at ages eleven and seventeen years old. The other character Amalia is a middle-aged Mexican woman who is Marisa's lover. With this female triadic matrix, Moraga can be seen to be both reworking the classic dramatic structure and the Freudian Oedipal triangle. This effectively challenges the heterosexism of dominant patterns of representation and instead suggests the dramatic possibilities of a woman centred system.

Each of the characters is recognisable by their own language, dress, psychic registers and gendered codes. Amalia's accent, Indio looks and fuller body type clearly mark her Mexicano heritage and cultural background. Marisa and Corky embody the role of the butch; Amalia their opposite embodies the femme. Amalia's Spanish is more lyrical than either Marisa's or Corky's; her appearance is said to be "soft"; her clothes give the impression of being draped, as opposed to worn: "Shawl- over-blouse- over skirt all of Mexican Indian design. Her hair is long and worn down or loosely braided." (Introduction) Although men are marginal to the narrative, Amalia's past male lovers, Alejandro and Carlos, haunt her, to the extent that they constantly interrupt the development of a fully erotic relationship with her lover Marisa. At the opening of the play Marisa declares that the figure of the male lover "is a ghost/ always haunting her...lingering" (Moraga 1986, 3). And again later in Act One when Amalia learns of Alejandro's death she simultaneously feels her womanhood leave her and his ghost being born in her:

> When I learned of Alejandro's death,
> I died too, weeks later.
> I just started bleeding and the blood wouldn't stop,
> not until his ghost had passed through me
> or was born in me
> I don't know which.
>
> (pause) Except since then,
> I feel him living in me

Every time I touch *la Marisa*
I felt my womanhood leave me.
Does this make sense?
And it was Alejandro being born in me. (Moraga 1986, 27)

Judith Butler might call the reappearance of Amalia's lovers "the normative phantasm of a compulsory heterosexuality," which in the play re-emerges like the "return of the repressed" to haunt Marisa and Amalia's relationship (Arrizón 1999, 137). The sense of entrapment within this symbolic order is contextualised through the strong association established between heterosexuality and loss and melancholia. Amalia later refers to the men who have used her sexually as "un río de cuerpos muertos" (a river of dead corpses) (Moraga 1987, 24) and through repeated allusions the predominant tone associated with heterosexuality becomes one of silence, trauma and death:

i'd watch it move from outside the house
that crazy espíritu of hers had been out making tracks.
i'd watch it come inside through the door
watch it travel all through her own private miseries
and finally settle itself right there in the room with us. (Moraga 1986, 57)

Unlike Amalia's male ghosts, the ghost Marisa must relinquish is that of her younger self, Corky. When Corky first appears she is dressed in the "chuca" style of the 1960s, she also speaks in calo and is generally depicted as a street wise, defiant, and dangerous character:

the smarter I get the older I get the meaner I get
    tough ...
    sometimes I even pack a blade no one knows
    I never use it or nut'ing but can feel it there
        there in my pants pocket run the pad of my thumb over it
to remind me I carry some'ting am sharp secretly. (Moraga 1986, 4)

Despite this cool and tough exterior, Corky and her experiences of rape and oppression is one of the ghosts to be given up in Moraga's play. The memory of these experiences as a young girl haunt her older self Marisa in the form of a pain that disables her, making her legs feel "like they got rocks in em" (Moraga 1986, 7). The dramatic action borders the past and recovers the anger and dispossession that lead to this state of symbolic disempowerment. As the ghosts appear and embody these repressed events, the play can be said to enact a kind of psycho epic. (Neate 1998, 205) The dramatic time of *Giving up the Ghost* mimics

psychological time, it is unpredictable, moving in and out of the present
and the past paralleling the retrospective process of uncovering the
repressed. Focusing upon the play's lack of normative temporality,
Yarbro-Bejarano analyses the ways in which the drama enacts the sense of
being haunted by a sinful and violent past, which demands exorcism
through a performance of memory. She states that "the monologues
...negate[s] chronology. They arise as memories arise, at times through
association..." (Yarbro-Bejarano 1987, 21) The psychological time space
is thus further emphasised through the displacement of a historicizing
narrative with several narratives that co-exist and at times conflict with
each other.

These narratives also present multiple interpretations of Chicana
identity politics. For instance the social roles of women and men are
constantly undermined through complex and ironic manipulations of
normative expectations about sexuality and gender. At one point during
Act One, Corky's older self Marisa declares that,

It's not that you don't want a man,
You just don't want a man in a man.
You want a man in a woman.
The woman-part goes without saying.
That's what you always learn to want first. (Moraga 1986, 29)

These gender transgressive positions can be read as a radical critique
of traditional designations of female sexuality, which promoted a binary
logic that legitimised the oppression of Chicana women. Marisa's
viewpoint in contrast is sexualised in a way that undermines normative
expectations. The interchangeably butch-femme relationship between
Amalia and Marisa present sexualities which are crucial to Moraga's
unsettling of the "violent hierarchy of the man-woman" dyad on a number
of different levels. In one sense they enact a performance that parodies the
entrenched inequalities of the phallic economy represented by the
traditional heterosexual partnership. But in a more culturally specific
sense their relationship, based as it is on "wanting the woman first", is
also a symbolic inversion of the Chicano cultural mandate of "putting the
male first" within Chicano families. Within this economy the mother is
the betrayer of the daughter by loving the males in the family more than
the females, thus bearing responsibility for the daughter's subordination
and abandonment. In her essay *A Long Line of Vendidas* Moraga states
this more explicitly, "You are a traitor to your race if you do not put the
man first. The potential accusation of 'traitor' or 'vendida' is what hangs
above the heads and beats in the hearts of most Chicanas." (Moraga 1983,

103) Under the pressure of the conflation of her sexuality with betrayal, the Chicana must prove her fidelity through commitment to the Chicano male, thereby initiating what Moraga famously terms "A Long Line of Vendidas." By putting women first in her dramatic productions, by excluding men from representation, and by imaging women as desiring subjects, Moraga represents the possibility of liberation from this "prison of sex."

Her strategies of female representation are an inherent part of this liberating project. Among the most significant is the simultaneous appropriation and critique of the symbolism associated with Mexican Catholicism. Inverting the church's inherently patriarchal ideology, it becomes an important source for a Chicana lesbian identity (Yarbro-Bejarano 2001: 90). During the play women and women centred relationships are often expressed in religious terms as a site of worship or as a "liberating angel" and are said to offer "salvation" and "redemption." At one point during the second act titled "La Salvadora" Marisa declares that "Sí. La Mujer es mi religion," and later she places her mother at its centre:

> "n' it was so nice to hear her voice
> so warm like she loved us a lot
> 'n' that night
> being cath-lic felt like my mom
> real warm 'n' dark 'n' kind. (Moraga 1986, 13)

In this scene Moraga shifts the relations of power from the patriarchal conventions normally associated with Mexican Catholicism, to Marisa's mother who is instead figured as the source of religiosity. This feminisation of religion subverts the macho ethic of aguantar (forbearance) and subservience normally associated with the church. The connection between the mother's faith and the daughter's faith in a vision of women bonding also disrupts the usual hierarchies established between god and the priest who exercises the secular control of religious power. By implication this also severs the ties that are normally established between the church's institutionalised authority and its enactment through daily sexual domination.

Closely related to this positive identification between women and religion are the passages that describe the love between the female characters. In these scenes the relations between women are often figured as fluid. As Yarbro-Bejarano states, Moraga's characters represent "non-binary giving and taking in sex within a butch-femme erotics" (Yarbro-Bejarano 2001, 89). These erotic exchanges occur particularly in the

scenes where Marisa and Amalia are collectively remembering the
discovery of their shared desire for each other. At one point Marisa asks
Amalia,

> was the beautiful woman
> in the mirror of the water
> you or me?
> who do I make love to?
> Who do I see in the ocean of our bed? (Moraga 1986, 27)

The breaking down of physical boundaries and the merging of one self
with another represents the paradoxical desire to sink into the other in
order to resolve fragmentation and division, while at the same time to be
without foundation or limits. This challenge to the concept of a unitary
sexual identity is highlighted through the fluid, shifting nature of desire
and pleasure in an undifferentiated sense of selfhood. The breaking down
of physical borders and the merging of one self with another represents a
link between a lack of boundaries and female sexuality that figures
throughout the play.

In keeping with this logic, when the action switches to an earlier
period, we are shown how as a younger woman, Marisa's sexual identity
then was also multiple and complex. At times this complexity is revealed
through the performance of what her younger self Corky calls her "movie
capture games" (Moraga 1986, 9).

> When I was a little kid I useta love the movies
> every Saturday you could find me there
> my eyeballs glued to the screen
>   then during the week my friend Tudy and me
>   we'd make up our own movies
>   one of our favourites was this cowboy one
>   where we'd be out in the desert
>   'n' we'd capture these chicks 'n' hold 'em up
>   for ransom we'd string 'em up 'n'
>   make 'em take their clothes off…
> strip we'd say to the wall
>   all cool-like
>   in my mind I was big 'n' tough 'n' a dude
>
>   in my mind I had all their freedom
>   the freedom to really see a girl
>   kinda the way you see
>   an animal you know? (Moraga 1986, 4-5)

In contrast to the female-to-female identification outlined previously, this scene depicts relationships between women based on patriarchal power differentials. Forced through lack of positive portrayals of Mexicans to turn to consumerised images of white male bravery in order to define herself, Corky further entrenches herself in the domination against which Chicanas stand. Her female "captives" signal a profound lack of personal liberty, whereas freedom is equated with masculinity and the penetrating force of the male gaze. The sexual politics of looking is therefore central to the above scene. Feminist criticism, especially psychosemiotic film criticism, has concentrated on the spectatorial position women occupy both on and off the screen. Corky's "captives" share the quality of "to-be-looked-at-ness," a phrase coined by Laura Mulvey in order to analyse systems of representation which position women as objects to be watched, gazed upon and the source of spectatorial pleasure:

In a world ordered by sexual imbalance, pleasure in looking has been split between active/male and passive/ female. The determining male gaze projects its fantasy on to the female figure, which is styled accordingly... women are simultaneously looked at and displayed, with their appearance coded for strong visual and erotic impact so that they can be said to connote to-be-looked-at-ness. (Mulvey 1989)

In Corky's fantasy women are stripped naked and possess no power and agency over their bodies, but occupy passive recipient positions. She simultaneously objectifies these women while identifying with the male subject of the action. Scripts of American entertainment provide Corky with a syntax and a location from which to forge her identity. Mainly locating her identity in an American "site of production" also enables her to signify on and appropriate the dominant position. She takes up the male gaze, in Freud's terms the "phallic activity linked to...sadistic mastery of the object"; so that the site of her desire is that of a man." (Alarcón 1988, 228) Within the symbolic order the action of the patriarchal subject is to objectify the woman and to deny her subjecthood. Partly because of her own experiences of patriarchy, Corky sees woman as "other", and "inscribes her erotic fantasies of women in contexts of violence and dominance"

As the drama unfolds it becomes clearer why Corky adopts an identity that necessitates the repression of her own femininity, as at the centre of the second act are graphic descriptions of her childhood rape that are retold through a mixture of comedy and pathos. Corky's speeches here, performed in opposition to the sanctity of patriarchal culture and religion, in effect restage a kind of secular confession that presents a radical shift in gendered power relations. Within Catholicism the vows of chastity and obedience function as church laws and any infringement of them has to be confessed to the father. As God's corporeal substitutes and emissaries, this father or the priest is invested with the power to mediate, punish or absolve. A mainstay of this power is the ritual of confession, which as Michel Foucault explains unfolds within a power relationship in which "the agency of domination does not reside in the one who speaks ... but in the one who listens and says nothing" (Trujillo 1998, 148). Moraga disrupts the patriarchal nature of these relations, as the point of address is not the symbolic father of the church or the priest, but the audience who act as Marisa's confessor. The following quotation clearly illustrates this point:

> Got raped once.
> When I was a kid.
>> Taken me a long time to say that was exactly what happened.
>> but that was exactly what happened.
>> Makes you more aware than ever that you are one hunerd percent
>> female, just in case you had any doubts
>> one hunerd percent female whether you act it or like it or not.
>> (Moraga 1986, 36)

De Lauretis argues that it is especially meaningful for Marisa that this confession is directed toward the audience. She states that

> it is of crucial significance that the restaging, the performance, is accomplished for and with the people, a Chicana community who act as both the play's point of address and the point of Marisa's transference; for it is their presence, their participation in the staging, and their recognition of the fantasy that provide the Chicana subject with a meaning and a narcissistically empowered image of her self. (De Lauretis 1994, 57-58)

Corky's speech therefore also poses fundamental questions about constructions of gender identity in the Chicana/o context. Her insight into gender as a performative mode during her confession underscores this. Up until the moment of rape she thought that it would never happen to her because of her appropriated masculinity and denied femininity. But the guilt and shame the rape mobilises is also strongly associated with the myth of Malinche, a central icon within Mexican American culture that contributed to what Alarcón (1989) calls "the extensive ideological sedimentation of the ... [silent] ... good woman and the bad woman archetypes that enabled the cultural nationalistic and paternalistic 'communal modes of power'" (McClintock *et al* 1997, 278). According to tradition Malinche was the mujer mala (the bad woman), whose sexual union with Hernan Cortes made possible the defeat of the Aztec nation. Moraga states that she is thus viewed not, "[as] innocent victim, but ... [as] ... the guilty party ... ultimately responsible for her own sexual victimisation" (Moraga 1983, 118). Each Chicana inherits and transmits this cultural legacy that situates her as "la india/ the whore, la vendida (sell out/betrayer) and la chingada (the fucked one)".

Octavio Paz (1967) was one of the first to note the link between Malinche and the epithet la chingada. He asserts that the verb chingar is masculine, active and cruel, "it stings, wounds, gashes, stains" and "provokes a bitter, resentful satisfaction" (Paz 1967, 77). The object that suffers this action is passive, la chingada, in contrast to the active, aggressive subject who inflicts it. Paz asserted that the passivity of the violated, or la chingada, found its analogy in Malinche. This passivity accordingly causes her "to lose her identity, to lose her name/ she is no-one/ she disappears into nothingness/she is nothingness" (Paz 1967, 77). Taking these factors in to consideration, it is particularly significant that Corky states after the rape that "HE MADE ME A HOLE!" and Marisa later comments in reflection that "He only convinced me of my own name" (Moraga 1986, 43).

Analysing the stereotyping tendencies of this discourse Emma Pérez (1993) argues how the contempt for Chicanas within their own culture began with the Oedipal conquest triangle, within which the indigenous male was castrated and lost his language to that of the white rapist father (De la Torre and Pesquera 1993, 57-71). It is significant then that Corky's violator is white, rapes her while speaking both English and Spanish, and is associated with an Oedipal subtext that clearly demonstrates his paternal signification:

> 'n' I kept getting him confused in my mind this man 'n' his arm
> with my father kept imagining him my father returned
> come back
> I wanted to cry *"papá papá"*...
> *"¿Dónde 'stás papá?"*
> *"¿Dónde 'stás?"*
> 'n' finally i imagine the man answering
> *"aquí estoy. soy tu papá"*
> 'n' this gives me permission to go 'head
> to not hafta fight. (Moraga 1986, 41)

Subliminally imaging these paternal relations, Corky's experiences
establish their point of origin in the primal scene of colonial rape. Rather
than suggesting a continuum in the economy of the masculinist myth that
effectively silenced and marginalized women, her very speech disrupts the
previously repressive coding given to Malinche's cultural legacy. This
successfully enables a reconciliation of self and past experience for her
older self, Marisa. According to de Lauretis (1994) this 'performance' also

> Enacts her simultaneous recrossing of the 'stages' of psychic development
> toward subjectivity and subjecthood ... from primary narcissism and
> autoeroticism to the disavowal of castration and a new body ego. (de
> Lauretis 1994, 57-8)

The staging of Marisa's confession therefore functions as a performative
re-enactment of the mirror stage, in which the audience act as the other in
the mirror. Overall, the multiple facets of all the characters clearly reflect
this, not only challenging the repression of female identity specifically
within the Chicano or Mexican American context, but also providing
Moraga with a specific vantage point from which to criticise and disrupt
the politics, language and institution of psychoanalysis too.

Bibliography

Alarcón, Norma. 1988. Making 'Familia' from Scratch: Split
    Subjectivities in the Work of Helena Maria Viramontes and Cherríe
    Moraga. In *Chicana Creativity and Criticism: Charting New Frontiers
    in American Literature*. eds. Maria Herrera-Sobek, Helena Maria
    Viramontes, 220-232. Houston: Arte Publico Press.
—. 1990. The Theoretical Subject[s] of This Bridge Called My Back and
    Anglo-American Feminism. In *Making Face, Making Soul: Haciendo
    Caras: Creative and Critical Perspectives By Feminists of Color*. ed.
    Gloria Anzaldúa, 356-369. San Francisco: Aunt Lute Books.
—. 1996. Anzaldúa's *Frontera:* Inscribing Gynetics. In *Displacement,
    Diaspora, and Geographies Of Identity*. eds. S. Lavie and T.
    Swedenbourg, 41-54. Durham: Duke University Press.
—. 1997. Traddutora, Traditora: A Paradigmatic Figure of Chicana
    Feminism. In *Dangerous Liasons: Gender, Nation and Postcolonial
    Perspectives*. ed. Anne McClintock, Aamir Mufti, and Ella Shohat,
    278-297. Minneapolis: University of Minnesota Press.
Anzaldúa, Gloria. 1987. *Borderlands/ La Frontera The New Mestiza*. San
    Francisco: Aunt Lute Books.

Arrizón, Alicia. 1999. *Latina Performance: Traversing the Stage.* Bloomington and Indianapolis: Indiana University Press.

Cixous, Hélénè. 1980. Sorties. In *New French Feminisms.* eds. E. Marks and I. De Courtivon, 366-71. Amherst, Mass.: University of Massachusetts Press.

de Lauretis, Theresa. .1994. *The Practice of Love: Lesbian Sexuality and Perverse Desire.* Bloomington and Indianapolis: Indiana University Press.

Gaspar de Alba, Alicia. 1995. The Alter-native grain: theorising Chicana/o popular culture. In *Culture and Difference: Critical Perspectives on the Bi-Cultural Experience in the United States.* ed. Antonia Darder, 105-115. Westport, Connecticut: Bergin and Garvey.

—. 1998. The Politics of Location of the Tenth Muse of America: An Interview with Sor Juana Inés de la Cruz. In *Living Chicana Theory.* ed. Carla Trujillo, 136-165. Berkeley: Third Woman Press.

Moraga, Cherríe. 1986. *Giving Up The Ghost.* Los Angeles: West End Press.

—. 1983. *Loving in the War Years/ lo nunca pasó por sus labios.* Boston: South End Press.

Mulvey, Laura. 1989. *Visual and Other Pleasures*, London: Macmillan.

Neate, Wilson. 1998. *Tolerating Ambiguity: Ethnicity and Community in Chicano/a Writing,* New York: Peter Lang Publishing.

Paz, Octavio. 1967. *The Labyrinth of Solitude,* trans. Lysander Kemp London: Penguin.

Perez, Emma. 1993. Speaking from the Margin: Uninvited Discourse on Sexuality and Power. In *Building With Our Own Hands: New Directions in Chicana Studies.* ed. Andela de la Torre and Beatriz Pesquera, 57-71. Berkeley: University Of California Press.

Yarbro-Bejarano, Yvonne. 1987. Cherríe Moraga's Giving Up the Ghost and Feminist Theory. *Critical Approaches to Hispanic Women's Literature.* Norma Alarcón ed. Houston: Arte Publico Press.

—. 2001. *The Wounded Heart: Writing on Cherríe Moraga.* Austin: University of Texas Press.

CHAPTER EIGHT

CARL LAVERY

NARRATIVE, WALKING
AND PERFORMATIVE CRITICISM

Performative Writing and the Need for Narrative

For the past decade or so, the US theorist Peggy Phelan has championed the practice of what she calls "performative writing", a type of criticism that writes about performance in such a way as to acknowledge both the body of the critic and the intense ephemerality of performance art itself:

> Performative writing is different from personal criticism or autobiographical essay, although it owes a lot to both genres. Performative writing is an attempt to find a form 'for what philosophy wishes all the same to say'. Rather than describing the performance event in direct signification, a task I believe to be impossible and not terrifically interesting, I want this writing to enact the affective force of the performance event itself….(1997, 12)

For Phelan, performative writing's blend of autobiography and theory articulates a very definite form of textual politics, situated somewhere between Brecht and Derrida[1]:

> Performance theory and criticism have tended to respond to the loss of the object by adapting a primarily conservative and conserving method. Writing about performance has largely been dedicated to describing in exhaustive detail the mise-en-scène, the physical gestures, the voice, the score, the action of the performance event. This dedication stems from the knowledge that the reader may not have seen the event and therefore the critic must record it. This urge to record has given rise to an odd situation in which some of the most radical and troubling art of our cultural moment has inspired some of the most conservative and even reactionary critical

commentary. The desire to preserve and represent the performance event is
a desire we should resist. For what one otherwise preserves is an illustrated
corpse, a pop-up anatomical drawing that stands in for the thing that one
most wants to save, the embodied performance. (3)

According to Phelan, the autobiographical nature of performative
writing dispels an essentially authoritarian myth: the sense that a given
work supposedly possesses a transhistorical or metaphysical meaning that
holds good for any space or time. In this way, Phelan claims that she is
able to historicize not only the work in question, but also the act of writing
about it:

> As I attempted to make clear in *Unmarked*, one of the deepest challenges
> of writing about performance is that the object of one's meditation, the
> performance itself, disappears. In this sense, performance theory and
> criticism are instances of writing history. (3)

Phelan's historiography is radical historiography. Unlike bourgeois or
patriarchal critics (and Michael Fried immediately comes to mind here),[2]
Phelan has little interesting in denying history. On the contrary, she
deliberately draws attention to the contingency of her writing. Mimicking
the transience of performance itself, performative writing invests in an
ethics of disappearance, an affirmation of loss. It accepts its own death:

> Mimicry, I am more and more certain, is the fundamental performance of
> this cultural moment. At the heart of mimicry is a fear that the match will
> not hold and the 'thing itself' (you, me, love, art) will disappear before we
> can reproduce it. So we hurl ourselves headlong toward copy machines,
> computers, newspapers, cloning labs. The clichés (among other things) of
> critical prose are themselves symptoms (among other things) of this longed
> for assurance that we are saying something that someone might some day
> hear. I want less to describe and preserve performances than to enact and
> mimic the losses that beat away within them. In this mimicry, loss itself
> helps transform the repetitive force of trauma and might bring about a way
> to overcome it. (12).

Phelan's notion of performative writing has had a major impact on the
way that critics and practitioners think about and document performance.
And since its appearance in the mid-1990s, it has effectively changed the
critical landscape of Performance and Theatre Studies in the UK and US
by legitimising what might otherwise have been dismissed as a marginal,
or perhaps even pretentious, critical practice.[3] However, despite its
influence, there is something lacking in Phelan's idea of performative

writing, which, in my view, needs to be rectified. The importance that
Phelan attaches to mimicry, autobiography and theory has meant that the
function of narrative has tended to be either overlooked and/or
underestimated. While this may be of little relevance to performance
which strenuously resists telling stories, it starts to pose problems in
certain forms of contemporary site-based performance that send their
audiences on journeys and walks through various types of landscape.

Practitioners and companies such as Fiona Templeton (*You-the City*),
Graeme Miller (*Linked*), Deborah Warner (*The Angel Project*), and
Wrights & Sites (*Mis-Guide to Anywhere* (2006)) structure their walks
narratologically. That is to say, they ask their audiences to follow a set
itinerary in which a pre-determined sequence of events unfolds in real time
and place. In each case, the spectator/walker is encouraged to navigate
his/her way through the site or landscape in much the same way that a
reader might read a novel. Like the reader, moreover, the spectator/walker
is obsessed by a teleological desire. S/he needs to finish the story, to get to
the end of the path, for it is only when the last step has been made that s/he
can make sense of the totality of his/her experience.

In order then to write performatively about this genre of site-based
work, it is important to practice a different kind of textual strategy. Where
Phelan is concerned with developing a poetic style, the critic interested in
itinerant performance concentrates on form.[4] For this critic, the focus is
not so much on fashioning a mode of writing that would "mimic" the
ephemeral nature of performance. Rather, s/he is more attuned to
"hermeneutics", to constructing or organizing a way of telling that would
respond to the durational aspects of performance s/he has walked.[5] In what
follows, I will provide a practical demonstration of how a narrative-based
mode of performative writing might function by concentrating on Graeme
Miller's work *Linked*, which I walked in the summer of 2004.

Narrating *Linked*

Graeme Miller's performance work *Linked* was installed in 2003 in the
scruffy, unglamorous corridor of urban land that runs from Lee Valley,
Hackney to Walthamstow in East London. The walk follows the M11 link
road and covers about 4 miles in total. The piece is a sonic memorial to
two communities: the local residents who were forcibly evicted in order to
make way for the link road in the mid-1990s, and the road protestors who
fought in vain to resist the contractors and bailiffs acting on the orders of
the then Tory government.[6] In the terminology of the Marxian philosopher
Henri Lefebvre, *Linked* is a "spatial representation" (1991, 38-39) – it

intervenes into and contests contemporary spatial practice by reminding us, albeit melancholically, that we have a "right to the city" (1996, 147-59). *Linked* articulates and performs a complex urban politics: it witnesses, accuses and resists. It is both representation and praxis. To experience the work, you have to walk the work.

Linked's embeddedness in the urban landscape insists upon a different way of telling. The walk punctures the work, and at all times you are aware of at least two realities. First (and always) the city, the stuff of the real, out there in front of you; and second, the voices of the evicted, the occupants of ghost houses, fading in and out as the signal, emitted from the transmitters, waxes or wanes. *Linked* is not only durational in its content (the past haunts the present); it is durational in its effects, as well, in the way that it performs on your body and consciousness in and after the event. *Linked* imposes cuts, brakes, schisms; it stops and starts; it disconnects and reconnects; it makes you think in broken rhythms. And because of that, thought becomes, like the fragmentary, sampled voices you hear on the headset, ephipinal, intense, a series of dislocated moments.

The fragmentary and durational nature of *Linked* provokes key aesthetic and formal questions: How do you narrate a work in which the vicissitudes of memory constantly dislocate the reality of the present? What is the best way to describe a walk that is a work? And how do you go about communicating and representing a sense of radical disjunction in body, space and time? My solution – and it is *my* solution – was to structure my account of *Linked* according to the principles of pilgrimage, a journey marked by stations that partake in, but stand out from, the linearity of a walk from A to B. In keeping with the logic of the pilgrimage, I used the stations for purposes of respite, reflection and meditation. By adopting this structure as a device, I hoped to transmit a sense of my own thoughts on, and theories about, the work as I walked from Hackney to Wanstead.[7] I take it for granted that no one will think that I simply transcribed these "moments" from raw experience to the stage – they have been edited, rewritten and reconfigured long after the event. Nevertheless they do try to convey some sense of the experience I had while walking and thinking about *Linked*. Discomfort and dislocation are crucial terms.

Station One

11 AM
Standing outside of Leytonstone Library: The Time of Expectation

In *Wanderlust: A History of Walking*, Rebecca Solnit talks of pilgrimage in a way that would be familiar to anyone interested in performance theory:

> In going on a pilgrimage, one has left behind the complications of one's place in the world – family, attachments, rank duties – and become a walker among walkers...The Turners talk about pilgrimage as a liminal state – a state of being between one's past and future identities and thus outside the established order, in a state of possibility. (2001, 51)

For Solnit, pilgrimage is performative: it produces self-transformation through a "doing", through a walk that allows the walker to encounter liminality. In keeping with the Turners' notion of ritual (a couple she cites), liminality, according to Solnit, is a threshold state, a way of leaving reality and identity behind, and contacting the sacred, what she refers to as "a state of possibility".

Like Solnit, I'm interested in walking that affects you, in walking that makes you feel different, but, despite that, I'm dubious about the type of sacred experience she desires. I'm not after *communitas*, society as a single, fused body; I'm after a spectral community, a collective where you never feel as one, and in which belonging is not defined in purely spatial or linguistic terms. In *Strangers to Ourselves* (1991), Julia Kristeva terms this "the impossible community", and, in his book *The Space of Encounter*, the architect Daniel Libeskind, calls this "homelessness", an experience that is always, and forever, dislocating (2001, 21-22). Although it is making a comeback in some circles – I'm thinking here of Jill Dolan's recent work on performance and utopia (2005) – I wonder if *communitas* is the right word to describe what is happening in contemporary performance. It seems to me that artists today are interested in something more humble. They simply want us to relate to others, to take a step beyond the "cocoon" of the privatised family and home (Augé, 1995, 119). This is not the mystical stuff of poor theatre or paratheatre, as it was for practitioners, such as Jerzy Grotowski, in the 1960s and 1970s. On the contrary, this is an appeal that some form of "relationality" might occur, no matter how brief and fleeting (Bourriaud, 2004, 43-9).

Station Two

11.20
Walking to Lee Valley Park

In a recent essay, Graeme Miller said:

> All present moments are haunted by their absence. I'm not sure what the
> official duration of the moment is, but it is certainly something which can
> be halved 100 times and still exist. The moment is shadowed by the past
> and future but is of neither. It seems to be made up of pure place: a Place
> sandwich in Time bread. Place seems to share the inherent poignancy of a
> musical moment – its instant death at the second of its birth. (2006, 110)

Station Three

11.30
Sitting on empty ground in Lee Valley Park

There's no one here. It's Friday mid-morning, the sky is overcast. It looks
like they are building something on the wasteland in the near distance: a
leisure centre, a flyover, an Olympic village. Who can tell? At any rate,
it's deserted now, except for the security guard from Dumfries, with the
unionist tattoos on his forceps, guarding the site. I sit on the pavement, and
listen to the cars on the A12 Eastway funnelling down to the M11. I take
the time to try out the headset, and look at the map of *Linked*: Hackney
Wick, Leyton, Leytonstone High Road, Greenman Roundabout, Wanstead,
Redbridge. I lived in Leytonstone in 1987, and remember very little of it
except the Thursday night on 16 October when the "Great Hurricane"
struck, flattening most of the trees in South-East England.

Station Four

11.45
Quartermile Lane: The Road to the First Transmitter

Something strange is happening on British television and cinema these
days – all the films, all the programmes seem so dark and sinister. An
obvious response would be to see this in terms of the Iraq War. But maybe
that's too easy. Perhaps what's really happening is that the filmmakers are
creating narratives that reflect their unconscious experience of the misery

of urban space in Britain. Maybe their real interest is not in the stories they tell but in documenting the monstrous excrescence of motorways, retail parks, storage units that seem to have hatched out of nowhere during the past decade or so. I dream of software that would allow me to erase all of the actors from the following films: *Shaun of the Dead* (2004), *Dead Man's Shoes* (2004), *Once Upon a Time in The Midlands* (2002), *The Football Factory* (2004). Once done, we'd be left with films of cities, total dilapidation, pure misery. As I walk through East London, I see lots of cars and meet no one. At the end of Quartermile Lane, a huge Asda looms on the horizon.

Station Five

12.00
Listening to Testimony on Ruckholt Road

In the much under-valued and little read essay 'The Strange Word Urb', published in 1967 in the avant-garde journal *Tel Quel*, Jean Genet argues that theatre, in an age of televisual media, needs to reject the constraining walls of the auditorium, and to site itself in a grave-yard instead.

> In today's cities, the only place – unfortunately, only near the outskirts – where a theater could be built is the cemetery. The choice will benefit both the cemetery and the theater. [...] I'm not speaking of a dead cemetery, but a live one, not the kind where only a few gravestones remain. I'm speaking of a cemetery where graves would continue to be dug and the dead buried. (2003, 107-8)

And what is the point of this theatre for the dead, this performance in a graveyard? For Genet it is simple: to open a wound in the spectator, what he calls *une blessure*. According to Genet, *la blessure* is a blessing; it produces a breathtaking liberation' (104), which, for him, has the potential to emancipate the spectator from Western notions of time and to contest capital's disenchantment of the world. Genet's desire to re-enchant, to retheatricalize the city, is inseparable from an uncanny encounter. It can only be brought about through an encounter with death:

> That strange word "urbanism", whether it comes from a Pope Urban or from the City, will maybe no longer be concerned with the dead. The living will get rid of their corpses... as one gets rid of a shameful thought. By hurrying them to the crematorium furnace, the urbanized world will rid itself of a great theatrical aid, and perhaps of theatre itself. [...] If the

crematoria in cities are made to disappear or are reduced to the dimension of a grocery store, the theater will die. (103)

Station Six

12.30
The corner at the start of Grove Green Road

The voices on the headphones are talking about snow in the city and laughing, and how they built the shed in the garden, and how the police burst through the door during the road protests, and how the barricades went up, and how the kids took control of the land, and how the cat, Maybeline, wandered into a dinner party with a huge rat in her mouth. (All text in italics is reconstructed from *Linked*)

It's muggy in London, and the asphalt's hot. I'm sweating, and the sun is failing to burn through the thin layer of ozone. I'm listening to voices on the headset speaking blind in the present. The voices blend into one. They have no names. Are they a collective voice, the expanded soul of the departed? Genet's dream has come alive. *Linked* is performance as séance, a way of listening to the dead, a sonic graveyard.

I try to situate myself; I want to get a handle on this performance. What's my role? What am I supposed to be? I think immediately of Mike Pearson's and Michael Shanks' taxonomy of performative pedestrianism in *Theatre/Archaeology*: the walker (de Certeau); the *flâneur* (Benjamin); the nomad (Deleuze and Guattari); the rambler (Jane Rendell) (2001, 148-50). I like *Theatre/Archaeology* very much but it's not helping me here. None of the categories really fit with my experience of *Linked*. I feel more like a pilgrim. I'm walking with a purpose, lost in the memories of others, tracing the footprints of the departed. But why do I feel so strange? What's going on here?

Station Seven

1.15
The Middle of Grove Green Road

The voices are talking of nightclubs and I hear cowbells. One of them talks of London burning from stead to stern in the Blitz, and of watching his Dad get emotional. And of fire-engines coming from Glasgow and Blackpool and asking "Where's London"?, "Where's London"?

If the encounter with every angel is terrible, then the encounter with every ghost, as Derrida argues in *The Spectres of Marx: the State of the Debt, the Work of Mourning, and the New International* is ethical. To meet a ghost is to be held responsible, to undergo an interpellation, to be called to task:

> If I am getting ready to speak about ghosts…it is in the name of justice. Of justice where it is not yet, not yet there, where it is no longer, let us understand where it is no longer present…(1994, xviii).

Derrida's words are illuminating. They suggest that every spectre, every haunting, is discomforting. But how, and in what way? The discomfort of the ghost is not Rilkean discomfort or Artaudian discomfort – it's discomfort as dislocation. A discomfort that takes you away from who you think you are and opens you up to what is perhaps your humanness, your being in the world. The more I experience landscape, the more I think that psychoanalysis is mistaken about its notion of the uncanny. There's no cure for the uncanny, it's part of our experience of living, hardwired into the brain.

Station Eight

2.00
The end of Grove Green Road

A voice talks about being born and his mother receiving £10 on the first day of the National Health System and how "It was a brilliant place, absolutely brilliant", and how "My mother had black hair like a raven's wing" and "my Dad worked on the railway at Stratford".

The stories, sounds and sampled music that Miller has assembled and broadcast alter consciousness. The memories and events entering my ear conflict with the data processed by my eye. Where my ear recreates a vanished world of gardens, children playing in the street, bluebells and greenfinches, my eye stubbornly insists on what is still there: the motorway. Time and space are "out of joint". I have the sensation of belonging to the world and yet also being outside it. I'm more attuned to absence (the voices on the headset) than presence (the pedestrians that passed me). I'm feeling uncomfortable.

Station Nine

Kingswood Road
2.30

The voices say "a house isn't just bricks and mortar" and "I've been offered compensation" and "The house exists in my brain, and the community exists in my heart" and "The sheriff said what you have to remember is that this isn't your property it's the Crowns".

The word *comfort* combines the Latin prefix *com* (meaning *with*) with the noun *fortis* (meaning *strength*). To be comfortable translates literally as being strong. In spatial terms, this signifies being rooted, centred, attached.

In *Counterpath: Traveling with Jacques Derrida* (1999), Derrida, in the first of his postcards to his reader and co-author Catherine Malabou, offers another interpretation of comfort. He reminds us that *com* signifies *being-with*, in communion, being part of a distinct social group. So using the ontological and religious connotations that Derrida has teased out, we can say that being comfortable has a definite sense of being rooted in a self-confident community, a community sure of itself, a community with identity. Accordingly, then, to be uncomfortable is to be dislocated, lost, not part of things, and, as I think this, I wonder if dislocation might not be a precondition of reception – the thing that opens you to the Other.

Station Ten

3.00
Outside of the new Tesco at Leytsonstone

The voices talk of being on the roof and waiting for the bailiffs to come, and of witnessing an exodus of people. They are suspended in music. Remembering the occupants of a demolished house, one of them says "I don't know who they were, they were a family".

In the essay "The Metropolis and Mental Life", the German sociologist Georg Simmel argues that "metropolitan individuality" is inherently discomforting. In his view, "the swift and continuous shift of external and internal stimuli" combined with "the rapid telescoping of changing images" threatens to drown the subject in affect (2002, 11). As a way of protecting himself/herself against this unbearable sensory assault, the metropolitan subject adopts what Simmel calls "a blasé outlook" (14) and, by doing so, reifies those around her/him into things. If discomfort, *jouissance*, is what we protect ourselves from, then *Linked*, to the extent to which it provokes discomfort, would appear to strip away the reification we undergo in the city. Can we talk here of a beyond of *jouissance*? A fundamental commitment to Others? Is *Linked* really a love letter, or an invitation to love?

Station Eleven

3.30
Blake Road

I hear a sampled, stuttering female voice, repeating they "DJ'd the music", they "DJ'd the music". And then she talks of the Flamingo Club, and "dancing from 9 and until 2 in the morning", and never wanting to come home and of " just waiting for the next Friday to come".

Site-based performances that have taken place in cities in the past two decades have consciously attempted to disrupt the blasé attitude, to re-humanize the urban landscape. The influence of Situationism is palpable. In Fiona Templeton's work *You-The City*, individual participants or clients were guided through various sites in Manhattan by a number of strategically placed performers. In the "Afterword" to the scripted version of *You-The City*, Templeton explains that she wanted the work to re-active human relations in New York, which she thought – and it is hard to disagree with her – were increasingly under threat from mass-media communication. As the society of the spectacle morphs into the society of the console, the notion of *civitas*, the foundation of politics, is in crisis. There is no one on the streets to talk to. This is what Templeton's piece militates against. She wanted to produce discomfort as a way of producing a new *civitas*, of reminding us of the presence of the other. This, for her, is the essence of performance:

> Theatre is the art of relationship…a realized moment of performance is the meeting of as many as are present, performers and audiences. *You-The City* personifies such meetings at a level of necessity, intention directly addressing interpretation, as You. The word "you" is the pronoun of recognition, of reply, of accusation…; beyond the visual, animate, returnable; "you" assumes and creates relation. (1990, 139)

According to Emanuel Levinas intimacy, the presentness of the face-to-face encounter is the core of ethics, the very stuff of responsibility (2001, 218). What happens when you lose this? Do we cease to care? Fail to love? In an age of spectacular separation, is the title of *Linked* ironic?

Station Twelve

4.00
Draycot Road

The voices talk of the Territorial Army Centre and radios, and getting off the 101 bus at Wanstead Road, and the drill parade and cobwebs, and getting haircuts, and entering the main gates of an oblong building with a frontage as a radio is trying to tune itself in.

Although situated in the concrete reality of twenty-first century London, *Linked*, unlike *You-The City*, does not seek to activate, at least not consciously, the face-to-face encounter. The whole work is a sonic memorial to a community that is no longer there, and a testament to a protest movement that failed. But still, as much as Templeton's piece, the work is ethical. The difference here, as I have argued above, is that the ethical call comes from the ghost, from the spectre, from the voices that haunt the airwaves. Crucially, this ethical injunction emerges from a sense of dislocation, a blast of uncanniness, an experience of melting. The power of *Linked*, its capacity to haunt you, is caused by the solitary nature of the performance. *Linked* has to be walked alone. It is an intimate performance that encourages you to give yourself up – to give yourself over? – to the voices on the headset. And when you do that, you belong more to the dead than to the living.

Station Thirteen

4.45
Wanstead Common

The voices talk of snow and being blessed and sharing a drink with the enemy, the security guards, between 6 and 8, on a cold night, and running workshops after the battle for Leytonstonia and meeting a security guard who is now a social worker in Harrow, and living in a treehouse along the route of the campaign, and smelling chestnuts coming into fruition and getting whiskey, and squirrels, and sleeping well, like a baby, and creating a letterbox in a treehouse and delaying the inevitable, the destruction of the common.

In *Specters of Marx*, Derrida makes the following critical point about the ghost:

> The last one to whom a specter can appear, address itself, or pay attention is a spectator...at the theater or at school. The reasons for this are essential. As theoreticians or witnesses, spectators, observers, intellectual, scholars, believe that looking is sufficient. (1994, 11)

Linked is a work that refuses the closed space of the theatre. There are no spectators because there is nothing to see. To experience *Linked*, you have to perform it. You have to become an actor, a participant. As Derrida points out, this is the only way of encountering the ghost, the only way of undergoing dislocation. And this is also the reason why Miller's sonic walk is ultimately a pilgrimage. This walk through real space is a work of mourning, a performance that points to the future, a sleepwalk that wakes you up. For, as Derrida reminds us, the riddle posed by the ghost – "what does it mean to live"? - is inseparable from questions of "where"?, "where tomorrow"?, "whither"? (xiii-ix).

Station Fourteen

4.45
Yorkshire Sculpture Gardens, 8 October, 2006

This narrative, like the walk itself, is made up of stations, moments of reflection, in which the flotsam and jetsam of sensation is stilled, stopped and silenced. Returning to something I mentioned earlier, I'd say that my narrative is essentially mimetic – I wanted to express how I experienced the work in early June 2004. Two years after my experience of the work, and as I sit in James Turrell's installation *Deer Shelter* watching an ever-changing patch of sky, I think I understand how and where I can situate the work. *Linked* is part of a trend in contemporary site-based work that, by struggling against the increasing spectacularity of existence, strives to impart significance (and perhaps wonder) to the everyday. This site-based art is an art of relationality, an art that gets us back into the world, an art that stuns us into 'presentness' by using moments to stop the onward flow of time. But what are these moments? And how do they function? Henri Lefebvre provides a good explanation of this in his autobiography *La Somme et le reste* when he explains how moments 'introduce an intelligible and practical structure into the Heraclitean flux of becoming' and thus, in his view, situate the subject within a series of communal, local and ultimately cosmic narratives (1959, 235; my translation). For Lefebvre, there is something dialectical about the moment - its fragmentary quality, its stopping of time, is what allows us to get a total or global perspective on events, and, importantly, to reengage with history. Why? Because the moment, argues Lefebvre, always points beyond itself and demands to be included within larger social, political and spatio-temporal frameworks. The moment, then, is never isolated; rather, like Graeme Miller's work, it is always and already linked, always and already part of a collective body of stories.

Notes

1 This is my understanding of performative writing. The influence of Brecht is apparent, I think, in the self-conscious theatricality of Phelan's strategy; Derrida's presence is evident in the way that performative writing collapses rigid distinctions between creative writing and criticism.
2 See Fried (1980)
3 Performative writing has experienced a more controversial reception in departments of English Studies and Art History. See Payne and Schad (2004) and Butt (2005)
4 This is evident when Phelan mentions how performative writing is characterized by a blend of autobiography and theory. In other words, Phelan is interested in the specific "poetics" of these two very different style of writing, especially when they are combined together
4 The word *hermeneutics* here refers specifically to Roland Barthes' use of the term "the hermeneutic code" in *S/Z* (1974).
5 I find Jen Harvie's notion of "ephemeral monumentality" very useful here. For Harvie, Steve McQueen's video installation *Caribs' Leap/Western Deep* is a visible, but non non-static, monument working to do undo the 'triumphant, enormous, concrete memorials' that celebrate and mark London's colonialist past (2005, 213).
6 The theoretical nature of my reflections can be explained by the fact that I am an academic interested in cities, performance and landscape.
7 The theoretical nature of my reflections can be explained by the fact that I am an academic interested in cities, performance and landscape.

108   Chapter Eight

Bibliography

Augé, Marc. 1995. *Non-Places: Introduction to An Anthropology of Supermodernity*, trans. J. Howe. London: Verso.

Barthes, Roland. 1974. *S/Z*, trans. Richard Howard. New York: Hill and Wang.

Butt, Gavin, ed. 2005. *After Criticism: New Responses to Art and Performance*. Oxford: Blackwell.

Bourriaud, Nicolas. 2004. Berlin Letter About Relational Aesthetics. In *From Studio to Situation*, ed. Claire Doherty. 43-50. London: Black Dog.

Derrida, Jacques. 1994. *Specters of Marx: The State of the Debt, The Work of the International& the New International*, trans. Peggy Kamuf. London: Routledge.

Derrida, Jacques and Catherine Malabou. 1997. *Counterpath: Traveling with Jacques Derrida.* Trans. David Wills. Stanford: Stanford University Press.

Dolan, Jill. 2005. *Utopian in Performance: Finding Hope at the Theater.* Ann Arbor: University of Michigan Press.

Fried, Michael. 1980. Art and Objecthood. In *Aesthetics Today*, revised edn., eds, Morris Philipson and Paul J. Gudel. 214-239. New York: New American Library.

Genet, Jean. 2005. That Strange Word. In *Fragments of the Artwork*, trans. Charlotte Mandell, 103-112. Stanford: Stanford University Press.

Harvie, Jen. 2005. *Staging the UK*. Manchester: Manchester University Press.

Kristeva, Julia. 1991. *Strangers to Ourselves*, trans. L. Roudiez. Hemel Hempstead: Harvester Wheatsheaf.

Lefevbre, Henri. 1959. *La Somme et le reste*. Paris: La Nef.

—. 1991. *The Production of Space*, trans. D. Nicholson. Oxford: Blackwell, 1991

—. 1996. *Writings on Cities*, trans. E. Kofman and E. Lebas. Oxford Blackwell.

Levinas, Emmanuel. 2001. *Totalité et infinié: essai sur l'extériorité*. Paris: Livre de Poche.

Libeskind, Daniel. 2001. *The Space of Encounter*. London: Thames & Hudson.

Miller, Graeme. *Linked* (on going)

—. 2006. Through the Wrong End of the Telescope. In *Performance and Place*, eds, Leslie. Hill and Helen Paris, 104-122. Basingstoke: Palgrave Macmillan.

Pearson, Mike and Michael Shanks. 2001. *Theatre/ Archaeology.* London: Routledge.

Phelan, Peggy. 1993. *Unmarked: The Politics of Performance.* London: Routledge.

—. 1997. *Mourning Sex: Performing Public Memories.* London: Routledge.

Payne, Michael and John Schad, eds. 2003. *Life.After.Theory.* London: Continuum.

Simmel, Georg. 2002. The Metropolis and Mental Life. *The Blackwell City Reader,* eds. Gary Bridge and Sophie Watson, 11-19. Oxford: Blackwell.

Solnit, Rebecca. 2001. *Wanderlust: A Short History of Walking.* London:Verso.

Templeton, Fiona. 1990. *You-the City.* New York: Roof Books.

Wrights&Sites. 2006. *A Mis-Guide to Anywhere.* Exeter: Arts Council.

Chapter Nine

Chris Megson

"The State We're In": Tribunal Theatre and British Politics in the 1990s

"Replay Culture"

In *The Routledge Reader in Politics and Performance*, published in 2000, Lizbeth Goodman draws attention to the marked ascendancy of what she terms "replay culture [. . .] in which the ability to fast forward and replay [. . .] has altered our everyday ways of being in and seeing the world" (288). Her observation provides both an appropriate and evocative stimulus for thinking about the explosion of documentary modes of playwriting in the past two decades, and, in particular, about the notable proliferation of plays that draw upon verbatim or "found" testimony in order to reconstruct actual historical or contemporaneous events. This essay focuses on a particular modality of verbatim performance that came to prominence in British theatre culture of the 1990s - the so-called Tribunal plays that have been staged intermittently at the Tricycle Theatre in North London and elsewhere since 1994, under the stewardship of Nicolas Kent, the artistic director of the venue, and Richard Norton-Taylor, the journalist for the *Guardian* newspaper. Drawing on established traditions of documentary theatre practice, Tribunal productions have offered a forensic re-enactment of the official proceedings of various inquiries into miscarriages of justice or malpractice within British legal, judicial and political institutions. Often staged synchronously with the inquiries that they simulate, these productions have sought to illuminate the effects and implications of endemic structural weaknesses within the British state. The first Tribunal play, *Half the Picture* in 1994, offered a dramatic re-enactment of the explosive Scott Arms-to-Iraq Inquiry that spavined John Major's Conservative government. This was followed two years later by

Nuremburg, a staging of the 1946 War Crimes Trial, together with *Srebrenica*, which dramatized the Hague "Rule 61" Hearings in the aftermath of the conflict in former Yugoslavia. *The Colour of Justice*, in 1999, re-enacted testimony to the Inquiry into the racist murder of Stephen Lawrence. In 2004, the Tricycle staged *Justifying War: Scenes from the Hutton Inquiry* followed, in 2005, by *Bloody Sunday: Scenes from the Saville Inquiry*. I will be focusing on the two Iraq-related interventions - *Half the Picture* from 1994 and *Justifying War* staged ten years later - arguing that the theatrical re-playing, in edited form, of these seminal inquiries has exposed audiences to the internal workings of government, raising crucial questions about parliamentary accountability, the ideological manipulation of state institutions and, in particular, the lack of transparency in Whitehall decision-making. I will begin by placing Tribunal theatre in a broader conceptual and political framework, before identifying some of the more problematic issues that have arisen from the Tribunal plays' engagement with documentary theatre methods.[1]

British institutional malaise in the 1990s

At this point, it is worth shifting emphasis slightly to introduce two important studies of the British state, one published in 1980 (during the embryonic months of the first Thatcher government), the other, dating from 1995, which surveyed British society after sixteen years of Conservative rule. I wish to start with this broader canvas in order to demonstrate how and why the Tribunal plays articulate with a set of intensifying concerns, widespread on the left in the 1990s, about a perceived intractable malaise in British state institutions.

Kenneth Dyson sets out an overview of various approaches to thinking about the state in his book, *The State Tradition in Western Europe*, published in 1980. In this, he argues that:

> "State" societies display a particular sensitivity to the requirements of institutions and to the internalization of their standards for cultural survival [. . .] [The state] represents not only a particular manner of arranging political and administrative affairs and regulating relationships of authority but also a cultural phenomenon which binds people together in terms of a common mode of interpreting the world. (6, 18)

Dyson's principal argument is that state societies consist of both conceptual and material properties: they manifest certain ethical "values" which can find a concrete "embodiment" in institutional structures (206). He routinely associates his definition of the state with the values of a

presiding "political community"; in other words, for him, notions of state
are impermanent, not transcendent and immutable (206). He also makes
clear that the apparatus of state, including its political and civic
institutions, should ideally promote a sense of "depersonalized" power in
marked contradistinction to the ebb and flow of party politics in liberal
democracy (206). What becomes apparent from his broad geopolitical
survey, however, is the acidic commentary he reserves for the British state
in particular:

> In Britain an attempt is made to avoid a fundamental reappraisal of
> institutions [. . .] in two ways: by an almost excessive tinkering with the
> formal working arrangements of discrete institutions (as in "machinery of
> government" reform); and, particularly, by taking institutions less
> seriously, by assuming that informal, fluid processes of élite consensus-
> seeking [. . .] will provide a satisfactory [. . .] way of accommodating
> problems and that personal moral virtues of the individuals who take part
> in institutions are the foundation of good government. (280)

For Dyson, state institutions in Britain are bastions of élite and class
privilege, unaccountable and mired in a gentle reformism that forever
stymies the possibility of radical structural change. It is this institutional
landscape, of course, that was colonised and distinctly unsettled by
Thatcherite ideologues in the 1980s.

The debate about the legacy of Thatcherism, about the need to reform
Britain's antiquated and beleaguered public institutions, gathered
momentum in the early 1990s. This was galvanized in part by the Labour
Party's fourth successive defeat in the General Election of 1992 and the
perceived deleterious effects of the Thatcherite revolution, not least the
widespread assumption in the early 1990s that standards in public life
were in moribund decline. This debate arguably reached an apotheosis
with the publication of Will Hutton's *The State We're In* in 1995. In this
landmark text, Hutton argues that Conservative hegemony has subjected
the British state to structural deformity and, above all, politicisation. His
primary concern is that the British government needs to conceive of what
he calls a "different institutional matrix", to engage in a period of
"creative institution-building", in order to reverse the process of decline
(xxix).[2] In the context of the Tribunal plays, it is significant that he
reserves particular rhetorical firepower for those who administer the
"machinery of government" in Whitehall and the Civil Service. As Hutton
puts it:

The rot starts at the top. The political system is malfunctioning, bringing politicians and civil servants into disrepute and discrediting the very notion of the public realm in which national renewal might be attempted. Instead, the state is the handmaiden of the process of loss. [. . .] The already confused boundaries between public, government and party interest have been blurred even further, with senior officials as committed to partisan policies as their ministerial bosses. [. . .] This is a weakness that has been thoroughly exploited - as the ministerial and official testimony to the Scott Inquiry showed so dramatically. (3, 4)

In this context, it is pertinent to recall that British theatre in the early 1990s was engaging with the "rot at the top", articulating this "process of loss" in a series of landmark dramatic interventions that placed Britain's "institutional matrix" under theatrical scrutiny. Indeed, much of this work actually pre-dates Hutton by a year or two. Of these, the most redoubtable is the *David Hare Trilogy*, staged at the National in 1993, and which has itself been glossed as a series of "institution plays".[3] Hare has, as David Pattie has shown, moved from a position of outright hostility towards British institutions in the 1970s to a position in 1993 where he could proclaim:

The one thing I have learnt and understood from five years study is that British society need not abolish its institutions, but refresh them. For, if not through institutions, how do we express the common good? (Quoted in Pattie 1999, 363)

Hare's valorisation of the "common good" echoes an aspect of Dyson's argument - namely, that state institutions "embody" shared values - and certainly echoes Hutton's impassioned conviction that "the *institutions* we have generate the *values* we have".[4]

It is in the precise framework of this debate that the Tricycle's forensic documentary "replays" first emerged in 1994, at a time when British institutions were widely held to be in a state of crisis. In theatrically re-enacting the testimonies of officials, ministers and other implicated individuals, these plays "re-play" the "confused boundaries between public, government and party interest" (4) that so enraged Hutton - whose own book was published the year after *Half the Picture* was first performed. The Tricycle's approach, then, is to annex the resources of documentary theatre to expose the democratic deficit in the wider political culture.

Two Case Studies: *Half the Picture* and *Justifying War*

The Tribunal plays achieve this by selectively interweaving traditions of documentary and verbatim theatre in Britain that stretch back to the 1960s counter-culture and beyond to the innovations of Piscator. Its direct antecedents include, variously, Peter Cheeseman's documentary work at the Victoria Theatre in Stoke from 1965; David Edgar's 1974 television drama *I Know What I Meant* which was comprised of edited transcripts of White House recordings at the time of Watergate, and more recent verbatim television drama productions such as *Black and Blue* (which re-enacted the Industrial Tribunal of PC Surinder Singh) in 1990, and *Whitehall on Trial* (which focused on the Scott Inquiry) in 1993.[5]

However, it was Derek Paget who, in a prescient article published in 1987, first identified the growing significance of verbatim practices in British theatre culture, and identified aspects of its historical development and provenance. His definition of the form is illuminating:

> [Verbatim theatre is] firmly predicated upon the taping of and subsequent transcription of interviews with "ordinary" people, done in the context of research into a particular region, subject area, issue, event, or combination of these things. This primary source is then transformed into a text which is acted, usually by the performers who collected the material in the first place. (Paget 1987, 317)

Tribunal theatre clearly departs from Paget's model in significant respects since the text for each production is edited more or less verbatim from the published transcripts of the official inquiry. Indeed, the style of these pieces has been described, sometimes rather witheringly, as deliberately unemphatic - foregoing razzle-dazzle, "shock-and-awe" theatricality in favour of a meticulous reproduction of the inquiry's setting, disputations and formal procedures. In his analysis of realism in film, Bill Nichols notes that documentary tends to be constituted by what he terms "discourses of sobriety" (29) of which "literalism" (27) and "denotative authenticity" (28) are key characteristics. If classic naturalist theatre aspires to the condition of the photograph, then Tribunal theatre aspires to the condition of live television coverage: indeed, the initial rationale for staging *Half the Picture* was to compensate the public for the banning of TV cameras from the Scott, and later Hutton, Inquiries, and to draw attention to the fact that, during each, only around ten lay members of the public were allowed to observe each session.

However, the utopian reach for what might be termed "unmediated verisimilitude" in Tribunal theatre belies subtle variations in approach that are brought into particular focus if *Half the Picture* and *Justifying War* are compared. In this respect, Peter Weiss's landmark definition of what he terms "Theatre of Actuality", published in the first edition of *Theatre Quarterly* in 1971, is instructive. Weiss conceives of documentary theatre as a "critique of concealment", "distortion", "lies" and the "artificial fog" generated by mass media and government (41):

> The strength of Documentary Theatre lies in its ability to shape a useful pattern from fragments of reality, to build a model of actual occurrences. It is not at the centre of events, it is in the position of spectator and analyst. It emphasizes, through montage, significant details in the chaos of external reality. [. . .] Documentary theatre takes sides. (42)

Weiss argues that, in order to "take sides", documentary practitioners might usefully incorporate reflections, monologues, flashbacks, parody, mime and songs in order to "lay bare the basic problem" (43). His argument is that a dominance of naturalism in theatrical documentary will inevitably but misguidedly place the focus on human interest and psychology of character, rather than the changing historical forces that shape circumstance and situation, and make social agency possible.

In this light, it becomes apparent that *Half the Picture* and *Justifying War* each demonstrates differently-nuanced inflections of the documentary mode. The former, in 1994, incorporates a range of strategic non-naturalistic devices. In this piece, Norton-Taylor collaborated with the late John McGrath: the former edited the transcripts of the inquiry while the latter wrote a series of fictionalised monologues that were interpolated within the enactment of the inquiry and addressed directly to the audience. These monologues were spoken by "composite" or representative characters ranging from Colette, an office worker at the Matrix Churchill firm, to Mustafa, a Kurd in Iraq whose people were devastated by British-made bombs.[6] The laconic former Defence Minister, Alan Clark, who reviewed the Tricycle production and himself gave evidence to the Scott Inquiry, witheringly denigrated these vignettes as "soliloquies of a Joan-Littlewood-Memorial-Plaque kind" yet, to be sure, they served to broaden and deepen the audience's perspective on issues raised in the play, and to place the deliberations and ramifications of the Scott Inquiry in a wider socio-political context.[7] In addition to McGrath's material, the production featured an electronic display placed above the stage that provided further factual and contextual information, such as the number of people killed in the Iran-Iraq War. *Half the Picture* concluded rather strikingly with a montage of voices that reiterated excerpts from the inquiry; cumulatively, these amount to a fierce indictment of the then

Conservative government's cover-up. In this light, *Half the Picture* can be understood as edging towards Weiss's model of documentary theatre, one that is both "spectator and analyst" of its subject matter. Its polemical orientation is evidenced by the remarkable fact that the show became the first play ever to be staged in the Houses of Parliament: it was performed in the Grand Committee Room at the behest of a Labour Party rallying together in July 1994, only two months after the sudden death of its leader, John Smith. This marked the play's final appropriation as a piece of barnstorming anti-Tory polemic.

However, if *Half the Picture* is suggestive of an explicitly interventionist paradigm of documentary, *Justifying War* is more ambivalent in effect. In the latter, there is no theatrical equivalent to McGrath's "composite" monologues and so no interruption of the play's seamless illusionism. In fact, the inherent artifices that attend and suffuse theatrical production were distinctly downplayed in the production. The piece started with strategic understatement, as a couple of minor officials entered the onstage Inquiry room preparing for the arrival of Hutton and his team. In the best tradition of André Antoine, the actors playing the legal counsels had their backs turned to the audience as they speak. At the end, there were no bows from the cast, no acknowledgement at all that the audience had witnessed actors playing rôles. Norton-Taylor's editorial decision to alter the actual chronology of the Hutton inquiry by relocating, to the end of the play, Janice Kelly's heartbreaking testimony about her husband's suicide, works to spotlight the very human cost of the whole WMD debacle. This emphasis in performance is, perhaps, symptomatic of the controversially limited remit of the Inquiry itself, which was set up to "investigate the circumstances surrounding the death of Dr Kelly" (quoted in Norton-Taylor 2003, 9).

Justifying War, then, unlike *Half the Picture*, leaves the audience to draw its own conclusions. The programme for the production is so brimful of copied documents and transcripts that it resembles a ministerial briefing. The audience was surrounded by television screens that flashed up the requisite evidence at the moment when it was referred to onstage. This amounts to spectating as jury service, in a play that has been compared to "a courtroom drama without the verdict".[8] As one reviewer whimsically put it, *Justifying War* is analogous to *An Inspector Calls*, because representatives from Downing Street, government, Whitehall and the BBC are questioned, express their condolences about Kelly's suicide and dutifully pass the buck, one to the other.[9]

Yet, in spite of the differences between *Half the Picture* and *Justifying War*, there is clearly a general orientation towards hardcore illusionism in much Tribunal theatre. However, this approach to staging contemporary news events raises a thorny issue, one that is, I argue, exacerbated when actors portray living politicians onstage.

Staging "Stars of Decision"

What kind of theatrical dynamic is established in a Tribunal performance when the testimony of a well-known politician or public figure is replayed by an actor, before an audience, "as if for real"? Earlier, I noted Dyson's conviction that British institutions have stagnated because of their adherence to liberal reformism and a patrician conviction that the "personal moral virtues of the individuals who take part in institutions" uphold the "foundation[s] of good government". Dyson's reference to "personal moral virtues" resonates, intriguingly, with the focus of Max Weber's 1968 treatise *On Charisma and Institution Building*. In this important study, Weber argues that institutions are founded on three general systems of rule: the first, *rational* or legal authority; the second is *traditional* authority, dependent on "an established belief in the sanctity of immemorial traditions", and, finally, *charismatic* authority: "[which] rest[s] on devotion to the specific and exceptional sanctity, heroism or exemplary character of an individual person, and of the normative patterns or order revealed or ordained by him [*sic*]" (46). In outlining the careful interplay of these three elements - the legal, the traditional and the charismatic - in each institutional ecosystem, Weber proceeds to make the vital point that charismatic leadership is precariously dependent on the "personal trust" placed in the leader; this trust, as Weber notes, can generate complex "emotional" reactions in those who invest hope and aspiration in the charismatic leader (47). In this respect:

> The only basis for legitimacy [of charismatic authority] is personal charisma, so long as it is proved; that is, as long as it receives recognition and is able to satisfy the followers or disciples. But this lasts only so long as the belief in its charismatic inspiration remains. (52)

The point here is that the perceived institutional malaise that so preoccupied Hutton, and other commentators from the early 1990s onwards, derives not only from a despair with British reformism and Conservative malpractice, but also from a sense that politicians are no longer able or willing to provide the leadership necessary for institutional rejuvenation. This is partly because they have subordinated political vision to the need to solicit trust through a careful process of media image construction. There are, of course, a number of plays dating from this period that give a precise theatrical expression to these very concerns. David Hare's *The Absence of War* (1993), for example, focuses on an attempt by a political party, during a General Election campaign, to bolster the charismatic appeal of George Jones, the Labour leader and aspirant Prime Minister in the play, and to project his image as a compelling, humane and eminently trustworthy - and, therefore, marketable - politician. What is apparent, however, is the play's mission to *expose* the strategic processes of political "charisma-building", and to illuminate the severe restrictions on open political debate which result from such processes. When considered alongside Weber's analysis of leadership within institutions, it is notable that Hare's writings also engage repeatedly with the importance of political charisma and its public mediation. His introduction to the published text of *Paris by Night* in 1988, registers bewilderment that so few "plays and films" have addressed "the characteristics and personalities of those who have ruled over us during these last eight years" (Hare 1988, vii). Hare problematized the issue of political charisma with reference to contemporary parliamentarians: "I've learnt," he says, "in the long years of Heath and Callaghan and Thatcher, that a country may despise its leader with one part of its brain, and obey him or her with the other." (Hare 1991, 19). It is in *Asking Around*, however, a compilation of the hands-on research that informed his trilogy, that Hare focuses on the attempts by party officials to project or contrive the charismatic qualities of political leaders. For example, he documents his reactions to a Conservative election rally:

> I find myself for the first time disliking John Major. You suddenly realize that he depends for our esteem on being what he seems: a genuinely decent man who has become Prime Minister. But this necessarily means he is hopeless at personal abuse. The more he attempts it, the more distasteful it becomes. He looks like a weak man whose advisers have talked him into being unpleasant. (Hare 1993b, 216)

If the Tories sought to fortify Major's charisma in 1992 by formulating a more aggressive rhetorical register, Hare also notes the attempts by the Labour Party to make Neil Kinnock, the then Labour leader, appear "statesmanlike" (165). Crucially, according to Hare, part of this process involved restricting the Labour leader's tone and subject of speech: as Kinnock complains in one private outburst documented by Hare, "I'm the only man wearing a bloody corset over his mouth" (221).

In interview with Hare after the election, Julie Hall, Kinnock's press officer, stated:

> Ever since I joined, that was my message. Be yourself. But there were also pressures on [Kinnock] not to be his natural self, to hold himself in. So we didn't get the real Neil across. And the fact is, the more people saw the real Neil - the more they got to know him - the more they liked him. (227)

While claiming that Major has been badly advised, Hare nevertheless contends that Major's appeal resides in "being what he seems"; in contrast, Hall is convinced that the "real" Kinnock was never manifest to the electorate in the 1992 campaign - the campaign on which *The Absence of War* is based. These formulations posit a fixed, stable and individuated charismatic persona that is available for identification in each party leader: Major "is" what he "seems to be" while Kinnock is required to shackle his "natural" charisma in a doomed endeavour to appear "statesmanlike". In this respect, John Bull is correct to note that "[w]hat chiefly preoccupies Hare is the analogy between public life and acting" (1984, 66). In *Asking Around*, Hare makes this connection explicit:

> All the politicians in this election are pretending to be bank managers. John Smith is very definitely trying to be area manager, and what's more, with Barclays, not the Midland. (1993, 174)

This sardonic humour belies Hare's identification of the performative aspects of political charisma, and its problematic mediation by news technology. What is clear from the published text of *The Absence of War* is that Hare signals George Jones's charisma in a variety of ways but, most often, through his frequent insertion of stage directions. These function not only as triggers for the actor's approach to character work but also to indicate how other elements of the performance are organized: spatial configurations and groupings, aspects of visual composition, and properties of lighting and costume. While Hare's use of stage directions may be unremarkable in this respect, I argue that, in this play, they function primarily to denote Jones's charismatic leadership. For instance, Jones's first entrance in the playtext is marked by an authorial comment observing "the quiet sparkle in his manner" (Hare 1993a, 9). This is specific to Jones and is, of course, the signature of his charisma. What is remarkable, of course, is that this comment offers no tangible indication of how such a "quiet sparkle" might be actualized in live performance. Needless to say, it functions in this context solely as metaphor – a sign of charisma - and similar formulations circulate freely in the published text.

The problem with the play is that it both celebrates the force of Jones's quietly sparkling charisma - placing it at the centre of the theatrical experience - while bemoaning the indubitable fact that "character" or "personality" *has become the issue* in a contemporary political culture driven by focus groups, image consultants and spin doctors.

Given this, it is intriguing to note that the critical reception of Tribunal theatre - and, indeed, of other verbatim pieces that feature contemporary politicians - is marked by an insistent preoccupation with the *manner* in which discourses of authenticity are constituted within the documentary performance itself. This preoccupation focuses intransigently on the work of the actors. If we look at the reception of *Half the Picture*, Michael Billington's review is indicative: "Part of the pleasure, of course, lies in watching the play of personality [. . .] the star turn, needless to say, is Lady Thatcher (Sylvia Syms) who comes on like a Wildean dowager addressing a class of backward infants [. . .]."[10] A small army of critics label the appearance of Sylvia Syms as Mrs Thatcher as the "star turn" or "star event" of the production.[11] This mesmerising and talismanic theatrical presence is not the preserve of Thatcher alone. One perceptive reviewer fears that the play is "too kind" to Alan Clark: "[He] has become a cult figure even with a predominantly left wing audience in Kilburn. Played by Jeremy Clyde he is almost cheered for his outrageous nonchalance."[12] William Hoyland, who played John Major in *Half the Picture*, is reported as saying that "we did sometimes feel the audience was egging us on to be funny."[13] This has led Danny O'Brien to comment that *Half the Picture* felt like "a panto for responsible members of the community [. . .]" and, indeed, he notes that one spectator shouted out "what a terrible man!" when the actor playing Alan Clark appeared onstage to give evidence.[14]

If we turn to *Justifying War*, at least three critics bemoaned the exclusion of Tony Blair from the play, one observing rather pithily that leaving Blair out of the show left it "as gripping as an old pair of barrister's briefs" - the equivalent of staging *Hamlet* without the Prince.[15] But Norton-Taylor's omission of the Prime Minister's evidence may be strategic: as Carole Woddis recognised, his portrayal may have overwhelmed the production, turning it into "Blair Witch II".[16]

The double-edged sword, then, is that charismatic politicians may indeed steal the show. It is invariably the case that the presence of actors portraying public figures onstage generates a scintillating theatrical frisson. Yet there is some evidence from the reception of the Tribunal plays that the actorly figuration of Thatcher, Major, Clark, Alastair Campbell and so on resulted in a critical fetishization of political personality. This might work against the broader institutional critique that is the mission of Tribunal theatre, as I suggested earlier. It is important to remember that, at least in part, Norton-Taylor's motivation for staging his verbatim plays is to critique "the Whitehall machine and the Whitehall culture, embracing civil servants and ministers alike" (Norton-Taylor 1995, 209). Yet, to a significant degree, responses to this work are less focused on the "machine" and the "culture" than on Billington's seductive "play of personality" and Weber's "charismatic leadership". This raises questions about the extent to which incisive, systemic critique of institutional structures can be articulated in a mode of performance that sometimes ends up reifying dazzling political charisma. It seems that, following Weiss, the visual registers of documentary performance need to rupture illusionism if the aims of Tribunal theatre are to be realized more effectively.

In *Justifying War*, David Kelly is quoted as saying to one of his BBC contacts, "the word-smithing is actually quite important" - and, indeed, the composition of these plays sets up an opportunity for audiences to scrutinise, as one quoted source puts it in *Justifying War*, the "spin merchants of [Labour's] administration" (Norton-Taylor 2003, 28, 81). This focus on words rather than dynamic physical action characterises many of the Tribunal-inspired productions staged in the past few years: as one spectator stated after seeing *Beyond Belief*, Dennis Woolf's Tribunal play focused on the Inquiry into the Harold Shipman murders and produced at the Manchester Library Theatre in 2004, "there is no action as such and you find yourself listening so carefully to every word".[17] This replaying of events or spoken testimony retrieves a sense of the complexity of issues that have been too easily turned into digestible or sensational headlines. Alternatively, other modalities of verbatim playmaking allow for the theatrical evocation of what John Pilger has called the "distant voices" - of marginalised individuals, peoples and classes - excluded from mainstream political processes.[18] *The Unprotected*, for example, staged at the Liverpool Everyman in 2006, was written in response to the city's proposed establishment of a legal zone for street sex workers and is based on interviews with a range of individuals and groups affected by the controversial proposals, while Tanika Gupta's *Gladiator Games*, performed at the Theatre Royal Stratford East in 2006, traces the background to the racist murder of Zahid Mubarek, in March 2000, at Feltham Young Offenders' Institute and its staging was timed to coincide with the report of the public inquiry into Zahid's death (an inquiry resisted by the then Home Secretary, David Blunkett).

Despite the enormous range and diversity of these rapid-response interventions, they may occasionally seduce us with the modes of identification that are made available to audiences. While the Tricycle may have restored to theatre a sense of civic purpose, the dominant discourse of verisimilitude in production - what Derek Paget has described, in witty shorthand, as "lookylikey naturalism"[19] - and, above all, the marked attentiveness to political celebrity in critical reception, might jeopardize the proper disruptive potential of Tribunal Theatre by narrowing the horizon of expectation established for the play and eclipsing the object of critique: that is, the endemic and systemic flaws in the institutions of Whitehall. What is achieved in these instances is not a rupturing of the political spectacle but a reification of what the Situationists disparagingly called its "stars of decision".[20] This problem becomes, perhaps, particularly apparent when well-known public figures perform key roles in verbatim productions. Perhaps the most bizarre example of this occurred when, quite remarkably, a famous member of the Guantánamo Human Rights Commission, none other than Desmond Tutu, guest acted the role of Lord Justice Steyn in two performances of the verbatim play by Victoria Brittain and Gillian Slovo, *Guantánamo: Honour Bound to Defend Freedom*, when it transferred from the Tricycle Theatre to the Culture Project, Greenwich Village, in August 2004.[21]

Impact

Whatever the relative merits of its approach to documentary performance, the impact of Tribunal theatre has been felt in the wider culture: some of the plays have toured or transferred, been adapted for television and radio, and been published.[22] As one journalist recently put it: "It's increasingly the case that no official inquiry can be considered complete until it has been transcribed, condensed and turned into a piece of verbatim theatre".[23] It is significant that, in searching for a theatrical form in which to lay bare complex political issues for his audience, David Hare has gravitated increasingly towards verbatim address and, indeed, personal testimony (in *The Permanent Way* (2003) and *Via Dolorosa* (1998), respectively). Other notable examples include *My Name is Rachel Corrie*, compiled by Katharine Vine of the *Guardian* newspaper and the actor Alan Rickman. First performed at the Royal Court in April 2005, it consists of collated excerpts from the diaries of an American activist killed by an Israeli bulldozer in the Gaza Strip in 2003. A cluster of verbatim plays have responded to the provenance and repercussions of the "War on Terror": Robin Soans's *Talking to Terrorists* toured nationally and to

critical acclaim in 2005, while *Yesterday Was A Weird Day*, performed by
Look Left Look Right Theatre Company at the Edinburgh Fringe in 2005
and, in revised form, at the Battersea Arts Centre in 2006, included video
and audio excerpts alongside verbatim interviews in order to calibrate the
impact of the suicide bombings in London.

Much of this work is clearly and directly responsive to a deeply-felt
unease not only about the dubious morality of the Iraq conflict, and the
provenance and apparently infinite longevity of the "War on Terror", but
also about the abdication of news reporting from serious political analysis
in an era of infotainment. As Hare observes:

> Audiences, at this time of global unease, urgently feel the need for a place
> where things can be put under scrutiny. They want the facts, but they also
> want chance to look at the facts together, and in some depth. Everyone is
> aware that television and newspapers have decisively disillusioned us, in a
> way which seems beyond repair, by their trivial and partial coverage of
> seismic issues of war and peace. (2004, 28)

Dennis Woolf, who has written a number of verbatim plays based on
official hearings, has noted that this style of playwriting furnishes the
audience with "an accessible overview [. . .] with many of the marathon
inquiries that I've attended, I've been struck by the way in which press
attention falters in direct relation to the length of the hearing".[24] On a
similar note, for David Edgar: "Verbatim theatre fills the hole left by the
current inadequacy of TV documentary, perished under the tanktracks of
Reality TV".[25]

Most strikingly, these productions enable their audiences to undertake
a collective act of bearing witness: *Justifying War* opens with a poignant
minute's silence for David Kelly, a theatrical "quoting" of the silence that
opened the Hutton Inquiry itself, while *The Colour of Justice*, in contrast,
concluded with a minute's silence - this time, of course, for Stephen
Lawrence. There are reports of audience members standing up respectfully
when the actor playing the Judge entered onstage at the start of *Beyond
Belief*.[26] In this sense, we might conceive of these Tribunal simulacra as
acts of reclamation - an opening up of institutional processes normally
hidden from view or submerged within a deluge of newsprint.

The achievement of Tribunal theatre is to offer audiences synchronous
"re-play" of forensic inquisitorial examination, the cumulative effect of
which is to indict the "rot at the top". It is part of a broader concern,
reflected in a range of cultural practices over the past two decades, to
refresh British institutions, to promote greater freedom of information and
accountability, to assess "the state we're in". Nicolas Kent, reflecting on

his work at the Tricycle, puts it rather well: "in ten years", he says, "we have progressed from selling arms to Iraq to trying to find them there." And he adds, rather tellingly, "it seems Britain has defined itself against Iraq."[27]

Notes

1 Some of the observations in this essay are developed from a short contribution to the Backpages section of *Contemporary Theatre Review*. See Chris Megson, "'This is all theatre': Iraq Centrestage". *Contemporary Theatre Review*. 15, 3 (2005), pp.369-371.
2 The term "different institutional matrix" was transcribed by the author from a speech by Hutton at the Almeida Theatre on February 29 1996.
3 See, for example, John J. Su, "Nostalgic Rapture: Interpreting Moral Commitments in David Hare's Drama", *Modern Drama*, XL, 1 (Spring 1997), p.24. See also David Hare's note to *Murmuring Judges* (London: Faber and Faber, 1991), n.pag.
4 This comment is transcribed by the author from a speech by Hutton at the Almeida Theatre, February 29 1996. The italics reflect his spoken emphasis.
5 *I Know What I Meant* was produced by Granada TV and broadcast on July 10 1974, directed by Jack Gold and featuring Nicol Williamson as Richard Nixon. See David Edgar, "On Drama Documentary", in *The Second Time as Farce - Reflections on the Drama of Mean Times* (London: Lawrence and Wishart, 1988), pp.62-63.
6 The term "composite" is Richard Norton-Taylor's, transcribed from a telephone interview with the author (June 18 1996).
7 Alan Clark, "The other half", *Guardian* (July 1 1994).
8 Roly Keating, Controller of BBC4, quoted in *Huddersfield Daily Examiner* (December 11 2003).
9 Review by Philip Fisher for *The British Theatre Guide*: <http://www.britishtheatreguide.info/reviews/justifyingwar-rev.htm> Accessed: April 6 2004.
10 Michael Billington, "Truth upstages fiction", *Guardian* (June 14 1994).
11 See, for example, John Peter in the *Sunday Times* (June 26 1994) or Michael Coveney in the *Observer* (June 19 1994).
12 Malcolm Rutherford, "Scott Inquiry takes centre stage", *Financial Times* (June 17 1994).
13 William Hoyland, quoted by Vera Lustig, "Playing for Real", *Theatre*, 1, 2 (November/December 1995), p.18.
14 Danny O'Brien, *Guardian* (July 16 1994).
15 See, for example, Charles Spencer, *Daily Telegraph* (November 6 2003); Paul Taylor, *Independent* (November 6 2003) and Michael Coveney, *Daily Mail* (November 5 2003). The underwear simile is Roger Foss's, from *What's On* (November 12 2003).
16 Carole Woddis, *Herald* (November 10 2003).

17 Quoted in "It opened my eyes", *The Guardian* (October 27 2004).
18 John Pilger, *Distant Voices* (London: Vintage, 1992; revised 1994).
19 Email correspondence with the author, April 21 2004.
20 See Guy Debord, *The Society of the Spectacle*, trans. David Nicholson-Smith (New York: Zone Press, 1994).
21 See "My first night in Guantánamo", *Guardian* (October 6 2004).
22 Indeed, the *Independent* newspaper reported in early 2006 that the Tricycle's Tribunal productions have been seen, in their theatrical and televised incarnations, by 25 million people worldwide. See Joan Bakewell, 'Why we need the arts more than ever: political theatre is flourishing in the teeth, or rather the encouragement, of daily events', *Independent* (March 17 2006).
23 Alfred Hickling, "Beyond Belief", *Guardian* (October 28 2004).
24 Quoted in "Shipman play aims to shed new light on tragedy", *Guardian* (October 22 2004).
25 Quoted in Kate Kellaway, "Theatre of War", *The Observer* (August 29 2004).
26 Hickling, *op.cit.*
27 Quoted by Richard Whitaker, "Tony Blair doesn't cut it", *Independent on Sunday* (October 26 2003).

Bibliography

Bull, John. 1984. *New British Political Dramatists*. London: Macmillan.
Dyson, Kenneth H. F. 1980. *The State Tradition in Western Europe - A Study of an Idea and Institution*. Oxford: Martin Robertson.
Goodman, Lizbeth. 2000. "Chapter 46: The Politics of Performativity in the Age of Replay Culture". In *The Routledge Reader in Politics and Performance*, ed. Lizbeth Goodman with Jane de Gay, 288-294. London: Routledge.
Hare, David. 1993a. *The Absence of War*. London: Faber and Faber.
——. 1993b. *Asking Around: Background to the David Hare Trilogy*. London: Faber and Faber.
——. 2004. *Obedience, Struggle & Revolt: Lectures on Theatre*. London: Faber and Faber.
——. 1988. *Paris by Night*. London: Faber and Faber.
——. 1991. *Writing Left-Handed*. London: Faber and Faber.
Hutton, Will. 1995. *The State We're In*. Revised edition 1996. London: Vintage.
Nichols, Bill. 1991. *Representing Reality: Issues and Concepts in Documentary*. Indiana: Indiana University Press.
Norton-Taylor, Richard. 2003. *Justifying War: Scenes from the Hutton Inquiry*. London: Oberon Books.
——. 1995. *Truth is a Difficult Concept: Inside the Scott Inquiry*. London: Fourth Estate.

Paget, Derek. 1987. "'Verbatim Theatre': Oral History and Documentary Techniques". *New Theatre Quarterly* III, 12 (November 1987): 317-336.

Pattie, David. 1999. "The Common Good: The Hare Trilogy". *Modern Drama* XLII, 3 (Fall): 363-374.

Weber, Max. 1968. *On Charisma and Institution Building.* S. N. Eisenstadt, ed. Chicago: University of Chicago Press.

Weiss, Peter. 1971. "The Material and the Models: Notes Towards a Definition of Documentary Theatre." Trans. Heinz Bernard. *Theatre Quarterly.* I, 1 (January - March): 41-43.

CHAPTER TEN

DANIEL MEYER-DINKGRÄFE

CONSCIOUSNESS (STUDIES) AND UTOPIAN PERFORMATIVES

Introduction

Jill Dolan points out that few dramatic / performative texts *about* utopia come to mind (2002, 496), which is why she prefers to understand utopian performatives as leading to fleeting glimpses, or an 'ephemeral feeling of what a better world might be like' (2003). Dolan's essay on multiple character solo performers and utopian performatives (2002) shows, though, that she shares the predominant understanding of utopia as a concept to describe a socio-political context considered in some ways better than the one we find ourselves living in at the time of developing such utopian ideas. Plato's *The State* and Thomas More's *Utopia* have been groundbreaking treatises on which that understanding is based. In my essay, I want to discuss the relevance of utopian performatives against the background of current consciousness studies. By adopting this approach I hope to demonstrate that utopia as an array of ideas of possible socio-political alternatives to the status quo represents only the second stage in the development of utopia from the first stage: higher stages of human development on an individual level as the building blocks of society. I then proceed to discuss the role utopian performatives can play to help achieve individual utopia.

Consciousness Studies: A Brief Survey

Many disciplines on their own, or in an interdisciplinary exchange, contribute to the study of consciousness, including philosophy, neurosciences, psychology, physics and biology, as well as experience-based approaches. The study of human consciousness has become sufficiently mainstream over the last ten to fifteen years to make two print journals (*Consciousness and Cognition* and *Journal of Consciousness Studies*), and numerous books by leading publishers such as OUP and MIT Press commercially successful. *The Center for Consciousness Studies* at the University of Arizona in Tucson, USA, has led the field, with its large bi-annual conferences (since 1994), and the *British Psychological Association* has approved new sections in *Transpersonal Psychology* and *Consciousness and Experiential Psychology* (each with annual conferences and their own peer-reviewed, though smaller scale journals) as late as 1997.

Whereas for a number of years most interdisciplinary research into human consciousness had been predominantly science-based, research into the relationship between consciousness and the humanities, including literature, theatre, fine arts and media arts, is clearly growing in strength. Thus, at the Tucson conferences, literature and the arts feature on the long list of consciousness-related topics. In 1997, Malekin and Yarrow published their seminal *Consciousness, Literature and Theatre: Theory and Beyond,* and in 1999 the forth and last issue of the short-lived peer-reviewed journal *Performing Arts International* was dedicated to *Performance and Consciousness.* In 2000, I founded a peer-reviewed web-journal, *Consciousness, Literature and the Arts* (http://www.aber.ac.uk/tfts/journal). The argument of this paper is thus located within an emerging discourse both in consciousness studies and in theatre studies.

The Vedic Model of the Mind

Just as every other academic who deals with consciousness studies, I, too, have chosen one model of consciousness from among the abundance of models available, on which to base my argument, because it has, for me, the strongest explanatory power. The model I chose is based on Indian Vedanta philosophy. According to this model, I distinguish, initially, between three basic states of consciousness, waking, dreaming and sleeping. During the waking state of consciousness, several *functions* of consciousness can be differentiated, including decision making, thinking, emotions, and intuition. Vedanta postulates a fourth state of consciousness which serves as the basis of the states of waking, dreaming and sleeping, and their related functions. The fourth state is without contents, but fully awake. It is referred to as *pure consciousness*, or *samadhi* in Sanskrit. It has been described, albeit in different terms, across cultures. W.T. Stace, for example, writes about *pure unitary consciousness* in the context of Christian mystic experiences (1960). If pure consciousness is experienced not only briefly, and 'just' on its own, but together with waking or dreaming or sleeping, according to Vedanta higher states of consciousness have been achieved.

Characteristics of higher states consciousness as characteristics of individual utopia

What are the experience and the benefits of higher states of consciousness like? Its experience is based on a body that is free from stress, strain, and any symptom of acute or even emerging or latent illness. It is a body that enjoys a state of perfect health: it is able to repel any viruses or bacteria before they can take adverse effect on the body. Individuals living in a higher state of consciousness will not (be able to) make mistakes. They function, permanently, from the level of pure consciousness, which in turn is the level from which the laws of nature operate. Thus all their actions will be in tune with natural law: they will be unable to act against natural law, and that means they will not be able to act in such as way as to harm either themselves, other people, other creatures, or their environment. To such people, an enemy will not even arise, and therefore there will be no need for them to fight an enemy. They will have developed their individual characteristics, abilities, strengths, talents, each to their full potential, thus achieving true unity in diversity (the very opposite of all becoming the same, equal). They will experience bliss, one of the characteristics of pure consciousness, throughout their daily activity and will not lose it even while asleep or dreaming.

For the majority of people reading this, such a higher state of consciousness must indeed come across as a genuine example of individual utopia. Empirical studies of meditation, claiming to enhance the development of higher states of consciousness, suggest that the majority of people practising such meditation experience the first stages of such a development towards higher states of consciousness: tests results, often statistically significant, show that their health improves, as does their mental potential and parameters of social life. There is at least an indication that higher states of consciousness, and their characteristics and implications for human life, are not issues of utopia (in the sense of something realistically unachievable), but are within the scope of what we can achieve, *if only we make the decision to make use, personally, of the means that are available to enhance development of consciousness*. As I will show in the next two sections, glimpses of higher states of consciousness, which have been known throughout history (see the descriptions of mystics, for example), also feature in drama (text) and theatre (performance).

Higher states of consciousness in theatre (drama)

A striking example of a desirable higher state of consciousness experienced by a character in drama is Athol Fugard's *The Road to Mecca*. The main character of this play, Miss Helen, is an elderly lady who has started creating strange sculptures in her garden not long after her husband's death. Inside her house she has created a highly exotic combination of mirrors, candles, and blue and golden walls to allow a remarkable display of light when the sun shines, or when the candles are lit. In the course of the play it turns out that all this creativity had been inspired by an experience characteristic of a higher state of consciousness on the evening of her husband's funeral. She had been alone in her room, staring at a candle, when suddenly the vision started. Miss Helen recounts her experience in the play to the play's two other characters, Elsa, a young teacher, and the village priest Marius:

> [*She looks around the room and speaks with authority*]
> Light the candles, Elsa. That one first.
> [*She indicates a candelabra that has been set up very prominently on a little table. ELSA lights it.*]
> And you know why, Marius? That is the East. Go out there into the yard and you'll see that all my Wise Men and their camels are travelling in that direction. Follow the candle on and one day you'll come to Mecca. Oh yes, Marius, it's true! I've done it. That is where I went that night and it was the candle you lit that led me there.
> [*She is radiantly alive with her vision*]
> A city, Marius! A city of light and colour more splendid than anything I had ever imagined.   There were palaces and beautiful buildings everywhere, with dazzling white walls and glittering minarets. Strange statues filled the courtyards. The streets were crowded with camels and turbaned men speaking a language I didn't understand, but that didn't matter because I knew, it was Mecca. And I was on my way to the grand temple. In the centre of Mecca there is a temple, and in the centre of the temple is a vast room with hundreds of mirrors on the walls and hanging lamps. And that is where the Wise Men of the East study the celestial geometry of light and colour. I became an apprentice that night. Light them all, Elsa, so that I can show Marius what I've learned.
> [*ELSA moves around the room lighting the candles, and as she does so its full magic and splendour is revealed.* (Fugard 1985, 71-2)

Miss Helen's vision happens unexpectedly, and her account of her experience comes across as genuine, devoid of sentimentality or mood-making. Miss Helen's experience in Fugard's *The Road to Mecca* shares many other characteristics of peak experiences described by Maslow (1962): Miss Helen was inspired to artistic creativity by her vision. Both the experience itself, and even her report of it several years later is full of joy and liveliness. The experience is mainly visual. After her husband's death, the experience gave her self-justification and affirmation; now, in the dramatised scene of the play the vivid recollection of the experience serves the same purpose: cornered by the village priest Marius to sign the documents needed to put her into an old people's home, the recollection gives her strength to refuse her signature. She also becomes able to accept that she is too old to manage on her own altogether, and will accept more help in the future.

A passage from Ronald Harwood's play *The Dresser* can illustrate the idea of *witnessing* one's activities from the perspective of pure consciousness in a theatrical context. The main character in the play is called "Sir". He is an old actor in the actor-manager tradition, allegedly based on Sir Donald Wolfit, whose dresser Ronald Harwood was at one time in his career. The play shows one day in Sir's life: he plays Lear at a provincial theatre, during the Second World War. He describes the following experience to his wife:

> Speaking "Reason not the need", I was suddenly detached from myself. My thoughts flew. And I was observing from a great height. Go on, you bastard, I seemed to be saying or hearing. Go on, you've more to give, don't hold back, more, more, more. And I was watching Lear. Each word he spoke was fresh invented. I had no knowledge of what came next, what fate awaited him. The agony was in the moment of acting created. I saw an old man, and the old man was me. And I knew there was more to come. But what? Bliss, partial recovery, more pain and death. All this I knew I had yet to see. Outside myself, do you understand? Outside myself. (Harwood 1980, 70).

According to the Vedanta model of consciousness, one characteristic of higher states of consciousness is that pure consciousness is by definition experienced as separate from the manifest levels of the mind (ego, feelings, mind, intellect, senses) and witnesses the experience on those manifest levels.

Higher states of consciousness in theatre (performance)

The experience of witnessing, characteristic of higher states of consciousness, is found not only in a fictional character, but also in real life. The actor Ray Reinhardt reports:

> There are two stages of having the audience in your hand. The first one is the one in which you bring them along, you make them laugh through sheer skill--they laughed at that, now watch me top it with this one. But, there's a step beyond that which I experienced, but only two or three times. It is the most--how can you use words like satisfying? It's more ultimate than ultimate: I seemed to be part of a presence that stood behind myself and was able to observe, not with my eyes, but with my total being, myself and the audience. It was a wonderful thing of leaving not only the character, but also this person who calls himself Ray Reinhardt. In a way, I was no longer acting actively, although things were happening: my arms moved independently, there was no effort required; my body was loose and very light. It was the closest I've ever come in a waking state to a mystical experience (Richard 1977, 43).

At least two aspects of this report are striking: it shows an infrequent, but clear experience suggestive of witnessing during activity. The experience itself is described as highly satisfying, and, at the same time, improving the performance.

I expect further research to yield more instances of utopian performatives understood as descriptions of glimpses of higher states of consciousness in drama and theatre. In the next section I want to turn to the utopian performatives understood as potential impact various processes involved in theatre practice can have on actors and spectators with regard to the development of higher states of consciousness.

Textual and performative means / tools of transformation

Development of consciousness is a process of transformation. Richard Schechner defines *transportation* in the context of theatre and performance as performances during which performers are 'taken somewhere', but after which they 're-enter ordinary life just about where they went in' (Schechner 1985, 125) to the performance mode:

> The performer goes from the "ordinary world" to the "performance world", from one time/space reference to another, from one personality to one or more others. He plays a character, battles demons, goes into trance, travels to the sky or under the sea or earth: he is transformed, able to do

things "in performance" he cannot do ordinarily. But when the performance is over, or even as a final phase of the performance, he returns to where he started. (125)

A long series of transportations, experienced over a large number of individual performances, may lead to *transformation* for the performer: the performers are changed without returning almost unchanged to their starting point (as in *transportation*). Originally, and still in many cases today, transformation occurs in ritual, where

> the attention of the transported [performers] and that of the spectators converge on the transformed. This convergence of attention—and the direct stakes spectators have in the performance—is why so many transformation performances use audience participation. (131)

The *change* referred to by Schechner may be of a significant dimension during performance for both *transformation* and *transportation*. In *transformation*, change is noticeable, immediate and lasting. In *transportation*, change is noticeable, immediate, but mainly restricted to the performance mode: only traces of such change are left in daily life outside performance; those traces, however, accumulate to reach the status of *transformation*. Aspects, or features of theatre that enable transformation of actors and spectators in the sense of constituting development of consciousness are utopian performatives. I want to locate such utopian performatives first in a general Western, and then in an Indian aesthetics context.

Orme-Johnson has claimed that contents and structure of a work of prose fiction or poetry may serve the function of leading the reader's mind to subtler levels of their mind, in the direction of pure consciousness ((1987). Malekin and Yarrow provide a detailed account of processes through which 'spirituality is made available to the receiver' in the context of theatre. (1997, 129). They identify three constitutive elements of theatre: performer, character and audience, and locate processes involving neutrality (pure consciousness in terms of Vedic Science), witnessing and play (characteristic of higher states of consciousness) for each of the elements, giving references to numerous relevant plays. To illustrate their argument with one example: neutrality for the character in theatre is a liminal state. Malekin and Yarrow explain:

> Deaths, displacements, demands to do the 'impossible' or resolve the unresolvable all present the character with the paradigm of the familiar and known, and of hesitation before a threshold of new forms of knowledge and being. (1997, 137)

Such liminality is represented by Vladimir and Estragon in Beckett's *Waiting for Godot*, two characters who are 'cut off from any obvious criteria of personality, geographical situation or function (1997, 137). Exposing the performers and spectators to those processes serves the function of heightened spirituality, of development of consciousness in terms of the Vedanta model of consciousness. Malekin and Yarrow have opened up a rich area of enquiry, which should particularly suit those who advocate looking within our own traditions for a revitalisation of today's theatre.

Since the main focus of Indian philosophy has been human consciousness and practical techniques for its development, it is worth looking at theatre aesthetics provided within the framework of Indian philosophy. The key text is the *Natyashastra*, attributed to Bharata, and written or compiled between the 2nd century AD and the 8th century BC. Towards the beginning of the text we find a passage describing how theatre was created: the golden age, in which all human beings enjoyed a state of enlightenment, complete health and fulfilment, had come to an end. The silver age had begun, and humans were afflicted by first symptoms of suffering. The gods, with Indra as their leader, were concerned and approached Brahma, the creator, asking him to devise a means allowing humans to regain their enlightenment, to restore the golden age. Indra specified that that means should be a fifth Vedic text, an addition to the four main texts of Indian (Vedic) philosophy (*Rig Veda*, *Sama Veda*, *Yajur Veda* and *Atharva Veda*). The fifth Veda should be both pleasing / entertaining and instructive, and should be accessible to the *shudras*, the lowest caste, because they were not allowed to read or listen to recitations of, the other Vedas. Brahma listened to Indra's request, immersed himself in meditation, and came up with *Natya*, *drama*, which he asked Indra and the gods to implement. Indra assured Brahma that the gods would be no good at this task, and so Brahma passed on his knowledge about *Natya* to the human sage Bharata, who in turn taught it to his 100 sons, who were thus the first actors. The knowledge imparted to Bharata by Brahma is contained in the text of the *Natyashastra* (*Shastra* is a holy text). Following the instructions for acting contained in this text be conducive to:

> duty (*dharma*), wealth (*artha*) as well as fame, will contain good counsel and collection [of other materials for human well-being], will give guidance to people of the future as well in all their actions, will be enriched by the teaching of all scriptures (*shastra*) and will give a review of all arts and crafts (*silpa*). (Ghosh, 3-4)

Theatre in this context thus has the direct and explicit function to restore the golden age, an age of utopia, for humankind, implying restoration of the state of perfection, liberation (*moksha*), enlightenment, higher states of consciousness for all people on earth.

The *Natyashastra* describes in substantial detail how the performers have to move their body in particular ways, depending on specific dramatic situations, to create specific emotional responses in themselves and in the audience. Specific emotional responses are conceptualised as *rasa*, translated as aesthetic experience, sentiment, taste, or flavour. The *Natyashastra* differentiates eight major emotional responses: the erotic, comic, pathetic, furious, heroic, terrible, odious, and marvellous. The mechanism of how to create these sentiments is complex (see table 1). The *Natyashastra* enumerates a range of specific situations in existing or potential theatre plays. Those situations (for example: the lover is yearning for her absent beloved) are called *determinant* (in Sanskrit: *vibhava*). For each such situation, determinant, the *Natyashastra* details the specific means of histrionic representation the actor uses to express the determinant. The means of acting (words, temperament, gestures, costume and make-up, see table 4 below) are called *consequents* (in Sanskrit, *anubhava*). Both the situation in the play text, and the means of acting that have to be used to express that specific situation, combine to create dominant emotional states (*sthayibhava*) in the spectator. There are eight dominant states, and they correspond to the eight sentiments (*rasa*). Those dominant states combine with transitory states (*vyabhicaribhava*) and temperamental states (*sattvikabhava*). There are thirty-three transitory states, such as discouragement, weakness, apprehension, envy, intoxication, and eight temperamental states: paralysis, perspiration, horripilation, change of voice, trembling, change of colour, weeping and fainting. The temperamental states refer to expressions of emotion usually considered to be in the domain of the autonomous nervous system and beyond the influence of the will (Ambardekar, 26)

The concept of *rasa* is clearly related to consciousness: its functioning is phrased in the *Natyashastra* in form of a short statement, a *sutra*: *Vibhava-anubhava-vyabhicaribhava-samyogad rasa-nispattih.* Ghosh translates the term *vibhava* from the expressed context of the theatrical situation as "determinant", given situations found in the playtext in which specific means of histrionic representation have to be used. In view of the fact that *santa rasa* is pure consciousness, and taking into consideration that *vibhava* also means "pure consciousness" (Shankar, 1992), the use of the term *vibhava* in the context of the *Natyashastra* refers to situations structured as possibilities in the dynamism of pure consciousness. Such latent situations, present as potentialities on the level of pure consciousness, take their shape in the theatrical context as *anubhava*. Ghosh again renders this term on the expressed level, as "consequent", means of histrionic representation doing justice to the "Determinants". *Anubhava* also means the experience of multitude after arising from pure consciousness (Shankar 1992). In other words, the actor, and in turn the spectator, experience the potentialities of *vibhava* as taking a specific shape in the theatrical context. Manifestation progresses further by "adding the ingredient" of *vyabhicaribhava*, translated by Ghosh as "transitory states [of emotion]". Indeed, *vyabhicaribhava* means the spreading, the expression of that experience of multitude implied by *anubhava* (Shankar, 1992). *Samyogad* has been translated by Ghosh as "combination", taking recourse to the illustration provided by the *Natyashastra* itself, which compares the functioning of the different elements in creating *rasa* to adding diverse ingredients to cook delicious food. *Samyogad*, however, means not so much a combination, an adding together, but implies a unity (Shankar 1992). Only when pure consciousness (*vibhava*), the experience of the multitude after coming out of pure consciousness (*anubhava*) and the spreading, or expression of that experience form a unity will *rasa* be produced in actor and spectator alike.

To summarise: *rasa* is an aesthetic experience for both actor and spectator, consisting in the coexistence of pure consciousness with aesthetic, theatre/performance-specific contents, sensory impressions, stimuli for the mind, the intellect, and the emotions. Repeated practice of acting in accordance with the *Natyashastra* for the actor implies repeated experience of *rasa*, and repeated exposure to such experiences will train both the actor and the spectator in responding to *rasa*-inducing stimuli faster, and to a larger degree. In due course, experiences of pure consciousness together with other (i.e. not necessarily aesthetic) contents of the expressed mind will be the natural consequence of the training process.

Exposure of actors and spectators to the experience of *rasa* implies an experience of pure consciousness, and some of this experience remains (*transformation*), and is not lost. Dip the cloth into the dye, and it soaks up the dye. Place it into the sunlight, and most of it fades out again. Repeat the process until the dye is firm and lasting. Expose people to theatre that induces higher states of consciousness, and they will soak that experience up. Then the experience fades, but a little bit of its effect remains. This is transformation (as opposed to transportation) in Schechner's sense.

Empirical implications

For those interested in empirical approaches to theatre, the current consciousness studies debate should offer a wide range of methods allowing to subject theories to empirical research. I want to conclude with one potential scenario: Some years ago, researchers discovered the phenomenon of mirror neurones. Vilanyanur S Ramachandran, 2003 BBC Reith lecturer for the BBC, called them possibly as groundbreaking in today's neuroscience as the discovery of DNA in its time (2003). When we see movements of another person, neurones in our brains start firing in such a way that we should immediately copy the observed movements. Sometimes we do mirror observed behaviour, as in yawning or laughter. Usually, however, at the same time, different neurones start firing as well, and their activity prevents the mirroring action (Votluk 2001). The following hypothesis results from this discovery: if the spectator in theatre sees the actor's movements, part of the reception or response process involves the firing the two sets of neurones: mirror neurones and those neurones that prevent an imitation of the observed movement. Although the spectator will not imitate most of the actor's observed movements, some impact of the neuronal activity related to mirror neurones could well have an impact on some part of the spectator's physiology, the immune system, for example. This hypothesis obviously also applies to the actors themselves, and the production team, anyone who is present during rehearsals and performances. Applied to utopian performatives: we could argue that utopian performatives have a physical component, and we could further identify and define that physical aspect of utopian performatives, by associating it with, say, movement that follows the *Natyashastra*. We could then use the mirror neuron hypothesis as a model to explain (at least part of) the impact the movement component of such *Natyashastra*-based theatre has on actors and spectators.

Conclusion

If we take higher states of consciousness as characteristics of individual utopia, and as such as the basis of social utopia, then theatre has the potential of developing utopia for the individual, and through the individual for society. The utopian performatives are various techniques, which can be located both in Western and, in my examples, Indian traditions of theatre texts and aesthetics. As I suggested, further research should lead to more details for each of those two traditions, and probably to comparable consciousness-related utopian performatives in other cultural traditions, based in Africa, Japan or China.

Notes

Relevant websites

Consciousness and Cognition: website
    www.apnet.com/www/journal/cc.htm
Journal of Consciousness Studies: website
    www.imprint.co.uk/Welcome.html
Centre for Consciousness Studies: www.consciousness.arizona.edu/
Association for the Scientific Study of Consciousness http://assc.caltech.edu/
Consciousness and Experiential Psychology www.warwick.ac.uk/cep/
The British Psychological Society's Transpersonal Psychology Section
    http://www.transpersonalpsychology.org.uk/
Consciousness, Literature and the Arts: http://www.aber.ac.uk/cla

Bibliography

Ambardekar, R. R.   1979. *Rasa Structure of the Meghaduta*. Bombay: Prakashan.
Fugard, Athol. 1985. The Road to Mecca. London, Faber.
Ghosh, Manomohan, ed. and transl., 1950. *The Natyasastra. A Treatise on Hindu Dramaturgy and Histrionics*. Calcutta: The Royal Asiatic Society of Bengal.
Harwood, Ronald. 1980. *The Dresser*. Ambergate: Amber Lane Press.
Malekin, Peter, and Ralph Yarrow. 1997. *Consciousness, Literature and Theatre: Theory and Beyond*. London/New York: MacMillan/ St.Martin's Press.
Maslow, Abraham H. 1962. *Towards a Psychology of Being*. New York: Van Nostrand.
Meyer-Dinkgräfe (ed.). 1999. *Performance and Consciousness, Performing Arts International* 1:4.
Orme-Johnson, Rhoda. 1987: "A Unified Field Theory of Literature", *Modern Science and Vedic Science* 1:3: 323-373.
Ramachandran, V.S. 'Mirror Neurons and imitation learning as the driving force behind 'the great leap forward' in human evolution'. Accessed on 27.03.2003 at
    http://www.edge.org/3rd_culture/ramachandran/ramachandran_index.html
Richards, G. 1977. "The world a stage: A conversation with Ray Reinhardt". *San Francisco Theater Magazine* Winter , 46.

Schechner, Richard. 1985. *Between Theatre and Anthropology*. Philadelphia: U of Pennsylvania Press.

Shankar, Yogashiromani Shri Shri Ravi. 1992. Interview with Daniel Meyer-Dinkgräfe, 5 August.

Stace, W.T. 1960. *Mysticism and Philosophy*. London: MacMillan.

Votluk, Alison. 2001. 'Mirror Minds Mirror Neurons'. *New Scientist*, 27.January (http://www.newscientist.com/)

CHAPTER ELEVEN

MICHELLE PIASECKA

CREATIVITY, LIVE ART AND THE PRIMARY SCHOOL CURRICULUM

What would happen if school curricula, like the production of performance art, consisted of playful, performative contradictions?
—Garoian, 1999, p.1.

Introduction

This chapter explores the creative and pedagogic potential of Live Art at Primary and Junior School level. Given that Live Art is not statutory requirement of the primary national curriculum in terms of subject provision or pedagogical processes and techniques, the theme will be sustained by an examination of current discourses informing the Primary Curriculum, predominantly those surrounding creativity and creative learning. My argument begins, therefore, with an examination of the term creativity. I then consider the economic and political implications of creative education in a local context. Finally, I look at the political, ethical, personal and social potential of Live Art, referring in particular to a project undertaken by year six children at a Junior School in Stoke-on-Trent.

The Creative Agenda

Creativity and creative learning is an emerging term in the Primary School Curriculum. While initially referring to art and craft-based subjects, it is now more commonly associated with a range of creative learning opportunities and appears to dominate current educational thinking and writing. Some examples include the QCA *National Primary Strategy for Creativity Across the Curriculum*, the merging of the Literacy and Numeracy Strategies, as part of the Excellence and Enjoyment strategy for Primary Schools (2003), 'Creative Partnerships' (2005) and 'Every Child Matters' (2005). The shift in emphasis from art-based activities and discreet disciplines such as dance, drama and music to a broader understanding of the term signals the transitory nature of the curriculum and follows heavily upon a series of educational reforms and initiatives: for example, 'learning styles, thinking skills' (Cowley, 2005, p.7) and more recently, personalised learning (Craft, 2005). In response to these developments Stronach and MacLure developed the notion of 'policy hysteria', referring in particular to the sheer number of educational policies dating from the 1980s. They write, 'UK educational change in the 1980s and 1990s was characterised by recurring waves of reform. These developed increasingly short-term patterns, based on three to five year cycles of development' (1997, p.87).

The wealth of recent publications exploring creative approaches to teaching and learning provides some indication of the growing interest in this area (Craft, 2005; Cowley, 2005; Winston, 2004). Creativity has re-surfaced in policy-making, in educational writing and research and at practice level. Central to this resurgence is the belief that creative approaches can be applied across the wider curriculum. Cowley (2005), for example, utilises fairly standard drama-based exercises, such as role-play, characterisation and fictional settings as a starting point for creative exploration. 'Our learning in science, maths, history, geography, and so on, will benefit from creative activities and approaches, and both from teacher and children getting into a creative frame of mind' (Cowley, 2005, p.2).[1] Heathcote (1995), arguably the forerunner of drama in the curriculum, offers a distinctive approach, referred to as *The Mantle of the Expert*.[2] O'Neill writes, ' [t]his is essentially an approach to the whole curriculum...it is a rare example of truly integrative teaching' (1995; cited in Heathcote and Bolton, p.viii). Other approaches include Sawyer (2004) 'disciplined improvisation' (cited in Craft, 2005, p.135) and Winston's (2004) blending of drama and English in the primary school curriculum. It appears then, that drama is generally perceived to be a valuable and useful tool for encouraging a broader application of creativity in the classroom.

Indeed, the distinction made by NACCCE (1999) report between teaching creatively and teaching for creativity is also a good indication of the perceived benefits of a broad approach to creativity. Craft, in her examination of the differences between 'high creativity' (Feldman, 1994; cited in Craft, 2005) and 'little c creativity' writes:

> little c creativity has been suggested to be the ordinary but lifewide attitude
> toward life that is driven by 'possibility thinking' but is about acting

effectively with flexibility, intelligence in the everyday rather than the extraordinary (2005, p.19).

Hence, there is a relationship between everyday, 'lifewide' creative approaches and personal, social development. Such arguments would also suggest that all children (and teachers) are capable of being creative. 'Every person has it within themselves to be creative, and we as teachers can play a key part in helping our students to map out their own individual journeys' (Cowley, 2005, p.20). But, as Craft point outs, 'if the fostering of creativity and culture are linked then the multiple perspectives which learners bring to this process are highly significant in terms of engagement, and this can pose practical and philosophical challenges' (2005, p.96). Such thinking invites teachers and educators with opportunities to contest dominant pedagogical practices and to explore new teaching and learning methodologies. Or, as Taylor (1996) would suggest, an opportunity to challenge neo-positivist approaches to creative learning and to engage in multi-centric and multiple-perspectival approaches to education that take into *greater* account the cultural, demographic and physical backgrounds of the children who make-up our school populations. Yet before an examination of these kinds of teaching and learning opportunities can occur, it is vitally important to examine creativity in a local economic and political context.

Setting the Local Context

The Arts Strategy (2005) for Stoke-on-Trent City Council is an example of the kinds of local discourses and practices surrounding creativity and economic, financial stability. The Arts Strategy, written partly as a response to 'Every Child Matters' seeks to place *creativity* and creative learning opportunities at the forefront of the city's five year strategic plan. Broadly, it aims to achieve the following:

1. a vibrant and harmonious city;
2. a safer city
3. health and independence;
4. better outcomes for children and young people

To understand the significance of the above it is necessary to understand the local context for Stoke-on-Trent. According to Bailey (2005) it is, statistically, the 17th most deprived city in the country, both economically and in an educational sense. Over the last few decades there has been a steady decline in 'traditional routes to employment' (Bailey, 2005, p.5), where the closure of Shelton Bar steelworks is one such example. In a city whose creative heritage, namely the potteries, has a long and prominent history, young people are least likely to set up small businesses in the creative sector than anywhere else in the country. In terms of the city's cultural make-up, ethnic minorities represent 15% of the school population and with approximately 46 languages spoken there is a real need for the city to find, 'a sense of time and place that reflects a relatively new and emerging population…traditional, new and developing' (Bailey, 2005, p.14). Hence, there is a symbolic attempt to drive a correlation between creative learning and politically led agendas in a local and national context. Thus, Collard's (National Director of Creative Partnerships) argument carries particular economic significance:

> *Creativity* is now at the top of the political agenda and recognised to be of fundamental importance to the future of this country. Creative skills are increasingly identified by employers as a key to the kinds of skills needed for young people to operate in the twenty-first century (Collard, n.d; cited in Bailey, 2005, p.10).

A structural reading of the above quotation would suggest an 'outside-in' (Dawson, 1994) perspective, where notions of an 'economy of performance' (Stronach *et al,* 2002), control of the curriculum and policy change at a local level are prominent. In such cases, national initiatives are the driving forces behind documents like the City's five-year strategic plan. Read differently, however, from a post-structural position, terms like 'creative' are not stable utterances. When we engage with the term *creativity* at a local level we are also engaging in a power struggle between locally driven contexts and wider national agendas. Such struggles are both constraining and enabling (Stronach *et al,* 2002; Craft, 2005). Moreover, for Collard, *creativity* is situated within a wider national, government-led context. Whereas educators we are faced with textbooks, documents, papers and ideas, which support the idea that language is fixed and unchangeable (Cherryholmes, 1997). Yet the emerging meaning of a term like creative surely shifts depending upon the historical, social, cultural, political and educational contexts in use. McGinn, writing of Wittgenstein, explains this argument in the following way:

> Language is essentially in structural activities that constitutes a 'form of life'. Almost all of the activities that human beings engage in are ones that are intrinsically concerned with, or somehow grounded in, our use of language; our form of life is everywhere shaped by the use of language,

and it is this I have tried to capture...by saying that our form of life is
fundamentally cultural in nature (1997, p.58).

For Stronach and MacLure, meaning not only has movement but
adjacency, hence meaning lies somewhere alongside and 'between rather
than within words' (1997, p.93). Hence, from a post-structural
Foucauldian perspective the term *creative* moves between a complex
engagement with technologies of power (what is expected and demanded
at a national level) and of the technologies of sign (how language is
constructed and interpreted in a local context), thus producing a number of
semiotic possibilities. These semiotic possibilities do not occupy a ground.
Neither are they endless, as they tend to be situated within the immediate
discourse (Piasecka, 2004).

Cunningham's (1988) view of curriculum history as curriculum theory
is a useful one here, as it illustrates the active relationship between
personal, social, cultural and political, economic contexts and would
suggest that any attempt to articulate an understanding of the creative
curriculum would need to recognise how its theory engages dialogically
with economic agendas driving reform. Cunningham referring to Reid,
describes this in the following way:

> Reid (1986) has elaborated this point by demonstrating the practical
> application of curriculum history insofar as it depicts curriculum change in
> terms of action in context [...] as opposed to general or universal
> propositions, and because it enables curriculum theory to be evaluated
> pragmatically rather than by its internal logic, enabling us to see the
> partiality and temporality of theories (1988, p.7).

Introducing Live Art

Arguably, approaching the term creative from such a position is a
useful one, since it allows us to foreground some of the tensions at play
within current educational discourses. However, discourses surrounding
creativity are perhaps, at best, ambiguous and are caught up within wider
issues surrounding professionalism (Stronach *et al*, 2002), performativity
(Lyotard, 1984), the audit culture (Strathern, 2000) and the universalised
concept of creativity (Craft, 2005). Craft asks, 'how does our creativity
engage with needs and rights both inwardly (home and personal) and
outwardly (work and public life). This balance [...] may be the biggest
challenge of all that creativity poses for us' (2005, p.150). This is an
important argument to make and is perhaps one of the most compelling
reasons for exploring mutiple-perspectival approaches to creativity, like

Live Art, since a feature of this kind of work is its relationship (albeit an uneasy one) between personal, social and cultural identities. Heathfield suggests that:

> [o]ne consequence of this work, amongst many others, is to explore in all of its intricate ramifications our psychological and social dependency upon naming and identity: the quest for stabilities through which to see oneself and others, and by which one may live (Heathfield, 2004, pp.9, 10).

Hence, because Live Art is situated within lived experiences it invites the child to work from the position of their own personal, psychological and intellectual selves within wider social, cultural and political contexts. It has the potential to offer the child valuable time and space in which to explore where she comes from and the kinds of issues and challenges to be faced: 'performance art repositions artists, teachers, and children to critique cultural discourses and practices that inhibit, restrict, or silence their identity formation, agency and creative production' (Gaorian, 1999, p.5). This strategy is more ontological than pedagogical in nature and proposes that learning in also bound up in culture, community and received understanding, and suggests that children approach learning not from a fixed position but construct meaning from particular ideological and cultural vantage points (Lynch, 2000).

Therefore, Live Art might have something unique to offer, beyond that of established drama-based approaches to creativity in the classroom. For the former the child reflects socio-historical, political and cultural discourses from the perspectives of the other (character/ role/teacher). In Live Art, practical application is a result of active engagement of the personal, social, political self in performance. The child performs as herself and in adopting a pre-determined position notions of process and performance are unfettered by character and fiction. Another way of looking at this argument is to suggest that Live Art praxis deals with realities and actualities, unlike drama, which tends to analogise in a fictional way.

The Politics of Live Art

The focus of this discussion, therefore, now needs shifting, from an initial exploration of the term creativity, to a closer examination of the pedagogic potential of Live Art. The study and practice of Live Art, however, raises some difficult and problematic issues and arguably the tensions created through Live Art are greater than those identified by Craft

(2005). In Live Art, tensions are greater because of the complexity and awkwardness of its praxis. Teachers need to articulate an account of Live Art, whose histories and approaches involve challenges to fixed art, creative and cultural boundaries, as Garoian asks, 'Could a performance art pedagogy make personal/political agency attainable for students' (1999, p.2)?

Such an examination would also, by necessity, question the appropriateness of Live Art at primary level, especially since Live Art has a tendency to fall between the planks of established disciplines and social norms of acceptability. By its very nature, Live Art is a transgressive and challenging art form. The teacher who decides to examine Live Art, in the primary curriculum, may be subject to some criticism, since according to Stronach *et al*, 'usually and enduringly the notion of the 'professional' has expressed a kind of over-investment in the professional as agent for good in society' (2002, p. 110). This may be the case when we consider the conservative fear of 'opening a can of worms' − a praxis that engages the *subjective* and infers a sensible handling of the ethical, so far as a teacher is concerned (once we invite a subjective response from the child we may not like what we hear). Live Art resists the 'safe territory' of objectivity by its very nature. The teacher/educator is caught then, between what she would like to teach and professional social, ethical and political codes of conduct(s).

Pedagogy and Live Art

A live Art performance project undertaken with year 6 school children from Stoke-on-Trent is an example of some of these issues. The project, performed in May 2006, explored, via praxis, transition from primary school to secondary school, drawing upon personal and social stories within fictional, imagined, historical and factual contexts. The project required the children to create and perform a guided tour of their school (Hodge *et al*, 2006). The focus of the project was to develop and document the children's own personal histories of their time at the school. For example, children wrote stories about the games they played (real and imagined), stories about haunted toilets and bell-towers and tales of friendships and fallouts.[3] The purpose for this was to enable the children to locate themselves as individuals within a broader context of the school's history. In short, they needed to locate themselves in the subject. An argument also shared by Pollard, he writes, '[s]ince understanding can only be constructed in the mind of the learner, it is essential that learners exercise a significant degree of control in the process' (ref).

Therefore, Live Art may be considered as a formative experience, in that it offers children the opportunity to extend, through practice, their own life experiences into new ways and modes of thinking. In Live Art, children are working from inside their own intellectual, psychological, cultural and spiritual selves and are required to enter into a meaning-making discourse, which is at once social, political and personal (Piasecka, 2004). Importantly, in the absence of script-based narratives, a practical application of Live Art encourages children both to develop and control their own voice within their work.

This project also raised important issues surrounding process, since Live Art is more about the process of mapping personal and task-based issues to performance works rather than being concerned with a polished outcome (Piasecka, 2004). From a pedagogic perspective, an inclination towards process, potentially, allows for greater equality between children and may counter current outcome driven agendas in the primary curriculum. The use of narrational devices (role-play, story-telling, script work) may improve literacy and communication for some children, but also may prevent other children from taking part. In Stoke-on-Trent ethnic minorities make-up 15% of the school population and whilst many of these children will be English speaking there will be a significant number who have English as a second language. Hence, Live Art may offer another differentiated entry point to learning.

Live Art also questions established notions of virtuosity (Piasecka, 2004). Because Live Art has a tendency to avoid, disrupt and challenge such notions, children are able to bring in whatever skills they have to their practice, including writing, visual art, movement and sound, without worrying too much about bench-marked standards. Historically, the idea that Live Art challenges notions of virtuosity is not new to the contemporary arts: as Banes writes of Judson Dance Theatre, '[o]ne way to draw attention away from matters of virtuosic technique is to demystify it by making dances that acknowledge their own process of being made' (1987, p.17). Although it would be easy to interpret a shift towards process with the criticism that some form of 'quality' is diminished, a counter-argument might point out that a virtuosic concern is particularly dependent on subjective bias and closed cannons of practice. It might also be argued that the introduction of personal discourse shifts the emphasis from the teacher figure to the child herself and this in itself raises a benchmark regarding the way that practice is imbued with personal knowledge and understanding. Virtuosity also relies upon the reproduction of the archetypal and the hegemonic skills and diminishes the individual as subject. In teaching culture dominated by league tables, SATS, Ofsted reports, Live Art may offer the child valuable time and space in which to explore where she comes from and the kinds of issues and challenges to be faced. This argument cannot be taken too lightly, as Holt ironically observes, 'school is a place where children learn to be stupid...Children come to school *curious;* within a few years most of that curiosity is dead, or at least silent' (2001; cited in Pollard and Bourne, p.9, *own emphasis*). Because Live Art is situated within lived experiences it invites the child to become curious again and because Live Art is difficult to assess we might find ourselves, like Holt (2001), in the remarkable position of asking children what *they* think about their work. It might be concluded therefore, that children learn best when learning is situated in the social, political and personal discourses that have informed their practice. Live Art, in replacing virtuosity for task-based activity, and outcome in favour of process, may offer an exceptional and unique vehicle in which to do so (Piasecka, 2004).

Some Conclusions

In exploring the social, political and personal in performance, Live Art invites us (teachers, children) to engage with the world we live in from perspectives, other than dominant Western modes and ways of thinking, and may encourage a return to the artistic-aesthetic curriculum, as voiced by Taylor. In a passionate attack of neo-positivism, he writes, '[d]o we [...] want to produce a generation of children who are incapable of seeing, hearing, and attending to the possibilities of arts works, but are adept at intellectualising over them (1996, p.11).

Live Art is an open dialogue and as the Live Art Development Agency has said, it is a place, 'where the disenfranchised and disembodied become visible, where the politics of difference are contested and complexity is confronted' (Live Art Development Agency, 2004, p.2). Live Art, with its resistance to category or academy, with its rejection of the virtuosic, rewards originality and personal experience as true achievement. Primary children in the more problematised areas of Stoke-on-Trent already consider themselves in negative contexts of failure. In this respect a role-play that positions itself on the virtuosities of performance is undone. Such children require the licence of their own position and it is this 'situated' potential of Live Art that creates a genuine relation to the self. The importance of this argument cannot be overstated. If, as Stronach and MacLure suggest (1997), power and knowledge are in constant movement, shifting between the local, national and global, Live Art can offer an artistic and creative platform, in which to explore some of these ideas.

Finally, perhaps, Live Art should be studied because it offers us (teachers), the opportunity (which Greene and Taylor have argued is becoming increasing difficult to sustain in the contemporary curriculum) '[t]o make possible a pluralism of visions, a multiplicity of realities. We may enable those we teach to rebel' (Greene, 1978; cited in Taylor, 1996, p.2).

Notes

1 For example: Cowley provides an example of a maths class looking at probability. Titled 'Horse Race', the classroom is set-up as a racetrack with various obstacles and volunteers are timed as they complete the course. Role-play and fictional settings are utilised as a way into the learning environment; suggested scenarios include scenes of crime, characters on trial, left luggage, Alice in Wonderland, Cinderella and Snow White. Cowley also identifies the role and use of physical warm-ups and improvisational games and exercises as part of the creative process.

2 Heathcote and Bolton illustrate *the Mantle of the Expert* approach through the topic of China. First using a fictional student teacher, they adopt a traditional approach to the subject area, describing classroom activities such as the production of a map, a Chinese dragon, menus, drawings, pictures and traditional myths and stories. Heathcote and Bolton refer to this as the *Topic Approach. The Mantle of the Expert,* however would approach the same topic from a different perspective and would require the teacher to consider the kinds of people who would need to know about China, i.e., experts in their own particular field, such as travel agents, media reporters, medical people, entrepreneurs, historians and TV producers. Through a rather complex process of elimination the teacher finally decides upon the following theme: the children are required to adopt the role of hotel experts, who specialise in training Chinese staff for Western tourists. Through extended role play the children would undertake, hence '[t]hey become experts – experts at learning' (O'Neill; cited in Heathcote and Bolton, 1999, p.ix).

3 As part of the guided tour the children performed a number of stories about the school. My favourites include performances about ghosts who supposedly haunt the bell-tower and the girls' toilets, a bench where one pupil was "dumped" by his girl friend and heroic playground adventures, featuring giant spiders, aliens and world-cup football. The project, which was fully supported by the teachers, despite considerable noise and disruption to the teaching week, provided the children with the opportunity to work across a range of creative approaches: for example, map-making, story-writing, story-telling, documentation, photography and performing.

Bibliography

Bailey, Paul. 2005. *Arts Strategy – Children and Young People Services*, Stoke-on-Trent City Council.

Banes, Sally. 1987. *Terpischore In Sneakers: Post-Modern Dance*, New Hampshire: Wesleyan University Press.

Cherryholmes, Cleo. 1988. *Power and Criticism: Poststructural Investigations in Education, Advances in Contemporary Educational Thought, Volume 2*, New York: Teachers College Press.

Cowley, Sue. 2005. *Letting The Buggers Be Creative*, London: Continuum.

Craft, Anna. 2005. *Creativity in Schools: Tensions and Dilemmas*, London: Routledge.

Cunningham, Peter. 1988. *Curriculum Change in the Primary School Since 1945*, London: The Falmer Press

Garoian, Charles. 1999. *Performing Pedagogy, Towards an Art of Politics*, New York: University of New York Press.

Heathfield, Adrian. (Ed). 2004. *Live: Art and Performance*, London: Tate Publishing.

Hodge, Stephen, Simon Persighetti, Phil Smith, Cathy Turner. 2006. About Mis-Guides. *http://www.mis-guide.com/ws.htm (accessed May 19, 2006)*.

Live Art Development Agency. 2004. What is Live Art? http://www.thisisliveart.co.uk/about-us/whatisliveart.htm (accessed July 8, 2004).

Lynch, Michael. 2000. Against Reflexivity as an Academic Virtue and Source of Privileged Knowledge. *Theory, Culture and Society*, 17 (3): 27-53.

McGinn, Maria. 1997. *Wittgenstein and the Philosophical Investigations*, London: Routledge.

O'Neill, Cecily, Dorothy Heathcote, Gavin Bolton. 1995. *Drama for Learning, Dorothy Heathcote's Mantle of the Expert Approach to Education*, Portsmouth, NH: Heinemann.

Lyotard, Jean-Francois. 1984. *The Postmodern Condition: A Report on Knowledge*, Manchester: Manchester University Press.

Piasecka, Michelle. 2004. *Live Art and the Post – 16 Curriculum*, MA (by Research): MMU.

Pollard, Andrew and Jill Bourne. 2001. (Ed) *Teaching and Learning in the Primary School*, London: Open University Press.

Sawyer, R. Keith. 2004. Creative Teaching: Collaborative Discussion as Disciplined Improvisation. *Educational Researcher 33 (2): 12-20*

Strathern, Marilyn. (Ed.). 2000. (*Audit Cultures, Anthropological Studies in Accountability, Ethics and the Academy,* London: Routledge.

Stronach, Ian, Brian Corbin, Olwen McNamara, Shelia Stark, Tony Warne. Towards an uncertain politics of professionalism: teacher and nurse identities in flux. 2002. *Journal of Educational Policy,* 17 (1): 109-138.

Stronach, Ian and Maggie MacLure. 1997. *Educational Research Undone: The Postmodern Embrace,* Buckingham: The Open University Press

Taylor, Philip. (Ed). 1996. *Researching Drama and Arts Education, Paradigms and Possibilities,* London: Falmer Press

Winston, Joe. 2004. *Drama and English at the Heart of the Curriculum: Primary and Middle Years,* London: David Fulton

CHAPTER TWELVE

SIMON PIASECKI

FREEDOM FROM RESTRICTION: THE PHENOMENON OF THE PRIMAL AND THE RATIONAL IN EARLY MODERNIST PERFORMANCE PRACTICE

In 1781, following a silence of a decade, Immanuel Kant published his *Critique of Pure Reason*. The work served as a fusion of the empirical and the rational and as such a unity of *a priori* knowledge, or knowledge which may be gained through rational analysis alone, and *a posteriori* knowledge, or knowledge that may only be gained through actual experience. It applied these categories in respect of representation, imagination, sensation, space, time and form.

This stricture of knowledge can be considered by analogy as embedded in many ideological struggles since because it infers the question of control; *a posteriori* experience is inherently formed by the external phenomena of events & objects in the sense world, as argued in the Empiricism of John Locke in the 17th Century (Scruton 1995, 79–whole chapter). But experience is formed by the perception of the external and contemporaries of Locke, such as the Reverend George Berkeley, posited that our perception was only proof for the argument of a greater perception or consciousness of God – the implicit warning being that the idea of an individual discourse as separate from God was a heresy (Russel 1991, 623).

This Universalist view suggests that we are beholden to that which is beyond the self and that our behaviour is therefore subject to a greater judgement. A priori knowledge on the other hand requires rationality – logical proof. This wasn't separate from the question of God however and rationalists since Descartes had tried to use a priori logic to prove his/her existence. Whilst the hegemony of the church was still an essential of social and educational acceptance this aim of rationalism would remain but it nevertheless constantly reinforced the context of the individual, since it held the relationship of the mind with the body at its core, and these were internal rather than external issues. This naturally created a foundation for the growth of the argument for Individualism. By fusing Rationalism and Empiricism, Kant therefore created the possibility for the emancipation of the artist, amongst others, from the patron, the state and the church.

But it was also the ingredient elements of Kant's critique – representation, imagination, sensation, space, time, and form that would be so vitally engaged by the early artists of the early 20th Century. Prior to this though, and whilst Hegel was perhaps the most influential philosopher of the early 19th Century, it was Kierkegaard who really reinforced the idea of individual choice against the Universalist view (Scruton 1995, 182) - surprising considering his status as a pastor – and then Nietzsche who expressed the final rational conclusion that God was either dying or dead, that we should be judged as individuals (Scruton 1995, 185).

One of the outstanding issues of the rationalists up until Nietzsche was their preoccupation with proving the existence of God. Whilst admiring Kant, Nietzsche pours scorn on this aspect (Russell 1991, 732). It is arguable that whilst Kant threw into some perspective the dualism of the Empirical and Rationalist views, something of the social 'street-level' context that his contemporary Voltaire said was an essential of any philosophy of worth, was missing until the question of God was overcome. It took an Industrial Revolution, an expedition on the Beagle, and a gender struggle to do so. Voltaire was also anti-Christian, but such a blasphemy was more likely to emerge with some influence during the social upheavals of the following (19th) century and particularly in Germany with its various fragmentary principalities reducing the hegemony of a single academy.

The ramifications of the Kantian fusion can therefore form the basis of a phenomenological understanding of the social upheavals since the Industrial revolution; the move to the urban, the rise of the working classes, Darwinism and the struggle of science and religion, Marxism and the class struggle, the Women's' Movement and psychoanalysis, arriving rather neatly at the melting pot of Vienna just following the *fin de siècle*. This is where the debate of Universalism versus Individualism became most clearly focussed in the lectures of Franz Brentano. Ostensibly Brentano attempted to employ scientific methodology to prove the existence of God and his lectures were widely attended, influencing the emergence of Husserl's Phenomenology and Von Ehrenfels' Gestalt theory amongst others (Watson 2000, 31). It is not the answer to this debate that is indicative of a crucial zeitgeist of the period but rather the spirit of Kant in its proving of the Empirical with the Rational. Its primary impact was certainly not religious, however, but much more qualitatively present in the Café discussions of the Viennese cultural and scientific elite. There are many ways to view this new objectivity and most of them infer conflict – individual or God, the industrial or the agricultural, production or craft, tradition or progress, Semite or Anti-Semite, male or female. The latter question of gender found an unfortunate combination with fashionable anti-Semitism in the work of Otto Weininger, another follower of Brentano. Weininger's *Geschlecht und Character*, a baseless but scientifically presented publication, suggested that positive protoplasm (male) was responsible for all the great events, arts and inventions of civilisation, whilst the presence of negative protoplasm (essentially female) was destructive and most dominant in the Jewish race (Watson 2000, 33). The book was a best seller and sent shockwaves of interest through Viennese society for some time.

Jung was already well aware of a relationship between the rational and spiritual, the male and the female, the self and the external world. At a young age he was aware of a relationship between his logical and conservative No.1 self to its opposite in the subjective and spiritual No.2, terms which had first been introduced into his life by his deeply troubled mother. His analysis of this relationship, which would also develop – perhaps more positively – into an analysis of male and female, introvert and extrovert, continued to embrace the primal and spiritual contexts. In this regard it is more applicable to a view of artistic practice, at least, than Freud's demystification of the symbol. (McKlynn 1996, 18)

Many of the influential thinkers and artists of Vienna congregated in the Ringstrasse at the famous Café Griensteidl. Amongst them was the composer Schoenberg. As an autodidact, Schoenberg was in a good position to free his technique from the traditional canon. Watson suggests that since he was impressed by the visual artists' attempt "to make visible the distorted and raw forms unleashed by the modern world and analysed and ordered by Freud" (56 Terrible Beauty), he would try to do the same for music; in his own words he aspired to 'the emancipation of dissonance' (Schoenberg cited in Watson 2000, 56). The wording in itself is revealing – emancipation being that drive of the moderns to break with the past, dissonance stating that this would be a brutal declaration, a rational cacophony and a violent departure.

Schoenberg was quickly declared 'insane' by the media for his brutal application of atonality in composition and particularly following the performance of his String Quartet #2, op.10 in 1908. Watson suggests that for Schoenberg atonality finally arrived whilst composing the third and fourth movements (Watson 2000, 57), by leaving out all six sharps of the key signature and this is where Schoenberg arguably begins to free himself from social convention through the imposition of a rule. Traditionally tonality of music was achieved because every note asserts its relationship to the key of the piece, so logically atonality could be achieved in the absence of a central key pitch. Whilst the leaving out of sharps was possibly creatively inspired by the dark poems of Stefan George that he was composing to, and therefore something initially felt, this is consequently translated into *a priori* rules that would allow the emergence of Serialism in the following decades.

Schoenberg had found his discourse and his modernist rebellion. Indeed the premiere of his Second String Quartet was a huge scandal, and Watson describes the audience blowing upon their keychain whistles in protest. The *New Vienna Daily* printed a review in the crime section of the paper. Whilst admitting this to be a dreadful experience, Schoenberg did not waver. His following compositions and operas smashed the remaining traditions of theme and repetition through works such as *Erwartung* and *Pierrot Lunaire,* and led to his development of the twelve-tone system, which he called a 'Method of Composing with Twelve Tones Which are Related Only One with Another.' (Stein 1975, 218) This basically ensured that one tone cannot dominate over any other and perfectly illustrates the stricture of a modernist, rational parameter that challenges the hegemony of the traditional canon.

Anarchic dissonance in itself might be a way to describe the non-movement formed by non-artists not far from Vienna, in neutral Zurich during the First World War. Dada, as it called itself is perhaps an exceptional phenomenon of this study in that it wholly rejected the rationalism of the modern.

Tsara, its founder, later said in his 1922 *Lecture on Dada,* that "the beginnings of Dada were not the beginnings of an art, but of a disgust. Disgust with the magnificence of philosophers who for 3000 years have been explaining everything to us (what for?)" (Tsara 1922; cited in Motherwell 1989, 246-51). Interestingly though its rejection of rules was ostensibly driven by other rules – it was against any bourgeois process of the art product and as such adopted the transience of performance and the montage of the cabaret. Cabaret Voltaire provides the link that will consolidate Dada's relevance to this study.

The use of Cabaret is, like the Dadaist photo-montages of Hannah Hoch, a gestalt bringing together of objects that, as a whole, equal something greater than the sum of their parts. The name Voltaire refers to the French philosopher, a contemporary of Kant, although more a follower of Locke. Tristan Tzara eschewed the production of philosophy and certainly that of the rational and yet named his Cabaret after Voltaire. Certainly the 'rationale', at the risk of being sardonic, was that Voltaire was anti-Christian and felt that philosophy was useless if it held no sway over the average life of the street, but Voltaire also expounded that moral virtues were to be reached through man's capacity for reason.

Dada's anger is easy to understand in retrospect, but it is fraught with contradiction so far as its rejection of Modernism is concerned and particularly in Tzara's manifesto statements regarding objectivity – he detests the 'greasy objectivity' of the scientist, and feels that 'Psychoanalysis is a dangerous disease' (certainly rejecting the Viennese circle), 'that puts to sleep the anti-objective impulses of men and systematizes the bourgeoisie'(Tsara 1918; cited in Motherwell 1989, 78-81), but his Manifesto is rife with observation and objective, rational declaration alongside unquestionable passion. Moral in its immoralities Dada eats itself and so far as this paper is concerned it provides a necessary vehicle rather than a select example.

Across the other Swiss border into Italy, Marinetti had published his first manifesto for Futurism in 1909. The proximity is an interesting indication of socio-cultural difference to the subsequent Dadaists, in that it is in some respects the antithetical movement – the first manifesto expounded the glory of war, the love of danger, the beauty of struggle and aggression, the disdain of women. This rhetoric though is suffused with just the same ingredients of the vital and the rational but in a rather opposite fashion to Dada – Futurism was fundamentally modern in its love of speed, the machine, of mass production. Marinetti described the roar of the motorcar as 'more beautiful than the Nike of Samothrace', the Hellenistic sculpture of winged Victory (Martin 2005, 8). Interestingly, the artist Charles Sykes designed his own figure, inspired by the Nike of Samothrace, as a mascot to adorn the Rolls Royce in 1910.

The Futurists rejected the past wholesale, feeling that tradition was the death of Italy. They drew upon the contemporary philosophy of Bergson and his theory of the *élan vital* as a constant state of becoming (Martin 2005, 14). This would emphasise a departure with the past. However, Futurism contained something of the primitive too and this is more latently present in the meta-language of rhetoric; love, roar and hate. This primal, misogynist and rather testosterone driven aggression was dangerously precipitated by rationality and, like Kubrick's vision of the stone age weapon (a bone) hurled into the air only to become transformed into a space station in *2001: a Space Odyssey*, the Futurist vision of technological advancement belied a savage resolve to overpower the weak. Here was Conrad's *Heart of Darkness*; a modern and imperial madness, Nietzsche's *Übermensch*, Kant's fusion in the shadow of a dead God.

It was hardly surprising that Futurism should find its other natural home in pre-revolutionary Russia, where the power of the proletariat was synonymous with the vision of a greater machine, a productivity, a necessary change and a march to the future. In 1913 this was rather purely envisioned in the production of the musical play *Victory over the Sun* with Zaumist texts by Kruchenyk (Zaum being a non-language of the Russian Futurists) and angular, mechanised designs by Malevich. Described as 'Cubo-futurist' by critics of the period, Malevich's costumes are described by Conrad (Peter not Joseph!) as a 'collision of elemental energies invoked by the Italian Futurists' (Conrad 1998, 231) and included a cuboid setting split between light and dark that created a telescopic illusion of space.

The work depicted Nietzsche's *Übermensch* in an ultimate victory over, in the absence of a God, divine nature. The 'Strongmen of the Future' reach up and steal the fiery sun from its very orbit, Prometheus-like, harnessing its energy. This huge display of control is at once a pagan ritual heresy and a presentiment of the coming Revolution; it is a primitive and savage act of violence, a taking of power but also a means to rational advancement. Conrad observes that whilst a means of production (object, a priori) is harnessed, this is also one of apocalyptic destruction (subject, a posteriori)(Conrad 1998, 231).

For some the stricture between the Modern and traditional paradigms was more of a personal struggle. The psychology of Konstantin Stanislavski's drive to connect mind and body, internal and external through his psycho-technique, perfectly declares the presence of a Kantian fusion. For Stanislavski this fusion was not necessarily a happy one – Mitter confirms that he 'was not a political sophisticate' (Mitter 1993, 235), and whilst he intellectually welcomed the Revolution, his comfortable background was in some respects the symbol of what it was against.

This stricture is present in his work. Whilst his theory is unashamedly a-political, if not Stalin's later use of it, his system declares a social consciousness that is a contemporary index to that very same debate of the Universalists and the Individualists. It is hardly surprising in some respects that he might have disagreed with Chekhov over whether *The Cherry Orchard* was a great comedy or tragedy (for Stanislavski this fictional collapse of aristocracy was tellingly the latter, despite the 'prospect of a

better life' that Chekhov suggests in the last act) (Simmons 1970, 606).
Like Brentano's attempt to rationalise the existence of God through
scientific methodology, Stanislavski rationalises the tradition of the
proscenium arch drama through a system that is at once insightful,
progressive and yet retains civility and concretises the domestic dramas of
the preceding century. Here there is a dichotomic struggle with truth and
pretence. Mitter recognises that Stanislavski accounts for the actuality of
the stage space and its various properties and having done that asserts that
their true significance is only born out of a meta-existence in the
imagination, because their actuality is crude and basic unto itself. He
makes a concession to the present, but this is not a resolution because it is
presented to the actor as a barrier to be overcome. In Mitter's words
"through a devastating combination of censorship and propaganda, the
actor may make believe" (Mitter 1993, 8).

Stanislavski's struggle is with Modernism, the irony being that his
answer is essentially modernist. He presents a system that analyses the
connectivity of experience – *a posteriori* – and logic – *a priori*. He
rationalises for example the way that we control our consciousness from
the external to the internal, from that which we cannot control to that
which we can (in Concentration of Attention), he objectifies the narratives
of a role in a teleological context (Units and Objectives), he builds a trap
for the unconsciousness of inner emotive forces (Emotion Memory)
and therefore so clearly illustrates the useful combination of Jungian
personalities with Freudian thresholds. However rational his system, it
remains romantically driven by something of tradition, something less than
Modern, the manifestation of which is always in the meta-world of his
chapter headings in *An Actor Prepares*: When Acting is an Art,
Imagination, Emotion Memory, Communion, Faith and a Sense of truth
(Stanislavski 1988 edition) all of which are just as indicative of the
Universalist as they are of the Individualist.

Even the form of his system is presented as a meta-narrative within the
classes of the fictional Tortsov. This form certainly makes the work
palatable to any student, but in some respects undermines the factual and
the rational that is at the heart of it. Young students often express
momentary dismay and confusion when they realise that they are reading
about events that seemingly never took place – this returns us to Mitter's
commentary concerning Stanislavski's difficult relationship with the
present, with actuality (Mitter 1993, 6-25).

Stanislavski intended that the creation of a meta-narrative in the form
of the fictional Tortsov, would present logic in the context of experience.
Whilst this systematic analysis was based upon many years of practice, it

aimed to provide the talented actor with a rational route to successful performance. The apparent contradiction here is that it is a pretence unto itself.

Meyerhold, a student of Stanislavski, was motivated to finally split from his former master because of this struggle of actuality. Leach asserts that the point of this disagreement was primarily based upon the performer's relationship to their audience; Stanislavski went to great lengths to resist the existence of the audience so far as a performer's attention was concerned. Meyerhold, as a young modernist, a Bolshevik and with some influence from Futurists and works such as *Victory over the Sun*, was much more interested in a positive confrontation of the actor with his audience (Leach 1989, 30).

His development of a system of *Biomechanics* for the actor was as a depiction of the *Strongman of the Future*, realised at the point of revolution. This was an expression of the pure strength found in release, a determined physical execution of one's individual freedom. Whilst a retrospective irony is difficult to resist, the work was a powerful study of the repetition of physical being, of mechanisms, production and negation (the reversal that suggests the future in the moment before it occurs – the withdrawal that precedes the lunge). Meyerhold's rational analysis of physicality in particular, placed a psycho-technique on the sleeve where Stanislavski had tried to internalise it – mental intention was boldly declared in the magnified exertions of the body. Meyerhold 'claimed to have reconciled theatrical technique and the 'industrial situation'' (Conrad 1998, 240) since his work applied the repetitive cycles of a factory labourer to the virtuosic realisation of art. Here was a bringing together of class, of physical commitment, of productivity and primal strength, of mind and body.

The threshold between mind and body was extended to that between body and space in the theory of a young and influential patron of the Dadaist Cabaret Voltaire in Zurich, Rudolph Laban. It is to Laban and his student Wigman that Dada provides the vehicle referred to earlier. The reality, or actuality, of the body in a space was an increasingly architectural concern and dancers such as Martha Graham would certainly relate the utility of movement to modern principles of architecture in an attempt to be free of the virtuosic traditions of ballet technique. Prior to this, however, Laban was to lay out some principle parameters for movement which were arguably influenced by his initial training in architecture. By the second decade of the 20th century, architecture was adopting a much more utilitarian feel, rejecting the falsely decorative references to a classical past and adopting instead a new and powerful solidity that was grounded and geometrical.

Laban recognised in this a combination of qualities, the analysis of which could be applied to a system of movement that truly integrated a body within its space. Here in essence was the actuality that Stanislavski had barely disguised his dislike for. But here too was yet another urban project that asserted the internal self and its control of an external present world. This demystification was crucial to the new dance. However, the context of demystification is misleading if taken as an indication of Laban's early motivation. Far from the intense rationality of Schoenberg, Laban propagated a cult of mystique around himself, and Foster biographically describes him as cavalier, romantic, a womaniser and certainly not rational (Foster 1977). This Bohemian image is somewhat at odds with the educationalist but the mystery of his earlier self was, as was said, somewhat propagated – a mask.

Herein lies a Jungian thread to Stanislavski; Laban was transcending a threshold between conscious technique and the imagination. Curl, cited in Foster, finds it "difficult to distinguish between actual and imagined events" in Laban's recollections of early life, "for he plays so freely across the line of fantasy and fact. Inner and Outer worlds become fused in a mythical play of demons, spirits and everyday folk" (Foster 1977, 13). Whilst this refers more to Laban than to his work, it introduces the aspect of primitivism into early Moderns' work. This aspect shall not be dwelt on here, but there are three points to be considered as relevant. Firstly the freedom to return to the primitive, or pagan, was a provocative confirmation of the individual spiritual freedom since Nietzsche killed God. Secondly it raised the issue of aesthetics and rejected Western paradigms of beauty. Thirdly it was licensed by Jung's personalities and Freud's dreams.

Placing aside Laban's 'cult', which he ritualised somewhat through quasi-Masonic practices, what emerged was indeed a rationalisation of movement that was systemised and whole and that fused the logical with the experienced, the objective with the subjective. Laban often later visualised his ideas graphically and one of the most concise of these diagrams appears in *Modern Educational Dance* as a star (Laban 1948, 34). The illustration connects *eight basic efforts* to *six movement elements*. The efforts are : wring, press, glide, float, flick, slash, punch and dab – all verbs to do -, whilst the elements have an adjective quality: firm, light, sustained, sudden, direct and flexible. Spatially the star has a vertically line dissecting its centre and representing *weight* (light to heavy), and a horizontal line representing *space* (direct to flexible). There is then an interesting temporal diagonal line representing *duration*, but not as a graduation; it is rather expressed either as *sudden* or *sustained*. The points of the star connect the efforts, elements and dissections as an impressive analysis of possibilities for the dancer. Whilst spatially expressed this also infers several sets of sequences and relates rather interestingly back to Schoenberg's twelve note system.

But it also connects very interestingly with Schlemmer's Bauhaus Theatre, in the context of a geometric connectivity betwixt body, space and duration. During this period Gropius was developing the Bauhaus as a centre of mass production and functional Modernist design. But in the introduction to the Theatre of the Bauhaus, Gropius reinforces the value of the individual and attributes to Schlemmer's geometry a primal level of signification, 'symbolising eternal types of human character and their different moods, serene or tragic, funny or serious' (Gropius 1961, 8). The word magical is often used to describe the onieric qualities of Schlemmer's Buehnenelemente (stage elements) alongside, again, that of architecture. The building in Dessau was an unquestionable influence, but there remains again a fascinating relationship between the imagined and the real, creativity and parameter, superstition and rationality. On the Bauhaus stage the primitive was presented with the crystal clear lines of the new physics.

Before Laban's principles were quite so concretely realised as the Bauhaus Stage, an early student was the expressionist dancer Mary Wigman. Whilst interested, as was the American Pioneer of Modern Dance, Ruth St Denis, in the spiritual transcendence of being and drawing therefore on Oriental forms and what was regarded as primitive ritualism. Wigman's dance was visceral and organic but also grounded, angular and subjective. This latter context is arguably of most relevance to this paper. Like Schoenberg, there was a provocation of traditional virtuosity. Ballet form, as arguably a male invention of the Renaissance period, trained the dancer in respect of archetypal virtuosity – that is they were to be objectified, homogenised, light and apparently fragile.

These qualities, for the viewer, once again transcended the actual and replaced it with the imaginary. But now it was a disguising of power and strength in the body and also of individual determination or subjective presence in the work. This suited a pre-women's movement view of the dancer since it removed from her the licence of artistic identity. During the fin de siècle Isadora Duncan and Louis Fuller had already developed a response to this, with the removal of shoes and the decodification of movement. Wigman, however, began to recodify, with her ritual and repetitive angularity, but also presenting herself as subject, as pathology and most importantly as a Modern female artist.

This process of recodification was both personal and as the object of Laban's development of a notation for dance. The relationship was not without a clash of interest important to this study – Wigman wrote that Laban would name dynamic qualities with words like 'wrath' that she would respond to by throwing herself immediately into a 'colossal rage' of swinging that 'virtually exploded in space'. Laban would respond with a sincere fury, complaining that his theory of harmony was ruined! 'I knew,' wrote Wigman, '...[that] I had to keep the balance between my emotional outburst and the merciless discipline of a super-personal control....the self imposed law of dance composition.' (Copeland & Cohen 1983, 304/5)

St Denis was also re-codifying but in somewhat colonial fashion, creating a dance school curriculum out of her own interpretation of ethnically derived techniques. A student of the school was Martha Graham, who retained the expressionism of Wigman, whilst eventually rejecting to an extent the influence of derivative styles – in her autobiography, Graham recalls how she would practice her own style at night in the dark of the Denishawn studios to avoid criticism.(Graham 1993, 66) Graham most powerfully asserted herself and her gender as subject by grounding the work, by moving rationally and with the influence of the new architectural philosophies that were based in utility; movement was justified and not superfluously pretty or falsely, objectively feminine. She constructed rules for movement that emphasised Wigman's angularity and asserted a particularly female physiological power in the use of contraction and release. From the feminist perspective the subjective domain in Dance was a crucial aspect in breaking the bonds of the male gaze in a history of art because it inferred a biography of actuality and self. This is certainly metaphorically true of Graham's themes and balances particularly well with an emergent technique. A perfectly defined example is possibly in her 1930/31 work *Lamentation*. Lamentation is literally concerned with the mourning of a women, but by restricting the body in a tube of fabric, traditional virtuosity is rejected, architectural angularity is encouraged, expressive dynamism magnified. *Lamentation* reflects the primitive, the evolved, the urban, the individual, the woman and the rational – in short it provides a diachronic line back to Kant's fusion of the Empirical and the Rational and this is richly encapsulated in Graham's self proclaimed mission to "chart the graph of the heart" (Teachout, 1998; http://www.time.com/time/time100/artists/profile/graham.html).   It is interesting that in Lamentation there is again that encounter with something being left, dead and in the brutal shadow of the new; the work was as much about the impact of the skyscraper, at least formally, as it was subjectively concerned with grief.

As *Lamentation* was first performed, in 1930-31, so too was the magnificent Empire State Building reaching its completion. It is difficult to avoid the subjectively romantic when one imagines following the gaze of Graham as she craned her neck to this edifice, this tombstone of the past, this herald of the future. Kant's fusion is even elegantly indexed in its powerful title – Empire, State and Building – something of traditional or inherited power, something of rational or revolutionary governance and the object that is also the verb for progress: building.

But the great and rational rush from the past contained a savage stowaway, looming ever larger in a cloud over Europe. The identity of this primitive interloper was never hidden actually, it was volt-faced and clearly manifested in the practice of just about every artistic movement since the *fin de siècle*– artistic consciousness expressed a mechanised savagery, not just a rational utopia and carefully propagated it. And this is the great and tragic wonderment of the early modernists, the 'Terrible Beauty' as Watson would have it; this is the relationship between the grieving subject of *Lamentation* and its architectural object, Kant's fusion of *a priori* and *a posteriori*. This is the struggle between light and dark in Malevich's designs for *Victory Over the Sun*, but also in the Modern individual who would, as Nietzsche predicted, become the judge of her own actions in the absence of God.

Bibliography

Conrad, Peter. *Modern times, Modern Places; Life and Art in the 20ᵗʰ Century*, London: Thames and Hudson, 1998
Copeland, C and Cohen, M (Eds.). *What is Dance?*, New York: Oxford University Press, 1983
Foster, John. *The Influences of Rudolph Laban*, London: Lepus Books, 1977
Graham, Martha. *Blood Memory; an Autobiography*, London: Sceptre/ Hodder and Stoughton, 1993
Gropius, Walter. *"Introduction"* in *The Theater of the Bauhaus*, edited by Gropius, Walter. Middletown, CT: Wesleyan Press, 1961
Laban, Rudolph. *Modern Educational Dance*, London: Macdonald & Evans, 1948
Leach, Robert. *Vsevolod Meyerhold*, Cambridge: Cambridge University Press, 1989

Martin, Sylvia. *Futurism*, Cologne:Taschen, 2005

McKlynn, Frank. *Carl Gustav Jung; a Biography*, London: Bantam Press/ Transworld Publishers, 1996

Mitter, Shomit. *Systems of Rehearsal*, London: Routledge 1993

Russell, Bertrand. *History of Western Philosophy*, London: Routledge, 1991

Scruton, Roger. *A Short History of Modern Philosophy*, London: Routledge, 1995

Simmons, Ernest J. *Chekhov: a Biography*, Chicago: University of Chicago Press, 1970

Stanislavski, Constantin. *An Actor Prepares*, London: Methuen Drama, 1988

Shoenberg, Arnold *Style & Idea; Selected Writings of Arnold Schoenberg*, edited by Stein, L.London: Faber & Faber, 1975

Tsara, Tristan. *"Lecture on Dada"* and *"Dadaist Manifesto"* in *The Dada Painters and Poets; an Anthology*, edited by Motherwell, Robert. Cambridge, Massachusetts: Harvard University Press, 1989

Teachout, Terry. "The Time 100: Artists and Entertainers: Martha Graham". *Time Magazine*, June 8, 1998.
http://www.time.com/time/time100/artists/profile/graham.html)

Watson, Peter. *A Terrible Beauty*, London: Weidenfeld & Nicholson, 2000

CHAPTER THIRTEEN

JURRIËN ROOD

STANISLAVSKI AND THE IMPORTANCE
OF MENTAL IMAGERY

Introduction

In my master's thesis 'Stanislavski meets Embodied Cognition' I compare a recent philosophical theory, Embodied Cognition, with a succesful acting practice from the theatre, established a century ago.[1] Both relate to fields of personal experience: the theory I encountered as part of my studies in philosophy, the Stanislavski practice I have known and used for years in my professional life, making films and theatre.[2] Embodied Cognition is a theory from the philosophical realm of epistemology and philosophy of mind. It's main claim is that there is an intricate connectedness between cognition and the human 'body'.[3] Exactly this connection, of mind and body, plays a central role in the basic exercises used in the Stanislavski System. The thesis explores the possibility of using the basic exercises from the System to put the epistemological theory to the test. I argue that such a test will show clearly what part of cognition is necessarily embodied, and that it will elucidate the reasons for the gradual disembodiment of other parts of cognition. I also argue that in the process epistemology/philosophy of mind may learn something from the Stanislavski practice about the nature of the relations between mind and body, a classic philosophical theme.

Here I will limit myself to a topic that is central to the thesis: the importance of mental imagery for the Stanislavksi System. First I will succinctly present the Stanislavski System, then I take a closer look at one of its basic exercises. I will schematize its workings to get to a basic formula, revealing the structure of the mind-body connection in question and the role of MI.in the process. The outcome is then connected with the results of recent neuropsychological research.

But first the reader can do something for him/herself: perform a practical exercise to get a taste of the subject matter. The exercise proceeds as follows:

- Stand up, move clear from obstructing objects.
- Throw your right arm out and freeze it somewhere in the air. Just freeze.
- Now look at it.
- Evoke an *image* in your mind of what you are doing with your arm like that. (Are you, for instance, picking grapes? Or maybe in the middle of a tennis-game?)
- As soon as you've found the image, adjust your body, so that it better expresses what you are doing.
- Do it once more, but throw out the left arm. Freeze, look, evoke an image. Adjust.

You can sit down now. What is remarkable is the slight change taking place in the body, as soon as the image is evoked. There is a certain automatic adjusting taking place, even before the conscious adjustment sets in.

This is the very first exercise of the Stanislavski System, known as the Justification exercise.[4] I will come back to it.

The Stanislavski System

Constantin Stanislavski, a Russian theatre actor and director working at the end of the nineteenth century, developed his System as a reaction against the ways of stage acting of his time. Acting as a craft was essentially external, only concerned with outside appearance: it meant adopting an outward pose, a certain mimicry and specific movements for every role and every emotion. Stanislavski considered this way of acting to be completely untruthful and leading to cliché. What he found missing was an internal side to acting. So he concentrated on the creation of such an inner, thruthful life on stage, aiming to find a controlled and repeatable method for the actor to achieve this.[5]

The essential discovery of the Stanislavski System is that the personal memories and emotions of the actor can and should be used to fill in the gap and provide the inner life. However, the emotions should never be approached directly, because then they will either hide or come out stilted. So the System provides a roundabout way to get to the emotions. It is done by a *conscious psychophysical technique*, built upon a series of basic exercises involving the body as much as the psyche. In this psychophysical technique a central role is played by the concept of the *mental image*.[6]

Developed at the Moscow Art Theatre in the first decades of the 20th century, the System then rapidly conquered the theatres of the western world. In America the Actor's Studio turned it into the Method and applied it to the cinema, where it proved even more useful.[7] One can safely say that today most screen acting in the western world is Stanislavski based. The creation of an inner life and the use of the personal emotions and memories of the actor have become standard practice. This in itself may stand as empirical evidence for the effectivity of this System. Recent neuropsychological research now may provide the grounds for a theoretical explanation of the System's efficacity and success, as will be shown in section 4.

Schematizing the System: the role of mental imagery

Let's take a closer look at the workings of the System. Most 'unschooled', amateur acting will proceed somewhat like this: The actor reads a text (Txt0) expressing a certain dramatic situation, or has it told to him in some form. The text is the scene to be played: say a certain prince (Hamlet) gets frightened by a ghost (his dead father). Now something happens in the Actor's mind. He might divide the information, meant to be enacted, in an external and internal part. He may think about externals to embody a Prince - a posture, a certain expression. As regards internals he will see it as his natural task to play the emotion of the character in the scene. Is Hamlet scared? Play fear. Is he angry? Play anger. He will want to play the emotions present in the scene.

Schematically we can present this approach to acting as follows:

(0) Txt0 $\rightarrow$ Mind/Ideas $\rightarrow$ 'Body' + 'Feelings'.

Let us call this the ground level, the 0-level of amateur acting. Note that the arrows do not represent causality, but just temporal sequence. The quotes are used to indicate that the end result is unsatisfactory. There certainly is an activating of feelings and of body apparatus. But it is an activation in general, producing 'stencils', as Stanislavski called them. This happens for two reasons. A.) This way of acting is based on generalities; 'a prince' and 'a fear' are both general ideas. B.) Truthful emotions can not be captured directly. It was this direct, generalized and external way of acting that Stanislavski sought to overcome.[8]

How? Let us look at a famous example from the System: the <u>Magical If</u>.[9] Confronted with the same basic text, depicting the prince in fear of the ghost, the actor now has to ask himself: *what if I* were in circumstances like these?

What if *I* were in some place (say: my room) and I would see a ghost? What would *I* do in these circumstances? Note that the question is emphatically not: what would I *feel* in these circumstances, but: what would I *do*?

In executing this exercise the actor is encouraged to be very specific. He should answer questions like: what place are you in exactly, what does it look like, why are you there? Then he should do the same for the ghostlike appearance: who is he/she? what does he look like? in what way is he related to you? etc. All this preparatory work is done in the imagination. The actor builds himself a complete background story, captured in specific inner images. This in turn will now motivate him to act in a certain way.

Let us call the 'magical if' assignment: Txt 1. Schematizing the process of the exercise we get:

(1) Txt0 + Txt1 → Mental Image (MI) + Action → Body + Feelings.

The question the actor asks himself is: "what would I do if I...?" Then first there is a mental image evoked. This is followed by Action, meaning the *intention to act*, expressible as a verb. In this example it could be 'to save myself from', or 'to make contact with' (the ghost). The term 'Action' is used here in its System sense, meaning inner activity, not outer.[10] Both the 3rd and the 4th steps are psychic phenomena, taking place in the Mind, and they are intricately connected. There are no quotes at the final stage. The result is not a stencil. The outcome is natural behavior spurred on by the imagination.

This is the roundabout way of the System: the Magical If is a mind-tool, which seems to get the body moving automatically. The emotional result then produces itself. It is the same automaticity we encountered in the justification exercise at the end of section 1. This one in fact follows the same basic scheme, but starting and ending with Body.

Now, looking back, also in amateur acting the text will lead to the creation of some mental image. In fact we should write thus:

(0a) Txt0 → Mental Image + Action → 'Feelings' + 'Body' (stencils).

But the image created here is a general one ('a prince', 'fear').
The difference with (1) lies in the personalization brought about by the question 'What if I...?'. This results in what may be called a *personal* mental image, as opposed to a general one. Specifying our formulas we get:

(0b) Txt0 → general Mental Image (MIg) + general Action → 'Body' + 'Feelings' (stencils).

(1a) Txt0+1 → personal Mental Image (MIp) + personal Action → Body + Feelings.

There seem to be two kinds of MI operative, a general and a personal variety. The difference is crucial, as we will see when we take a look at the causality that is at work here.

One might say a general image is the same thing as an 'Idea'. 'The fear of a prince' is such a general idea. It certainly has bodily associations, both 'fear' and 'prince' can evoke lively images in the actor's mind. The idea is a necessary condition for the ensuing bodily expressions, but it is not a sufficient condition, and hence fails to be a cause. The actor pondering a generality like 'the fear of the Danish prince' must still add his will to the process, before anything happens. He is not forced to act by the idea alone - as is witnessed by the fact that we can read Hamlet sitting in a chair, not moving at all.

This is different with the System and its use of a personal mental image. Here the actor is as it were forced to express himself bodily, driven by what is a sufficient causal connection. What happens after the personal MI is evoked (in connection with personal Action) is the unfolding of an automatic chain of events, which could only be stopped by an immense act of the will or intervening outside influences. The personal MI is not only a necessary but also a sufficient condition, and hence functions as a cause. We arrive at these general formulas:

(0b) Txt0 → gen Mental Image (MIg) + gen Action → 'Feelings' + 'Body' (stencils).

(1b) Txt0+1 → pers. Mental Image (MIp) + pers Action ⇒ Body + Feelings.

The double arrow represents a causal relationship. Scheme (1b) presents the organic law Stanislavski was looking for, involving a necessary and sufficient causality. Whenever the personal MI is evoked, the body will start to move. In my thesis I have investigated a number of other exercises used in the System, and I conclude that this basic scheme underlies all of them. The System workings depend essentially on the creation and use of 'personal' mental imagery - in connection with an intention to act. To put it in philosophical terms: the cognition that is the starting point, viz. the text, finds a direct, automatic bodily expression when it makes use of a certain category of mental imagery: the MIp. This empirical category of personal mental imagery is of course loosely characterized and still stands in need of further specification.

Mental Imagery and Neuropsychology

Stanislavski worked from experience and intuition; he did not investigate the phenomenon of mental imagery nor its subdivision in different categories, but simply used them. Interestingly his findings are confirmed in recent years by research of an Italian group of psychologists from the university of Padova – who are quite unaware of the Stanislavski system.[11] They investigated the existence and characteristics of different categories of mental imagery. The interesting result is that subjects do indeed spontaneously generate different kinds of mental images.

Using traditional psychological methods the Italian group found a three-partite division, consisting of *general, specific* and *episodic-autobiographic* mental imagery.[12] When confronted with a certain noun subjects first and foremost tend to form a *general* image in their mind. This is followed by the creation of a *specific* image (a single well-defined example), and lastly by the *episodic-autobiographic* image (an image involving the person him/herself). So given a certain noun, (DOG) a *general* image represents the concept without any specification or conscious reference to a particular example of it (A dog). A *specific* image represents a single well-defined example of the concept without reference to a specific episode (The neighbour's dog, my dog). An *autobiographic* image represents the occurrence of a single episode in the subject's life connected to the concept (My dog as it jumped from the balcony on a holiday in Italy).[13] Of these categories the general image is evoked and reactivated fastest. Supposedly it can consequently be turned into a specific image, which scores highest on vividness. The autobiographic image needs the most time to generate, but scores highest when it comes to exact recall.

All of this is a full corroboration of Stanislavski's intuition and the workings of the System, even more clearly so if you incorporate more System exercises. The basic subdivision of mental imagery pointed out by the psychological experiments, runs parallel to the basic split between two approaches to acting. Amateur acting is the default exactly because it uses the quickest and most accessible way of image generation: the general image. System practice on the other hand avoids the general level by always insisting on specification and the creation of specific imagery. That autobiographical images are hardest to generate but are best remembered once created, is mirrored by the special status of the Emotional Memory exercise within the System, and the comparatively long time span of its execution. (Emotional Memory uses a personal memory of an intense emotional nature, reconstructs it through concentration on very specific images concerning the event – and thus lets the actor re-live the memory and the emotions involved.)[13]

Recently the Italian group turned to neuropsychological research, applying fMRI brainscan methodology to the same research question.[14] The existence of a subdivision of mental imagery is confirmed. But what appears on the neural level is a two way division, rather than a three way one. General and specific mental images turn out to be generated with the support of two different neural pathways[15], while a neural similarity is found in the generation of specific and episodic-autobiographical mental imagery. So a fundamental distinction of MI actually can be made on the neural level, between categories of General on the one hand and Specific/Autobio-graphical on the other. The latter category then must coincide with what we so far have called 'personal'. A closer look at the results of the experiments of Gardini et al. suggests that this category, autobiographic MI, also involves a significant activation of so-called pre-motor areas in the brain, which are responsible for the activation of the body. This activation appears to be absent in general MI.[16] This could be the neural proof for the close, natural connection Stanislavski presupposed to exist between the personal Mental Image and the body. More generally, this investigation points out the neural basis that can account for the difference between two types of acting.

Finally these results from imagery research suggest a specification of the still loosely defined term 'personal'. The Autobiographic image is characterized as a special type of Specific image, one with 'personal involvement' added. It is not an image of a dog in general, nor is it one of a specific dog (that you might have seen a week ago). Rather, it is the image of the dog you owned as a child and that licked your face; or the image of the dog that bit you in the leg last summer, while running. The category of Episodic-Autobiographical mental imagery thus brings along elements not just of memory, but of one's own body and feelings.

> "Episodic memory has the unique characteristic of enabling individuals to project themselves back in the past and recollect previously *experienced* events as such, with a peculiar sense of re-*experience* (..)"[17]

Experience is the keyword here. What I've so far called 'personal' in fact always involves the experiential level, and necessarily involves one's own body. The 'general' category does not. The difference in two types of MI points to an essential difference of two types of cognition: generalized via ideas, and personalized via experience.

Conclusion

What the Stanislavski System essentially does, by evoking a certain type of mental imagery, is to bring the actor back to the level of direct experience, starting out from a more general level of cognition or 'knowing'. In my thesis I further explore this result, postulating two modes of functioning of the Mind: an experiencing mode and a generalizing, knowing mode. This results in a provisional sketch of the build-up of 'Mind' and its relations to Body.

All this follows from the basic investigation, which uses exercises from System practice as a testcase for the theory of Embodied Cognition. I hope to have shown at least that such a confrontation of philosophy and theatre practice can be fruitful.

Notes

1 see Rood 2006.

2 I graduated from the Dutch Film Academy as a writer/director in 1976 and have been working on a freelance basis since then, mainly on fiction projects involving actors. Later I moved into the theatre, again as a writer and director. The study of philosophy I did parttime, next to my professional work.

3 The two seminal books in the formulation of the theory of Embodied Cognition are written by Francisco Varela et al.; see bibliography.

4 For more information on this exercise and its place within the Stanislavski System see Moore 1979 p37-38 ao.

5 For a detailed account of Stanislavski's theatrical quest see his autobiography *My Life in Art*, Stanislavski 1924.

6 See bibliography for a selection of Stanislavski's writings. The System is expounded in three main works: *An Actor Prepares*, *Building a Character* and *Creating a Role*. Of these the first is by far the most well-known and influential.

7 For the Method's debts to and cricticism of Stanislavski see Strasberg 1989. For a history of the reception of Stanislavski in America, including misconceptions: Sharon Carnicke, *Stanislavsky in Focus*. London: Taylor and Francis, 1998

8 For a discussion of 'stencils' see Stanislavski 1924 p476, or Stanislavski 1936 p22 where they are called 'rubber stamps' and 'cliché's'.

9 First mentioned in Stanislavski 1936 p.44.

10 About Action: see Stanislavski 1936 chapter 3, Moore 1979 class 4, and Cohen 1981, sketching the use of this concept by director/teacher Eugene Lansky.

11 The group consists among others of Cesare Cornoldi, Rossana de Beni and Simona Gardini.

12 See Cornoldi 1989 p25, de Beni 1995 p 1359-1360. The American neuropsychologist Stephen Kosslyn uses a similar taxonomy, of *prototypical* and *exemplar* images; the autobiographical appears as a subdivision of the latter. See Kosslyn 1994.

13 See Cornoldi 1989 p26.
14 For Stanislavski's discussion of Emotional Memory see Stanislavski 1936 chapter 9. Easty 1981 gives a detailed presentation of the Method's version of the exercise. See also Strasberg 1989, Moore 1979.
15 See Gardini et al 2005 and 2006.
16 See Gardini et al 2005 p.445. 'The generation of general images seems to involve brain areas associated with the formation of global gestalt-like images (areas in the right hemisphere), while the generation of specific mental images appears to require additional support from areas involved in the retrieval of visual details (i.e., the right thalamus).'
17 This is not one of the main concerns of the Gardini research. Although far from being a specialist in the field, I have tried a quick comparison of their two fMRI experiments, as to any significant outcomes concerning the involvement of motor areas in the brain. Such a *significant activation* appears in the case of BA 6 (Brodmann area 6, the Pre-motor cortex including Supplementary motor area SMA). In motor hierarchy premotor areas come first, giving their information in turn to the motor cortex, BA 4, which moves the body. The latter connection will not function in a brainscan experiment because of immobilization of the participant. The significant activation of BA 6 always comes in conjunction with that of other areas.

Bibliography

Behrmann, Marlene, S. Kosslyn and Marc Jeannerod. (eds) 1995. *The Neuropsychology of Mental Imagery* Oxford: Elsevier Science Ltd.
de Beni, Rossana and Francesca Pazzaglia 1995 Memory for different kinds of mental images: role of contextual and autobiographic variables. *Neuropsychologia* 33:11: 1359-1371. Oxford: Elsevier Science Ltd.
Blair, Rhonda 2002 'Reconsidering Stanislavski: Feeling, Feminism, and the Actor' in: *Theatre Topics* - Vol.12; 2 September 2002 Baltimore: The John Hopkins University Press
Clark, Andy 1998 Embodiment and the philosophy of mind A. O'Hear (ed.) *Current Issues in Philosophy of Mind: Supplement 43* Cambridge: Cambridge University Press.
—. 1998b Where Brain, Body and World Collide *Daedalus: Journal of the American Academy of Arts and Sciences* (Special Issue on The Brain) 127 (2) Spring 1998
—. 1999 Visual Awareness and Visuomotor Action *Journal of Consciousness Studies* 6:(11-12) 1999
—. 2001 Visual Experience and Motor Action: Are the Bonds Too Tight? *Philosophical Review* 110 (4) October 2001

Cohen, Martin 1981 2 *study reports from the Stella Adler Conservatory of Acting* private publication

Cornoldi, Cesare, R. de Beni and A. Pra Baldi 1989 Generation and retrieval of general, specific and autobiographic images representing concrete nouns *Acta Psycholigica* 72 (1989) North Holland

Damasio, Antonio 1995 *Descartes' Error* New York: Avon books.

—. 2003 *Looking for Spinoza* New York/London: Harcourt Inc.

Denis, Michel, E. Mellet and S. Kosslyn 2004 Neuroimaging of mental imagery: an introduction *European Journal of Cognitive Psychology* 2004, 16 (5)

Dennett, Daniel 1991 *Consciousness Explained* New York: Little, Brown.

Easty, Edward Dwight 1981. *On Method Acting.* Orlando: The House of Collectibles.

Edie, James 1971 The problem of enactment *Journal of Aesthetics and Art Criticism* 71:29

Farah, Martha 1989 Is Visual Imagery Really Visual? Overlooked Evidence from Neuropsychology *Psychological Review* 95(3) p 307-317 July 1988

Finke, Ronald, S. Pinker and M. Farah 1989 Reinterpreting Visual Patterns in Mental Imagery *Cognitive Science* 13 (51-78)

Gardini, Simona, R. de Beni and C. Cornoldi. 2003 Can we have an image of a concept? The generation process of general and specific mental images *Imagination, Cognition and Personality* 23 (2-3)

Gardini, Simona, R. de Beni, C. Cornoldi, A. Bromiley and A. Venneri 2005 Different neural pathways support the generation of general and specific images *Neuroimage* 27:3, Elsevier

Gardini, Simona, R. de Beni, C. Cornoldi and A. Venneri 2006 Left mediotemporal structures mediate the retrieval of episodic autobiographical mental images *Neuroimage* 30:2, 645-655 Elsevier.

Johnson, Mark 1990 Embodied Reason *Perspectives on embodiment: the intersections of nature and culture* eds. G.Weiss & H. Fern Haber 1999 New York: Routledge

Kosslyn, Stephen 1994 *Image and Brain: The Resolution of the Imagery Debate.* Cambridge, MA: MIT Press.

—. 2005 Mental Images and the brain *Cognitive Neuropsychology*, 22 (3/4), pp.333–347

Kosslyn, Stephen, Ganis,G. and W. Thompson 2001 Neural foundations of mental imagery *Nature reviews, Neuroscience* sept. 2001

Kosslyn, Stephen and W. Thompson 2003 When is early visual cortex activated during visual mental imagery? *Psychological Bulletin,* 129, pp.723–746.

Lakoff, George and Mark Johnson 1999 *Philosophy in the flesh; the embodied mind and its challenge to western thought.* New York: Basic Books.

Moore, Sonia 1979 *Training an Actor - the Stanislavski System in Class* New York: Penguin Books,

Rood, Jurriën 2006 *Stanislavski meets Embodied Cognition.* University of Amsterdam, Faculty of Humanities.

Stanislavski, Constantin 1924 *My Life in Art.* (transl: J.J.Robbins) Boston: Little, Brown, and Company.

—. 1936 *An Actor Prepares* (transl E. Reynolds Hapgood) New York: Theatre Arts Books.

—. 1950 *Building a character* (transl: E. Reynolds Hapgood) London:.Eyre Methuen.

—. 1952 *Der Schauspielerische Weg zur Rolle.* Other articles by: W. Prokofjew, W.Toporkow, B. Sachawa. G. Gurjew. Berlin: Verlag Bruno Henschel und Sohn.

—. 1961 *Creating a Role* (transl E. Reynolds Hapgood) New York: Theatre Arts Books.

Strasberg, Lee 1989 *A dream of passion.* London: Methuen Drama.

Varela, Francisco and Umberto Maturana 1988 *The Tree of Knowledge* Boston: Shambhala.

Varela, Francisco, Eleanor Rosch and Evan Thompson 1991 *The Embodied Mind.* Cambridge Mass: The MIT Press.

CHAPTER FOURTEEN

DAVID SHIRLEY

WHERE IS MY CHARACTER? – ACTING AND PERFORMANCE IN THE UNASCRIBED PLAY

'Theatre is no longer a mass medium' proclaims German scholar Hans-Thies Lehmann in the prologue to his recent and much celebrated book *Postdramatic Theatre* (2006, 16). *'To deny this'* he continues *'becomes increasingly ridiculous, to reflect on it increasingly urgent'* (2006, 16).

Whilst most of us would willingly concede to the view that theatre has long since ceased to represent anything even remotely approaching a mass medium, the question of how far this realisation has prompted those working within the drama school sector to undertake a review of the numerous assumptions on which 'training' is based is perhaps a little more vexing.

Notwithstanding a postmodernist cultural zeitgeist that assures us that experience is indeterminate, that the stable and knowable self is obsolete, that linear narrative is archaic, that 'grand narratives' are fictitious and the undoubted disintegration of the notion of 'truth', or, for want of a better phrase, 'ultimate reality', it would appear that in most, if not all, British drama schools, the methodologies used in the training of young actors are indicative not so much of the drive to empower and enable new artists, but rather an inexplicable tendency to cling to old ideas and established conventions. Nowhere is this more apparent than in the immense importance that is attached to the notion of 'character'.

Whether or not the training on offer is based on one of the many Stanislavskian models or more closely resembles the British 'repertory' system that seeks to foster the development of a dependable *technique*, the absolute centrality of 'character' (in the most obvious and traditional sense) as a fundamental agency of dramatic structure would appear, at least, to represent a corner stone in British actor training.

The elevation of 'character' as a constituent of Western drama is, in itself, hardly surprising. The combination of the Renaissance/Humanist image of mankind as superior to all other living creatures and the Enlightenment's advocacy of rationalism, knowledge and understanding generated a culture reflecting an increased self-consciousness and a growing sense of self-importance in what appeared to be a knowable and definable universe. Small wonder, then, that since the Renaissance, dramatic writing and the realist/psychological acting techniques associated with it encapsulate an underlying appeal to a transcendent human nature. The moment Marlowe's Dr Faustus chooses – choice is important here – to abandon God in order to fully embrace the consequences of his own humanity is a significant one and, in theatrical terms, at least, marks the arrival on the stage of a character that is determined to be the architect of his own fate.

Although in *The Poetics*, character is certainly acknowledged as an important feature of drama, it is worth remembering that Aristotle urges the primacy of plot over all other elements: *'every play'* he asserts 'contains spectacular elements as well as character, plot, diction, song, and thought. But most important of all is the structure of the incidents.' (*Aristotle's Poetics*, translated by S.H. Butcher). Without wishing to over-generalise, it is perhaps not inaccurate to say that in much Greek drama, the fate of the characters does not tend to turn as much on complex psychological conditions as it does on the exigencies of plot and circumstance. To over- emphasise the personal and play Hecuba as hysterical or Medea as insane will not so much open up the personalities of the characters involved as undermine the moral impact of the plays in which they appear.

The arrival of Shakespeare and his contemporaries, however, marks a significant shift in the plot/character relationship. Whilst, on what might be termed a *horizontal* dimension, the plays certainly deliver plenty of interesting plots – involving conflict, fraught romance, mistaken identity, supernatural effects, political intrigue etc., -- it can be argued that beneath the level of plot, on what we might refer to as the *vertical* dimension of the plays, there is a profound and compelling interest in the 'personalities' of the central characters. Macbeth's inescapable sense of guilt, for instance, or Othello's feelings of inferiority are every bit as fascinating as the dramatic events surrounding them. Moreover, the 'interior' landscapes that these plays generate provide immense scope for actors to 'personalise' and offer distinctive 'individual' readings of particular roles. Indeed, for many of our 'great' actors, the artistry, insight and skill with which they are associated were crafted from the increasingly attractive opportunities afforded by the *psychological* dimensions through which it is possible to interpret Shakespeare's tragic heroes.

A key feature of the development of 'character' as it is taught in most British drama schools is its appeal to a kind of Cartesian dualism. Whilst Stanislavski and others may not actually go as far as to claim the independent existence of the soul/mind as distinct from the body/physicality, the discourses and pedagogical strategies used to describe and frame the student actor's experience proceed very much according to a dualist principle. Clues and 'indicators' of a character's personality/mental state can be gleaned from the outer physicality of the performer. The ordering of a flow of information between the inner and outer realms of experience aids the construction of the modern dramatic character and stimulates the processes of 'recognition' and 'empathy' that are often a source of pleasure for both the actor and the spectator. Like the plays in which they feature, conventional dramatic characters are made up of a series of narratives. Some of these, of course, are shaped by the dramatic action itself, but many more are determined by the kinds of artistic/interpretative choices that are made by individual actors from 'outside' of the written text. A famous example, of course, is the Stanislavskian *biography*. The influence of other kinds of narrative, however, chiefly those associated with the fields of psychology and psychiatry should not be underestimated when attempting to understand the role of actor as storyteller. How often are the 'personal' experiences of the performer used as a kind of barometer on which to measure and approve the 'authenticity' and 'accuracy' of the interpretative choices made in relation to the construction of an entirely fictitious personality?

If in the popular modern theatre the text is a 'story', then the chief function of the actor is that of a storyteller. As a means of *illustrating* the text, character represents an extremely powerful device for creating the illusion that the tightly structured (the play) is improvised and the carefully rehearsed (the performance) appears spontaneous. Indeed, by and large, it is the development of the performance conventions associated with this kind of theatre to which British actor training is addressed.

But what about those new and developing forms of theatre in which actors are not required to illustrate the text? Or where there are no characters, no sequence of linear events, no dualist assumptions and where the text does not offer itself as a story? Does such a theatre have a need for the kinds of technique we have been describing? Does the apparent decline of 'character' as a dramatic construct necessitate a redefinition of the role of the actor as we have come to understand it?

During the last three decades or so, the proliferation of new theories pointing to the fractured, multiple notion of selfhood and the discontinuous, indiscriminate nature of experience raise serious questions about the refinements and seemingly neat aesthetics of Stanislavskian/unified methodologies. If the idea of a stable identity is deemed a myth and events are considered random what is the usefulness of a representational system for which 'unity' is the guiding principle? Moreover, if, as Howard Barker (1993, 111) has argued, the ordering of experience is posterior, and not anterior, to the events witnessed what becomes of the humanist theatre's principle of truth?

The impact of postmodernism on the theatre has, of course, been well documented and it is unnecessary to list all of the theories associated with it here. There are, however, certain aspects of postmodernity that, in the light of the present discussion, are worthy of closer consideration.

In the 'classical' or 'dramatic' theatre, the performance event is subordinated to the primacy of the *written* text. That is to say that most, if not all, of the creative work undertaken addresses itself to the need to *illustrate* and *translate* that which is essentially literary into something that can be read as performance. The text functions as a script that generates speech which in turn serves to define human interaction and behaviour. Whilst it would prove foolhardy to ignore other non-verbal languages that the theatre makes available – dance, mime etc – it is also important to acknowledge that in our own theatrical tradition the authority of the written text itself – as the chief bearer of meaning has, until recently, remained unchallenged. How often, for instance, do we as tutors demand that our actors 'serve the text', or claim, for example, that Shakespeare gives us everything that we need to know in the text – 'let the text be your guide' we proclaim confident in the assertion that meaning in Shakespeare's texts is unified, stable and somehow independent of history, politics, culture!

Whilst at one level there is a strong tendency to fetishize the meanings that are encountered in the text, one of the primary aims of performance – as distinct from rehearsal - is to deny the literary processes that make it possible. The 'written text' is replaced by speech, or more accurately 'dialogue' which, when coupled with the idiosyncrasies of character and situational staging, produce an impression of spontaneity – something that renders the 'text/script' invisible.

The basic element of the theatre as we in the West have come to understand it has been that of transformation - from page to stage, from words to speech, from the actor to the character, from the time now to some past or future time, from the imagined to the seemingly real. It was both the spectator's and the artist's need for *illusion* that helped establish such a performance tradition and it is a growing sense of disillusionment with it – evidenced by the insatiable appetite for 'reality' in popular entertainment – that, in my view at least, accounts for its gradual decline into what many have described as the theatre's state of crisis.

A defining feature of much postmodernist theatre/performance is its rejection of the need to represent coherent human experience. Experience, that is, that offers itself as a 'map' onto which can be traced a series of linear and logical events. Freed from what Beckett referred to as the 'distortions of intelligibility', and having dispensed with the old vocabularies of character and plot, the post-modern theatre, at its best, offers a space for genuine experimentation and artistic innovation. Acutely aware of itself as 'performance', it is not unusual for this kind of theatre to manipulate, rearrange and play with processes of signification in ways that can often prove unnerving and disorientating. Everything, it seems is offered up for scrutiny – the actors performances, the setting, the technical effects, the structure of the material, even spectatorship itself is considered a worthy target for deconstructive analysis. One area that is of particular relevance to any attempt to reshape or extend an understanding of the imperatives of actor training is that of the actual written text itself.

Whereas earlier forms of theatre conspire to deny or 'hide' the literary processes that make it possible, a common feature of much new work is the importance it attaches to the visibility of the written text. As American critic, Elinor Fuchs (1996, 74), has pointed out, many new works foreground the previously banished importance of the written word. This 'textualising' process can take numerous forms so that the written (as opposed to the spoken) word appears as both subject and setting and, as such, provides a rich 'quotational' framework. One of the consequences of this switch in emphasis from the authority of the spoken to that of the written text, is the undermining effect it has on the notion of 'character', which, as Fuchs makes clear, reassumes its pre-psychological, cursive meaning – as a literary construct!

Of course, experimentation of this kind is not exactly new to the theatre. The techniques pioneered by Brecht, for instance, often involved revealing the text (usually the stage directions) via placards and projected images as a means of highlighting the constructed nature of the live performance. The aim here, however, was to reduce the degree of empathy on the part of the spectator and as such, it was used to serve a specific political purpose. The same is not true of more contemporary writers, many of whom seek to interrogate traditional ideas about form, content and language. Even the most cursory glance, for instance, at Peter Handke's *Kaspar* (1968), or Martin Crimp's *Attempts on Her Life* (1997), or Sarah Kane's *4.48 Psychosis* (1999) reveals a curious 'literalisation' of the page. In each case the blank spaces, the broken phrases, the intriguing black and white patterns, the numerous repetitions, even the punctuation – a collage of stops, dashes, commas and exclamation marks – serve to make us acutely aware not just of the actual text itself, but also the nature of interpretation. Indeed it is the very process of encoding and decoding meaning that forms the subject matter of many works of contemporary drama. In each of the aforementioned plays, the rejection of characters with designated lines and definable personalities destabilises conventional attempts at interpretation. Who, for instance is the Anne that is the subject of so much speculation in Martin Crimp's *Attempts On Her Life*? The title implies not just her possible demise as a consequence of murder or suicide, but also attempts to narrate, to reconstruct, to make visible. The provocatively titled scenarios – *1. ALL MESSAGES DELETED, 11. UNTITLED (100 WORDS) etc.*– and the clusters of enigmatic poetry, fragmented messages and the intriguing visual patterns in which the text is reproduced suggest that Anne can be whoever we want her to be. A tenuous/shadowy figure that is made up of a series of impressions - all of which are partial, incomplete and unstable - she becomes a kind of metaphor for our need to comprehend the incomprehensible.

Like Crimp's text, Sarah Kane's *4:48 Psychosis* is an ambitious attempt to reshape theatrical form. Interestingly, suicidal despair and impending death are also important constituents of the drama. In this play, form and content seem to merge creating a disorientating, moving and often violently charged emotional atmosphere. Once again there are no definable characters, but the striking poetic dynamism and the visual impact of the printed text prove highly arresting. In contrast to Crimp's play – which teasingly invites us to piece together remnants of ideas to form shadowy impressions of character and narrative - this text, which is positively overflowing with 'personalities' and 'events', confounds attempts at easy identification by assaulting our sensibilities with a multiplicity of tentative and unstable 'possibilities'. It's a case of having too much and too little in the same moment!

At this point it is worth taking a moment to reflect on the Absurdist's contribution to the theatre. Positioned, as it were, in the revolving door that moves between the modern and the postmodern periods, the *Theatre of the Absurd* is, in many respects, in complete denial of the transparency and coherence that characterises more conventional modes of drama.

Whilst Beckett, Ionesco, Pinter and others frequently depict humanity in an unknown and senseless universe where beginnings and endings are often non-existent, spatial and temporal experience is rendered untrustworthy and character is at best mechanical and comic and at worst unrecognizable, there is nonetheless a profound acknowledgement of the primacy of speech as a means of representing human experience. Who, for instance, can deny the richly iterative qualities of either Beckett's or Pinter's work? Moreover, despite the apparent denial of meaning that its name suggests, the *Theatre of the Absurd* is established on principles that draw attention to a very particular set of philosophical, political and literary ideas. Ideas that sprang from the uncertainty and disillusionment that was fuelled by human barbarity and cruelty in the middle of the 20th Century. It isn't so much the case that the movement avoided representing the world, but rather that it sought to represent it from a very particular vantage point where 'truths' about the nature of human experience could be considered in a new light.

In classic realist modes of theatrical performance the relationship between text and performance tends to be one of struggle, compromise and oppression. The live performance becomes the inevitable 'reconstruction' of the 'purer' more perfect literary text. The aim is to convey cursive meaning through the medium of action from the stage to the spectator.

More contemporary models of performance allow us to experience moments where forms of signification other than text are considered its equal. Such forms often, of course, include the environment itself – sound/lighting/stage design, the electronic/mediatised images, for instance, that are already finding there way onto the stage. But they must also refer to the image of the performer him/herself. In this model movement and gesture, voice and sound, even breath itself acquires a significance that takes it beyond the simply representational.

If the West's traditional approach to theatre positions the performer as a signifier of human frailty – fear, pain, disease, mental and physical difficulty, preservation, age etc., more contemporary/experimental approaches position him/her as, in Hans Lehmann's words, '...an *agent provocateur* of an experience without 'meaning', an experience aimed not at the realisation of a reality and meaning but at the experience of potentiality.' (2006, 162-163)). Rather than a theatre that seeks to transmit 'signs' and 'representations' Lehmann (2006, 150) calls for a theatre of *shared energies* in which the conventional relationships between space, time, body, text, spectator and performer are reconfigured so as to allow for an exploration of new impulses and drives in which the body of the actor - rather than functioning simply as a site on which to project a fictive/imagined textual representation of 'character' - has the potential to carry its own message – play out its own fantasies/desires/agonies/fears, test out its own limits and potential and perhaps most importantly of all begin to play a much more 'active' role in helping to shape the theatre of tomorrow.

If we are to enable tomorrow's actors to meet new challenges, then I believe that it is necessary to undertake a review of the principles on which training is based. The aim is not to suggest that we dispense with narrative, character, relationships or text but rather to encourage a closer consideration of less familiar, more experimental/innovative approaches that serve to expand our thinking and extend our imaginative processes. It goes without saying, of course, that it is absolutely essential to ensure that all of our students are highly skilled when it comes to the need to comfortably and confidently embody 'character' and 'narrative' and the teaching practices associated with such traditions must continue to be valued and protected. No less important, however, is the need to confront those moments when traditional notions of embodiment are challenged, disrupted, fractured or even rejected entirely! The space between the actor and the character has begun to reveal itself in such a way as to allow for new and exciting creative opportunities. It isn't the case, as I have often heard argued, that post-modern/experimental approaches to performance seek to reject more traditional methods. The skills that actors bring to the space are often hugely valued and respected – recall, for instance, the highly accomplished actors that are members of Elizabeth LeCompte's The Wooster Group. It's more a case of seeking to adapt such skills and utilise them in ways that allow us to reflect on and experiment with our fascination with narrative and fiction, with the relationship between form and content, with ideas and politics, with notions of identity and culture and, indeed, with the very notion and function of art itself! If the validity of acting as an art form is not to become passé, I believe it is vital to ensure that the training experiences we offer also equip our students not just with practical and vocational skills, but also the *imaginative, artistic* and *intellectual* resources necessary to create innovative, challenging and genuinely ground-breaking theatre.

Bibliography

Barker, Howard. 1993. *Arguments for a Theatre*. Manchester: MUP.

Fuchs, Elinor. 1996. *The Death of Character*. Bloomington: Indiana University Press.

Lehmann, Hans-Thies. 2006. *Postdramatic Theatre*. London: Routledge.

Schechner, Richard. 1982. *The End of Humanism* New York: Theatre Communications Group.

CONTRIBUTORS

Vasiliki (Vicky) Angelaki is currently writing her PhD thesis, which focuses on the work of Martin Crimp from 1985 to the present. She is based at the Department of Drama/Theatre in Royal Holloway, University of London and is supervised by Prof. Dan Rebellato and Dr. Chris Megson. She has received a Royal Holloway research studentship for the completion of this project and teaches Critical Theories in parallel to her studies. She has previously completed a BA in English (Aristotle University, 2003) and an MA in Research - Drama/Theatre (Royal Holloway, 2005).

Carina Bartleet has an MA in Biological Sciences from the University of Oxford and a PhD in Drama from the University of Exeter. She has been a Lecturer in Drama at the University of Glamorgan and currently teaches at the University of Reading.

Lilja Blumenfeld completed MA Scenography at CSM College of Art and Design, London (UAL) in 1996. Since 1999, she has been holding the post of a Professor, Head of Scenography at the Estonian Academy of Arts. She has designed more than 40 productions in different theatres of Estonia and recently designed a production of *Yerma* at Arcola Theatre, London. She has won domestic and international awards for her artwork. Her and her students' work has been exhibited in Prague Quadrennial; in WSD 2005, she presented her scenography for Hamlet (Drama 2005, Festival Award). Lilja has been an active member of OISTAT Education Commission since 1998, and was recently elected an interim chair for the History and Theory Commission; she joined TaPRA in 2006. Lilja is currently working on a doctorate at the School of Motion Picture, Television and Production Design/ELO, University of Art and Design, Helsinki (UIAH). Based on the The Merchant of Venice by Shakespeare, her doctoral research titled The CUT-Project: Cutting the Flesh of the Other is an interdisciplinary study of human reality and performance space, combining melodrama, silent film, and theatre. Drawing on the dominant „pound-of-flesh" theme, she explores the possible scenographic representations of the implied 'cut'-motif of the play, seeking new ways to express the dark comedy through the ridiculous and the tragic.

Elpida Sophia Christianaki was born in Thessaloniki, Greece, but has lived in Canterbury since the age of 21. She received the BA (Hons) in European Philosophy and Literature with English Language Studies from Anglia University in 2001. After gaining an Ma in Comparative Literary Studies in 2002 from The University of Kent she obtained a Ph.D in 2006, specialising in Comparative Literature. Following this she joined the English Literature Department at Pembroke, Maritime University and Mid Kebt College where she is presently doing her PGCE placement.

Laura Cull is an artist and PhD candidate in the Department of Drama at the University of Exeter. Her PhD research, on Gilles Deleuze and "presence" in contemporary live performance, is funded by the Performing Presence project (http://presence.stanford.edu/) led by Nick Kaye and Gabriella Giannachi (Exeter); Mel Slater (UCL) and Michael Shanks (Stanford). Prior to her PhD, Laura studied Fine Art at the Slade School; completed an MA Cultural Studies at Goldsmiths and worked as Project Officer for the PARIP project (Practice as Research in Performance) based at the University of Bristol. At Exeter, she is the founder and co-ordinator of -intersect- : a guest speaker series focussing on the discussion of philosophical themes in an interdisciplinary context. Laura's artistic practice encompasses a wide variety of media and processes including drawing, printmaking, photography, sculpture and performance. She has presented performances at Tate Britain (2003), the Zoo Art Fair (2004) and Studio Voltaire (2005) and is a member of the SpRoUt collective. Contact: lkc202@ex.ac.uk

Elizabeth Jacobs works in the Department of Theatre, Film and Television Studies at the University of Wales, Aberystwyth. She researches and publishes on Chicana and Chicano literature and visual culture and is the author of Mexican American Literature: The Politics of Identity (Routledge, 2006). She is currently working on a related study of theatre and film on the US-Mexico border.

Carl Lavery is lecturer in Theatre Studies at Lancaster Institute for Contemporay Arts, Lancaster University. He is co-editor of Jean Genet: Performance and Politics (Palgrave Macmillan, 2006); co-author of Walking, Autobiography and Performance Writing (Intellect, 2007, forthcoming); and co-author of Sacred Theatres (Intellect, forthcoming).

Chris Megson is a senior lecturer in the department Drama and Theatre at Royal Hollowy, University of London. His doctoral research explored the impact and legacy of 1968 on the development of political theatre practices in Britain. In the past, having worked for a Labour parliamentary candidate and trade union, and his PhD project enabled him to explore two related areas of interest: the negotiation of political critique in a range of theatre forms and, more specifically, the portrayal of topical political events and living parliamentarians in the work of a range of British theatre practitioners since 1968. He has also written on the plays of Howard Brenton, David Edgar and David Hare, and completed some research on British theatrical responses to the Cold War (Routledge) and the war in Iraq (*Contemporary Theatre Review*).

Daniel Meyer-Dinkgräfe studied English and Philosophy at the Universität Düsseldorf, Germany and trained as a teacher. In 1994 he obtained his Ph.D. at the Department of Drama, Theatre and Media Arts, Royal Holloway, University of London. His thesis on *Consciousness and the Actor* was published by Peter Lang (Frankfurt, 1996). From 1994 to 2007, he was a Lecturer and Senior Lecturer in the Department of Theatre, Film and Television Studies, University of Wales Aberystwyth. Since October 2007 he has been Professor of Drama at the Lincoln School of Performing Arts, University of Lincoln. For Routledge he edited *Who's Who in Contemporary World Theatre*, and published *Approaches to Acting, Past and Present* with Continuum in 2001. He has numerous publications on the topic of *Theatre and Consciousness* to his credit, most recently *Theatre and Consciousness (Studies): Explanatory Scope and Future Potential* (Intellect, 2005) and is founding editor of the peer-reviewed web-journal *Consciousness, Literature and the Arts*. See URL http://blackboard.lincoln.ac.uk/bbcswebdav/users/dmeyerdinkgrafe/index. htm

Michelle Piasecka is a senior lecturer at Staffordshire University. She has worked extensively as performer in the United Kingdom and Europe, including the National Review of Live Art, Glasgow, 2001 and the Third International Festival of Experimental Art, St Petersburg, Russia, 2000. She is currently working toward a PhD with Manchester Metropolitan University, exploring Live Art praxis and the Primary School Curriculum.

Simon Piasecki has worked as a performance artist and academic since 1989 and has been a member of the BET4 Artists collective since its inception in 1990 and exhibited/performed as artist and writer in Britain, Europe and Russia. Much of his artistic output throughout the nineties was connected by a discourse of displacement and identity where work manifested as travel, durational installation and interventionist action. Simon is currently a senior lecturer, research practitioner and course leader for the new BA Hons Art, Event, Performance at Leeds Metropolitan University, having previously written and implemented degrees for The University of Chester in Drama & Theatre Studies and Performance & New Media and was a committee member for the Centre for Practice as Research in the Arts (CPaRA).He has delivered conference papers with recent submissions and publications on the performance of belonging, strategies of documentation, the live art laboratory of BET4 and travelling performance. He is in the last third of a PhD with Roehampton University, supervised by Heathfield and Birringer, that considers the performance of self and other in a post-soviet era. Simon is married, a father of four and has just returned from trekking the Himalaya!

Jurriën Rood (51) is a Dutch film and theatre maker as well as philosopher, living in Amsterdam. He graduated from the Dutch Film Academy as writer/director, made films, television programmes and wrote film criticism. Then moved to the theatre working as director and writer, mostly in tragic-comedy, directing over 30 productions. He recently studied philosophy on a parttime basis, specializing in epistemology/philosophy of mind and metaphysics and graduating with honors. contact: johny.des@planet.nl

David Shirley trained as an actor at the Arts Educational Schools and has spent sixteen years working in theatre, film, TV and radio. Currently Head of Acting and Programme Leader for the BA Acting degree at the School of Theatre at Manchester Metropolitan University, David was formerly Head of Drama in the Department of Contemporary Arts. Prior to joining at MMU, David worked as a senior lecturer in Acting at Rose Bruford College. A regular visiting lecturer at the University of York and RADA, David has also taught in the USA. Research interests include Shakespeare on Film, the Theatre of Samuel Beckett, the Theatre of the Absurd and Contemporary Performance Practice.

Daniel Watt is a lecturer in English and Drama in the Department for English and Drama, Loughborough University. His research interests include philosophical and literary influences on theatre and performance in the twentieth century, particularly the work of Samuel Beckett and Tadeusz Kantor. His other research work is focused on literature and ethics (especially in relation to J.M. Coetzee), fragmentary writing, and the nature of the puppet, or abject object, in performance. He is co-convenor, with Daniel Meyer-Dinkgräfe of the Theatre, Performance and Philosophy working group at TaPRA.